The Power of Address

Dick Leith is Senior Lecturer in Linguistics and English Language at Birmingham Polytechnic. He has for many years been teaching linguistics courses to students of literature, education, communications studies and speech therapy, and is a founder member of the Linguistics and Politics Group. His publications include *A Social History of English* (RKP, 1983).

George Myerson is Lecturer in English at the University of Bristol, having previously taught at Birmingham Polytechnic and King's College, London.

The Power of Address
Explorations in Rhetoric

Dick Leith

George Myerson

R

Routledge

London and New York

First published 1989
by Routledge
11 New Fetter Lane, London EC4P 4EE
29 West 35th Street, New York, NY 10001

Typeset in 10/12 pt Times Linotron 202
by Input Typesetting Ltd, London
Printed in Great Britain by Richard Clay Ltd

British Library Cataloguing in Publication Data
Leith, Dick, *1947–*
   The power of address : explorations in
   rhetoric
   1. Rhetoric
   I. Title   II. Myerson, George, *1957–*
   808

Library of Congress Cataloguing in Publication Data
Leith, Dick, 1947–
      The power of address : explorations in rhetoric / Dick Leith,
   George Myerson.
         p.   cm
      Bibliography: p.
      Includes index.
      ISBN 0–415–02938–4 (pbk.) — ISBN 0–415–03932–0.
      1. Rhetoric.   I. Myerson, George, 1957–   .   II. Title.
   P301.L35   1989
   808—dc19   89–31169
                                                                      CIP

ISBN 0–415–02938–4 (pbk)
      0–415–03932–0 (csd)

Contents

Contents

List of texts discussed

Preface

Our main concern in writing this book has been to produce a readable text. We have kept notes and references out of the way, at the ends of chapters, and have generally tried to be as accessible and non-technical as possible. Our analyses are meant to promote discussion and argument rather than display elegance or 'rigour' as though these were ends in themselves. Behind them lie many different disciplines and fields of enquiry. Perhaps the most important influences are the works of Mikhail Bakhtin, Kenneth Burke, George Kennedy, William Labov, and Raymond Williams. Donald Russell's and Michael Winterbottom's *Ancient Literary Criticism* has also been especially valuable. Given the interdisciplinary nature of our project we necessarily owe a great debt to feminism, the major interdisciplinary initiative at the present time, and to numerous scholars in what today are called the humanities and social sciences (whom we acknowledge in our chapter notes). We hope that the book will be useful to students in those fields.

This book grew in part out of shared teaching on the Language and Criticism course at Birmingham Polytechnic. We would like to thank Kathy Southworth, the commanding presence behind this course, who was also kind enough to read part of the manuscript. We are very grateful to Ron Carter and Wendy Morris for their interest and encouragement, and to Sue Leith and Lorna Ziegler for their swift and immaculate preparation of the typescript. Conversations, even the briefest, with John Bowen, John Burrow, Debbie Cameron, Jenny Coates, Mick Comber, Barbara Crowther, Norman Fairclough (whose own forthcoming *Language and Power* was a great stimulus), Simon Frith, Peter Goodrich,

Eamon Grant, Stuart Hall, David Hopkins, Debbie Johnson, Paul Kenny, John Lyon, Angela Lloyd, Peter Mack, Clifford Myerson, Jonathan Rée, Yvonne Rydin, Peter Stallybrass, Carolyn Steedman, and with numerous colleagues in the Department of English and Communication Studies at Birmingham Polytechnic and the Department of English at the University of Bristol, have helped to shape the project. We would also like to acknowledge David Crystal and Longman Ltd for permission to reproduce the text of the sermon from *Investigating English Style* (1968) and Malcolm Taylor, librarian at Cecil Sharp House, for his help in tracking down information about Elizabeth Cronin, and for permission to reproduce the text of *Lord Gregory* from the *Journal of the English Folk Dance and Song Society* (1956).

Introduction

This is an introductory book about language. It is not a survey of theories and models, but it suggests a way of approaching language, a way which we feel is both practical and illuminating. Our book is aimed not at those specializing in linguistics but at anyone who, in the course of thinking about other things, has come up against the feeling that in language there is something material, something that cannot be overlooked or simply taken for granted. But unlike most textbooks in linguistics, this one will try not to be too exclusive about language – not to imply that politics, say, or history, or philosophy, or sociology, could be merely subordinated to it. We aim to be interdisciplinary in the sense that we wish the book to be used in a variety of ways by people from very different disciplinary backgrounds, and used, moreover, at different educational levels, from the sixth form upwards.

Our conception of language is not the same as any of those currently dominant in the field of linguistics. We do not see language as an abstract system of units or rules. We have tried to find a way of talking about language that is neither exclusively 'linguistic' nor 'literary'. Our sense of 'language' comes closest to the notion of *discourse* in some of its current senses, but we have avoided using this term because of its great difficulty. Instead, we prefer the term *utterance*, and at this point we would like to refer the reader to the Theoretical Postscript at the end of the book (p. 241), where we discuss the intellectual currents behind the use of this term.

Our approach may strike many people as a predominantly literary one. In some respects this is so, although we are not so much assuming the separation of the 'literary' from the 'non-literary' that is characteristic of much literary criticism as making it a question or problem. But we hope and expect that the book will be read and used by students of literature, who will perhaps recognize our tendency to use examples drawn from novels, plays, and poems not merely as *data* for the illustration of some point about language but as sources of understanding in their own right. It is an important part of our argument, however, that these are seen *in juxtaposition* with other kinds of texts; to make this easier we have often tried to keep our analyses suggestive rather than comprehensive or exhaustive (if this is possible). A major aim of the book is to encourage readers to examine, and question, the ways in which different kinds of texts are conventionally received and interpreted.

Our approach to language is, broadly speaking, a Rhetorical one. We do not, however, see Rhetoric as a system of rigid categories but as a *process* in the production, transmission and interpretation of utterances, spoken or written, scripted or unprepared. It is not the 'letter' of Rhetoric that we want to reactivate so much as what we see as central to its 'spirit'. If our interpretation of the Rhetorical tradition may seem somewhat idiosyncratic, it is necessary to point out that there are various ways of interpreting that long and complex tradition; many different stories can be told. Our Rhetorical approach is based on three principles:

1   **Address:** language is always 'addressed' to someone else, even if that someone is not immediately present, or is actually unknown or imagined. This term is preferable to **communication** since this word is often linked in people's minds with the unproblematic 'transfer' of 'information' from one person to another.

2   **Argument:** all utterances can be seen as 'replies' to other utterances. The opposing 'voice' can be verified historically but it can also be projected from the utterance itself. All utterances can accordingly be seen as opposing moves in a dialogue which in principle can go on forever.

3   **Play:** the meaning of an utterance will always go beyond the conscious control of the speaker or writer, and there will thus be a 'looseness' or play of meaning (just as we speak of the play of the bicycle wheel which is loose in its forks). But the material qualities of language themselves can also be consciously exploited

by both sender and receiver, in the interest of either pleasure or solemnity, and this constitutes another dimension of play.

As will be readily appreciated, all three words are to a greater or lesser extent ambiguous (*argument* for instance, retains in current usage the sense of a dispute between people and the sense of putting a case or thesis). We do not see this ambiguity as a weakness, however, since these are not 'terms' in the technical sense but foci, rather, for the posing of related questions. In short, our approach is open and exploratory rather than closed and 'rigorous' in any scientific sense. We are more interested in asking questions than formulating answers. We write in the conviction that there is no single truth about language, but many truths, and that these different truths to a large extent address different audiences. Central to this conviction is the feeling that our every-day experience of language cannot simply be repudiated or repressed in the name of scientific understanding, and that any account of how language works should consider 'ordinary' perceptions, unsystematic though they may be. Insight into language, above all, is not the monopoly of any particular discipline.

Our attempt to reaffirm the value of a Rhetorical approach is in fact partly a reaction against what we see as the imperialism of linguistics within the field of language study. In that it claims to provide scientific insight into the workings of language, linguistics can be seen as belonging to the historical moment known as the Enlightenment. To try to put it simply, the Enlightenment attitude believes that the world will become a better place if more and more knowledge is accumulated in the pursuit of Truth. The guarantor of this process is Science, which can unveil the Truth behind the layers of dogma (derived from ancient, pre-scientific Authority) and other forms of 'distortion'. In the twentieth century the True Nature of language has supposedly been revealed by linguistics. While we are not against linguistics as such – large parts of the book would have been impossible to write without it, as a glance at the Glossary of linguistic terms will show – we want to distance ourselves from some of its larger claims. In particular, although linguistics is invaluable for reminding us of the materiality of language, it can contribute little to the larger issue of meaning and interpretation – precisely the point where 'literary' interest tends to begin. For us, the issues of meaning and interpretation are the most interesting, the most urgent, and also the most open.

The Power of Address, then, can be seen as a 'post-Enlightenment' project, one which challenges the newer authority of science and reason. This is a familiar context for theorizing of the advanced kind – as in the so-called Grand Theory of such thinkers as Foucault – but an unfamiliar one for books which claim to be introductory. Since Rhetoric itself was a principal target for Enlightenment attitudes, our defence of it is polemical as well as introductory. In the first three chapters, for instance, we focus on concepts which during the last few hundred years have often been disparaged: oratory, performance, the 'popular', and argument. We believe that by taking these seriously we can say relevant and interesting things about language (and introduce, in so doing, some concepts and techniques from linguistics). The last three chapters, which the reader may find more demanding, could be described as adventuring within the framework established in the first three. We have deliberately tried to engage with a very wide range of texts and types of utterance, as a glance at the Contents page will show. Some of our examples may seem strange in a book purporting to take a Rhetorical approach, but we have tried to justify our selection as we proceed. Some of our omissions, also, may puzzle. We have not analysed advertisements, for instance, although they are texts ostensibly Rhetorical in that they set out to 'persuade'. The reason for this is that we do not want to reinforce the widespread Enlightenment assumption that Rhetoric is a special, and slightly underhand, use (or abuse) of language. *All* utterances can be seen at one level as attempts to persuade; but the precise mechanisms by which someone is persuaded to part with their money in exchange for a commodity, or to adopt a particular course of action (as in the public sphere of politics) cannot be discovered by concentrating solely on language. There is no 'linguistic' method for demonstrating a text's persuasiveness. Two recent events show the enigmatic character of persuasion. Against all expectations, and in a climate increasingly hostile to trade unions and their financial links with Labour, the major party of opposition, ordinary members of a number of trade unions were persuaded to vote in favour of setting up political funds. And in the most recent general election (1987) that same party was rejected by the populace for the third time running, despite a widespread feeling – especially, perhaps, among sections of the media and the party leadership itself – that Labour's television election campaign was not only the most 'persuasive' it had ever run, but the most effective of any of the three major parties in the election.

From a political perspective, our post-Enlightenment condition could be seen as ambiguous. If reason and science are felt to have hardened into an authoritarianism, one possible reaction is anarchism. Another would itself be a new and different kind of tyranny: reason has failed, so people must simply be *told* what to do and think. A third possibility, however, is to keep insisting on the place and value of argument. This would be to link the Rhetorical tradition with the growth of democratic ideas, an interpretation that may strike many as one-sided and even over-optimistic, but one that we feel it is important to make in the increasingly authoritarian atmosphere of Britain in the 1980s.

A note on the term *Rhetoric*

The term *Rhetoric* has gathered many different meanings in the course of its history. Throughout this book we have put a capital letter at the beginning of the word, extending this even to those compound forms such as *unRhetorical*. Though at times this may give the text a somewhat bizarre appearance, we feel it is necessary to alert readers to the particular meanings we are trying to pursue.

Chapter one

Performance I: some versions of oratory

. . . teachers conceive of this apprenticeship as a *school* or *college* for *orators, scholars*. They teach by meeting with the entire class (generally five to ten students) about a month before the scheduled . . . meeting. Usually . . . the students dress . . . as they will at the meeting. At that point they will have written out speeches, *lessons*, for each, which the professors will read aloud and discuss in terms of the theory of presentational principles, how to stand, speak loudly and clearly, handle the mockery of the audience, make counter-jokes, appropriately flatter the judges, and so on. They will ask the student orators to read them aloud, acting on the principles discussed. The *professor* will judge and comment along the way, correcting pronunciation, enunciation, misplaced emphases, and speaking rhythm. In other words, the professor is charged with the task of teaching not only the speeches but the proper manner of speech-making, especially in regard to the features which the judges will take into consideration. The criteria of judgement are primarily the manner of delivery, the fluency of speaking, and perhaps most important, the way in which the scholar keeps himself composed and thus is able to manipulate the audience more effectively.

This is not, as might be imagined, an account of the training of orators in classical Greece or Rome, or of learning disputation in a medieval grammar school. It describes the training in 'talking sweet' on the Caribbean island of St Vincent during the 1960s. The young orator is learning how to make a speech at a gathering known as a Tea Meeting, on a matter concerning the Gospels or Emancipation. He (the orators are invariably males) will be judged at the meeting by the chairman, a 'man of words' respected as an orator by the community for his ability to construct and deliver his speech and his capacity for handling the audience, particularly the attempts by 'pit boys' to put him off by *rapping* sticks and *ragging* (shouting rhymes) in the local creole (the speaker himself will use a 'cultivated', more standardized, version of English). When the aspiring orator has learned the knack of improvising on his feet, he can eventually hope to challenge the chairman and even become one himself.

Public speaking, or oratory, is one aspect of Rhetoric that will be familiar to many people in contemporary British and American society. In recent years, however, the concept of oratory has fallen into disrepute, particularly in Britain, but our St Vincent example shows not only that it flourishes in what might seem to many people a rather unlikely context, but that there are also contemporary traditions of *training* which appear almost as systematic and thorough, perhaps, as those associated with classical Greece and Rome. Indeed, from the earliest times innumerable handbooks and treatises have helped to codify and recommend the various strategies of oratory. One famous account from ancient Rome is that of the orator Cicero, who identified five processes in the training of the orator:

> [He] must first hit upon what to say; then manage and marshall his discoveries, not merely in orderly fashion, but with a discriminating eye for the exact weight . . . of each argument; next go on to array them in the adornments of style; after that keep them guarded in his memory; and in the end deliver them with effect and charm.

These five stages were respectively named *invention, arrangement, style, memory* and *delivery*, and it is noteworthy that they cover not only the form of a speech but its content as well. The assumption appears to be that you can be taught *what* to say as well as how to say it: Rhetoric includes the whole process.

In classical Greece and Rome, the orator would be trained to speak not at Tea Meetings but at a court of law, where he would present a 'proof' in defence or in prosecution; a political assembly, where he would try to persuade others to a particular course of action; or at a public ceremony, where he would praise or denounce the famous. Central to such training was the primacy of the audience. The oratory of law court and political assembly was the oratory of argument: the effective Rhetorician always formulated propositions with both eyes on the anticipated objections of an addressee. Rhetoric, then, can be seen as a style of thinking, one which employs a dialogue between speaker and listener (sometimes within the same individual). It is a style of thinking particularly appropriate to the public domains of legal and political dispute, since in these areas matters are seldom finally settled in an absolute sense. Debates involving the relative virtues of justice as opposed to mercy, or individual freedom versus the common good, hinge on questions of value rather than proof in the scientific or mathematical sense.

Underlying Rhetoric, then, is a sense of perpetual dialogue between speakers and listeners (who in turn can also speak), proposition and counter-proposition, question and answer. Any assertion promotes or inspires an alternative or opposed formulation; only when contrasts and alternatives have been clearly expressed can truth, as something provisional and relative rather than fixed and final, emerge.

Throughout this book we shall be developing and testing these notions in a wide variety of contexts. In the first two chapters, however, we shall be concentrating on the oratorical aspect of Rhetoric by subsuming it under the more general notion of *performance*, used here in the physical sense of a flesh-and-blood speaker addressing (in song as well as speech) the tangible forms of a real audience. In the present chapter we consider some obvious and not-so-obvious species of performance such as lecturing, preaching, making a political speech, telling a story of personal experience, and pleading in a court of law. In all these instances the performer can be said to have a large share of personal responsibility for the material presented; to a greater or lesser extent it is the performers themselves who have performed all the operations listed by Cicero. Our selection of examples cuts across any distinction between the professional and non-professional; indeed, we are concerned to show that we are *all* at times performers, even if we have learned to be so by a process of unconscious assimilation rather than systematic training. Performances follow patterns, even if at times both performers and audiences may not be aware of this. Finally, there is a logic to our ordering of examples in that the role of the audience becomes in various ways more salient as we proceed.

The term 'performance' tends to evoke the theatre or concert-hall, and before discussing the examples we need to spend some time analysing what we mean by the term, for there is an inevitable element of theatricality even in those interactions so often labelled 'ordinary' or 'everyday' (see Chapter 4). The role of addressee, for instance, has to be learned: you are supposed to *look* as if you are listening (even if you aren't really), make the right sorts of grunt, make the right kind of response (if your interlocutor makes a self-deprecating remark, you are supposed to counter it: 'Oh come on, your career hasn't been a *complete* failure . . .'). What distinguishes performances from other kinds of interaction? First of all, they need to be 'framed' in some way, marked off from the surrounding discourse. In some cases such framing is achieved by means of special settings, such as theatres or lecture-halls, which involve distinctive arrangements of space: in many cases performers are set above and physically distanced from audiences. In less 'institutionalized' situations performances may be framed by the use of verbal formulas, such as 'Have you heard the one about . . . ?' In such instances as joke-telling sessions, performances may *emerge* from the flow of conversation. Despite, however, this wide variety of situations, performances do occur when and where they may at least be expected or approved, against a background of expectations about genre and style shared by performers and audiences alike. Common to all is the partial suspension of the **turn-taking** routine of much informal conversation: performances are marked by a certain quality of attentiveness towards the performer and his or her words and gestures. Performers are the object of the audience's gaze; even the smallest and most involuntary of movements (such as scratching the head) or minutest detail of dress (trouser turn-ups of uneven depth) may become meaningful for the audience. If the performer pauses, the pause is interpreted as significant: either it is strategic (and waited out in silent anticipation) or results from loss of memory or script (in which case the audience response may be less indulgent). Finally, performances tend to have a once-and-once-only quality; they are always fleeting, and at times this may feel momentous. The different components of performance accordingly occur simultaneously, a characteristic which makes analysis of its effects difficult in the extreme.

This is not to suggest, however, that performance(s) can be easily abstracted from the flux of history. Performance styles, audience expectations, and even what qualifies as a candidate for performance are all subject to change; different social or cultural groups, moreover, may have expectations which clash with dominant ones within a given society. Neither should we assume that performance can be discussed without considering cross-cultural variations. Different cultures, for instance, have different ideas about what kinds of activities constitute performances, as we shall see.

In classical Greece a categorization of Rhetoric into legal (forensic), political (deliberative), and ceremonial (epideictic) branches by Aristotle was based on how an oration addressed its audience. It is this principle of address that we want to emphasize throughout this book. All utterances address somebody: audiences are accordingly a vital and indispensable component of any utterance. We stress this partly because there has been a strong tendency during the last three hundred years or so to dismiss audiences as at worst contemptible, at best something to be taken entirely for granted. The term 'audience', however, is every bit as elastic as performance. The focus of the term may shift from the sense of real faces at a particular place and time smiling, gasping, or weeping, to the sense of a more abstract and less clearly defined aggregate, such as the audience for Shakespeare's plays, or, more generally, the television audience; from here the term slides into that amorphous and supremely useless category of 'the masses' (with its equally unhelpful sub-divisions 'the public', 'the folk', or 'youth'). Audiences should never, however, be abstracted from particular contexts of performance, in which they might be relatively captive (as in the case of lectures), eager (as in the case of some church congregations), or occasional (as in some cases of story-telling). But one generalization we are entitled to make about audiences is that they are seldom, if ever, inactive participants. In some cultures audience participation is expressed both vocally and bodily, as in the St Vincent Tea Meeting and, as we shall see, in other genres of Afro-Caribbean performance. In other contexts audiences are enjoined to be silent except at very specific times (as in recitals of 'classical' music – compare spectators at the Wimbledon tennis tournament) or relatively immobile (as in theatres – compare spectators at soccer matches). But the expectations of audiences may at times clash with those of the proprietors and guardians of certain institutions. Just as many soccer followers today want to do more than just stand and watch the game, many theatre-goers in the seventeenth century spent time throwing oranges at one another (and at the actors) as well as actually watching the play. Perhaps the point could be made more strongly: audiences, it seems, have a strong *desire* to participate in performances, even though the approved ways of doing this may vary according to time and place.

To be an audience is to play a role, one that has to be learned; in lectures, at least in the British education system, we must learn not to interrupt or chat to our neighbour, and in theatres we must learn to make appreciative noises. The existence of approved audience behaviour brings us to another, final series of distinctions that need to be drawn in relation to the general concept of audience. The actual people physically present at a particular performance need to be distinguished from the audience envisaged by the performer on the one hand, and the writer of a script on the other. We can therefore speak of *actual* versus *intended* audiences. But there is a further complication here. The audience that a writer hopes to reach or create is not the same as that which he or she will have unconsciously addressed through the sheer act of composing in language. This last point, which demonstrates the complexity and subtlety of the notion of address, will be further explored and clarified in the chapters that follow.

Performances in general may be seen as *privileged* acts of utterance, ones which, as we have seen, attract a level of attentiveness not accorded less focused kinds of interaction. Part of this privileging derives from the status of performers themselves. Formally institutionalized roles such as that of the preacher or the lawyer derive much of their status from the authority of those institutions. In both these cases the performer speaks on behalf of a 'text' which has been privileged with a degree of 'sacredness' (see Chapter 4). In these and other professionalized performance roles such as that of lecturer there are approved (and sometimes recommended) behaviours: part of being a lecturer or preacher is *sounding* like one (and to some extent looking like one as well). Without the support of a professional institution, however, the 'occasional' storyteller has to rely much more on his or her own skills to impress or move audiences. An effective storyteller therefore wields a kind of power that has often been seen as subversive. In fact, most kinds of performers have been regarded as suspect at one time or another, partly because they may give voice to alternative positions, but more generally because a widespread contempt on the part of the guardians of 'morality' for audiences engenders a corresponding fear of the performer. If audiences are seen as supine and mindless, it follows that they can only be persuaded by some devious trickery – which for many people constitutes a working definition of Rhetoric itself!

In contemporary British and North American culture, the status of performers may be enhanced in another respect. There is a strong tendency to celebrate the performer as an 'individual'. This notion of individuality, which has been gathering force since the Renaissance, tends to see the human subject as a separable, discrete and unified entity, with a particular 'personality'. One of its manifestations in an age of cinema and television is the cult of stardom. Originally a 'star' was a Hollywood film actor or actress whose image and persona was sufficiently established to be exploited as a means of selling films. Now that television has widened the scope for the construction and dissemination of star images, chat-show hosts, newsreaders and occasionally academics such as David Bellamy can become 'personalities' and therefore stars of a kind. While the financial and social rewards of stardom are great, the price paid for them is that the star is the object of constant attention; people are encouraged, furthermore, to see every gesture, vocal mannerism, and detail of dress as an aspect of a unique individuality rather than as components of a performance role. In fact, any attempt to draw attention to a performer's *technique* is likely to be viewed with suspicion. Nowhere is this more evident than when political speeches are being discussed. Such oratory tends to attract the suspicion noted earlier, but today this reaction is inspired by expectations about human beings which relate to the concept of individuality. There is a feeling that political oratory cannot, and ought not, to be taught, because 'good' public speaking should be spontaneous rather than contrived. Spontaneity is seen as a guarantee of something often called 'sincerity', the authentic expression of one's true, unitary, individual self. Such views are based on assumptions not only about what it is to be human, but also about language, which we shall try to uncover as our argument proceeds.

What, then, are the components of the performer's technique? Uniting all the performance roles – from acting to preaching, political oratory to storytelling – are the resources of the body which are generally grouped under the term *delivery*. We may refer to these as *voice, posture, gesture* and *face*. Each of these carries signals to the audience, many of them simultaneous, often reinforcing certain meanings, but sometimes setting different meanings off against each other. All four categories can be subdivided further. The voice, for instance, is strikingly complex (and, as we shall see, particularly salient in contemporary British culture). Variations in pitch and vocal intensity convey the attitudes and feelings of the speaker and help to differentiate **new information** from that already assumed to be shared. Also meaningful are volume and accent, the latter indicating which social group(s) the speaker consciously or unconsciously identifies with. Finally, there are the permanent features of the voice quality (sometimes called *timbre*) brought about by the speaker's individual physiognomy and the manipulable ones associated with signalling such attitudes as scorn or incredulity. Combinations of some or all of these aspects give rise to overall impressions of 'tone of voice' which, in the most systematic of Rhetorical handbooks, may be assigned to particular Rhetorical purposes. Cicero, for instance, distinguished between a conversational tone, a contentious one (more suited to debate) and an amplified one – a deep, full tone likely to invoke pity. Posture includes details of stance (standing, sitting, erect, hunched, etc.) and gesture: a range of hand and arm movements, some of which may emphasize or reinforce what is being said, while others signal independent culture-specific meanings (waving the hand, sticking two fingers up, etc.). The face also has its own repertoire of lip, tongue and eye movements, some of them more consciously manipulable than others. The range and quality of all four components will vary according to the proximity of performers to audience.

So far in this account we have stressed the importance of audiences and have noted some aspects of the performer's role. In any performance there is always a relationship of address between performer and audience, even if the role of the audience is projected rather than filled by actual bodies. There is, however, a final relationship we have yet to consider – that existing between performers and the material they perform. Here an acute terminological problem arises. The most obvious term for this material – be it lecture, sermon, speech, or song – is *text*, but as we work through the actual examples, we shall find that the nature of the 'text' changes quite radically. The text of a Shakespeare play is today verbally fixed (though contested in some passages); the 'text' of a narrative of personal experience exists in the minds of speakers and hearers in a much more fluid form, unless a particular performance of that narrative is transcribed into written language. This last point raises an issue of great significance. When we think of texts, we think of words, but this association is really a product of literacy. Any spoken (or sung) utterance is more, much more, than a sequence of words. For a start, all the resources of the body outlined in the preceding paragraph contribute to the reception of a vocalized utterance. Speech, then, can be described as *multi-coded*: many different components operate simultaneously. It is also fleeting: as noted earlier, part of the effect, even the meaning, of a performance is its uniqueness. Writing down the verbal (= word) component of a performance gives it the illusion of fixity and permanence,and it is difficult not to privilege this and call it the 'text' of a performance. But this term could more properly be used to include all the bodily operations discussed above (some descriptions of dramatic and oral narrative performances have used systems for notating gestures, specific voice qualities, etc.). In any case, the fixity of the purely verbal 'text' is an illusion for yet another reason. The verbal component may have a fixed form, but its *meaning* can never be fixed, because at different times audiences in various places will bring their own frameworks of interpretation to it and make it mean something new – an issue discussed in Chapters 4 and 5.

For these reasons a three-fold distinction will be made in order to refer to the verbal component of a performance. The record of the actual words uttered in performance we shall call the *transcript*. The words that the performer has in front of him or her (if indeed there are any) we shall call the *script*. In those circumstances where either scripts or transcripts become the focus of prolonged analytical attention, we can refer to them as *texts*. Of course, such 'textualizing' is in effect what we shall be doing throughout the first two chapters of this book; but the need for the distinctions will, we hope, be clear.

What primarily concerns the performer, of course, is the script. In all cases of performance it is the performers themselves who give voice to, or *animate* (to use Goffman's term), the script. In some cases, however, the words of the script express values which the performer is supposed to uphold, as in the case of preaching or political oratory; here we can talk of the performer being a *principal* as well as an animator. Finally, as in the case of lecturing, we can say that performers have also 'authored' the words, composed scripts themselves, in which case we can speak of animators who are also *authors*. Sometimes the three roles co-occur in the same person, which may serve as a reminder of the argument that the role of performer, like that of speaker or listener, is complex, and should not be conflated with the notion of the 'individual' as described above.

Lecturing

'Today's lecture is called standardization in English. I want to make some general points about standardization as a very widespread phenomenon in languages across the world, but most of what I have to say will be specifically related to English. Basically I want to propose three arguments: first, that the standard variety is only *one* variety of a particular language, and therefore mustn't be confused with the language itself; second, although it is often considered to be the *best* variety of a language, there are no good reasons for assuming this to be so; and third, that there are no grounds at all for arguing that standard English, the particular case we'll be considering, arose from the need to have a kind of *lingua franca* variety available for speakers of different dialects of English. You might remember that we discussed some of these terms and issues in the lecture on Language and Nation last week.'

This is the opening section of a lecture regularly given by one of the authors of this book. We make no claim for its typicality (as with the other examples we discuss): there are a variety of lecturing styles, and lecturers themselves vary according to the audience's familiarity with the material and differing ideas on the part of lecturers about what they can achieve through the form. But our account is based to a large extent on personal (sometimes bitter) experience, both as lecturers and former students in various institutes of higher education, and it is assumed that readers of this book will have had at least some exposure to lectures which they can draw on.

The lecture is the most 'professionalized' of the performances discussed in the present chapter. For many people it is an emblem of the power relations underpinning the formal education system; the lecturer is paid to 'know' things and transmit them to an ignorant audience, and the vehicle for this process is the lecture. In theory, other kinds of lecturer-student interactions such as tutorials and seminars allow students to participate vocally, and are widely assumed to be therefore more 'democratic'; in lectures, traditionally speaking, the power relationship is transparent. Lecturers speak, students are supposed to listen and make notes. This sense of inequality is reinforced by the tendency of many students to see themselves as a 'captive' audience. Attendance at lectures is accordingly begrudged, unless perhaps the lecturer is a well-known celebrity (in which case people may turn out to witness the physical embodiment of a 'name').

The power of the lecturer is also manifested through the manipulation of physical space in the lecture room: students often grouped in rows to face the isolated (and usually older) lecturer, whose status in some cases may be confirmed by the wearing of academic dress. In some ways, therefore, the lecture reproduces the spatial – and also many of the interactional – features of the traditional classroom. Extensive research into classroom interaction during recent years has shown how important is the physical organization of classrooms in shaping language use. Many of the teacher's utterances are **directive** in function (aimed at getting somebody to do or say something) and have to do with organizing sometimes quite large numbers of pupils in a small space – for example, getting them to sit, stand, and leave the room itself only in specified instances. Speaking itself is something heavily controlled and maintained by the teacher, who will request silence, nominate particular pupils to speak (often insisting that they raise their hands to request the right to speak) and will generally have the right to control the amount of speech uttered by a pupil, confirm understanding of it, summarize, define, edit, and correct it, and exercise control over the topics spoken about. Many of the teacher's utterances take the form of questions (to which he or she already knows the answer). And very often the teacher-pupil interaction has a predictable structure: the teacher makes an initiation (perhaps a question), the pupil responds (perhaps with the required answer) and the teacher provides feedback (thereby retaining the interactional initiative). These patterns are so pervasive that they are clearly replicated when children play 'school' in their own time.

Lectures are often criticized not only for retaining their aura of hierarchy but because they are also felt to be an inefficient way of teaching. One of the curious features of lectures is that, like news programmes (see Chapter 6), they tend to occupy an arbitrary length of time, regardless of the amount of material the lecturer may wish to convey (usually they last between forty and sixty minutes). There is therefore an unproductive tension between filling the hour, and over-filling it. But this factor of time is also linked with certain behaviouristic notions about the attention span of listeners. A common argument is that people 'switch off' after about twenty minutes. This rather facile assumption about audiences may be put into perspective if we remember that one of the major problems with lectures is the clash of expectations on the part of both lecturers and students. The latter often take it upon themselves to write down everything the lecturer says; in effect they end up with a transcription of the lecture (sometimes this has hilarious results; see below). What the lecturer is more likely to want from the students is a summary of the key points. More important still is the inability of many lecturers to see lecturing as performance. They fail in 'delivery' by not exploiting the resources of the body listed above; indeed, they appear to try to erase them altogether, sacrificing audibility, eye-contact, and vocal colour. (In few other instances, perhaps, is our distrust of *trained* oratory so misplaced.) Students, on the other hand, usually claim the privilege of seeing the lecturer as performer in a rather negative sense by contemplating his undone fly-button, wondering why she stares at the ceiling more often than at them, or counting up the number of ways she asks 'OK?' at the end of each point. In this respect lecturers are like babies, who are also made into involuntary performers by their parents' applauding every gurgle, burp, or other bodily emission.

Some lecturers, however, seem to start with the assumption that their audiences bore easily by scanning faces for what they think are the appropriate signs of lapsed attention, engaging in direct eye-contact, cracking jokes (many of them recycled from the year before last), distancing themselves from their script by asides in what Goffman calls 'fresh talk', and *colluding* with the audience by directing scornful rebukes at absent (often deceased) scholars. But there is a limit to such 'playing to the gallery'. A lecturer has to sound, and look, the part, and this means demonstrating that you have given some thought to your material. Audiences do at least tend to expect a structure of arguments (even if they don't listen to them) and some reference to the work of other scholars in the field. Looking at our example, it should be clear that the lecturer has actually tried to draw attention to the first of these by listing arguments to which he will later return. He gives his audience a menu which they then expect to materialize; they will therefore have already made a contribution by *anticipating* what is to come. If we look more carefully at the language of the extract we might notice that the arguments are generally couched in the form of **propositions**, using simple present tense verbs ('want', 'is', etc.), and that the *connections* between propositions are occasionally signalled very clearly by the use of **connectives** like 'although' and 'however'. This kind of language and opening strategy is not unusual in lectures, but is perhaps less conventionalized than the ritual flattering of judges that usually introduces a St Vincent Tea Meeting speech or a legal oration as described by Cicero.

Another important aspect of the text's language is that it has been consciously scripted to be read aloud. The words 'one' and 'best' have been underlined so that the lecturer can give them extra vocal stress, and linger on them, to emphasize the point. In short, phrases have been constructed to allow the speaking voice to operate with all its resources. Writing for oral delivery also tends to avoid what linguists call **left-branching structures** (see glossary), in which the main verb is delayed by piling up qualifying information in front of it, since these apparently place a heavy burden on the short-term memory of listeners. Such a script allows room for the lecturer to pause between propositions and look up at the audience, repeat material for the benefit of latecomers, and slide into improvised asides as is felt appropriate. Thus the script itself constitutes only a part of what is actually said in the lecture. But lecturers rarely leave much to chance: even the most spontaneous-sounding aside is usually contrived, as Goffman argues. The advantage of this particular style of lecturing – which is probably learned more through trial and error than through training – is that it avoids the great problem associated with reading aloud a script that has been constructed as a piece of written prose: that of never raising your eyes from the paper in front of you for fear of losing your place. Audiences, it seems, generally prefer the illusion of being talked to rather than read at.

Despite what has been said above about written prose, there is a clear sense in which the utterances in our extract appeal to a process of understanding often associated with writing. Part of this process concerns the careful scrutiny and retention of notions embedded in one proposition so that the next proposition may be understood in the light of the first. An extreme example of the process is the *syllogism*. For instance, the proposition 'All bears north of the Arctic Circle are white' can be taken as having a truth-value that is applicable if we want to ask subsequent questions about the colour of bears in, say, Alaska. If we know that Alaska is within the Arctic Circle we can confidently say that bears there will be white: the inference follows logically from the initial proposition. Syllogistic reasoning demands that we see propositions as purely formal: the question 'What colour are bears in Alaska?' has to be seen as answerable from the information encoded in the first statement. An answer like 'I've never been to Alaska' or 'Why don't you go and see for yourself?' is therefore deemed inappropriate.

There is a very important issue at stake here, which we need to discuss at some length before demonstrating its relevance to our example. Logical operations of the kind discussed above have often been regarded by scholars as the prerequisite of rational thought, even of civilized life; responses of the 'inappropriate' kind have been seen as a mark of inferior intellect or 'primitive' culture. Underlying this view is the assumption that language can be, and in some way ought to be, divorced from its context of utterance. Thus syllogistic reasoning is often associated with writing, since that, too, is supposed by many to be capable of decontextualizing language. In fact, one influential school of thought has argued that syllogistic reasoning is only made possible once writing has been invented, since writing is capable of overcoming the transitoriness of speech referred to earlier: it therefore enables us to contemplate propositions more closely. Such claims about decontextualization are fallacious, however, since *all* statements, propositions, or whatever, are produced and interpreted within a particular context. Syllogisms, for instance, are part of a language-game, associated with formal education, of 'Let's assume that . . .' and participants have to know the rules of that particular game if they are to produce acceptable moves.

The association of writing and logical reasoning in fact tends to privilege one kind of writing only – that conventionally used for argumentative, scholarly, and abstract thought. It is a view of writing fostered by formal schooling, one that sees speech as in many ways imprecise and messy by comparison. One consequence of these views and associations is the tendency to imagine that meaning in language resides in the words alone (rather than also being present in the voice, gesture, face, and posture of the speaker). Writing can therefore be considered superior because its only resource is verbal. Lecturers who read from a script of written prose are in fact deferring to this notion: they are in effect asking their audience to listen to every single word. A further consequence of this view is the tendency to foreground certain functions of language at the expense of others. Schooling tends to emphasize both **metalingual** and **referential** (see glossary for definitions of both these terms) uses: the first denotes language used to talk about language itself – for example, discussing the meaning of a word or inquiring after its spelling; and the second denotes language used to name or make propositions about entities, events, and processes in the 'real world'. Thus the proposition 'oil floats on water' refers to realities that we can touch, smell, taste, etc. and also states a relation between them that we can test for ourselves. This second function is very important in scientific discourse, as we shall see later in this book.

Our lecture extract can be readily analysed in the light of these two functions. There is an obvious metalingual component in that the lecture uses language to talk about two terms which themselves denote aspects of language: the general, superordinate term 'language' and the more specific 'standard'. And there is an assumed understanding that these two terms refer to phenomena that in some way actually exist (even if they are felt to be constructions that are social rather than 'given' in the real world). Behind the extract is a syllogism, in the loose sense, that could be stated as: 'a language has many varieties; the standard is only one of those varieties; therefore the terms "standard" and "language" are not interchangeable.' In short, part of the lecture's address is the appeal to its listeners to co-operate in a particular language-game: one which discusses the ways words are used as part of a system of reference to a shared world.

Another vital ingredient of the lecture's address – where 'address' is understood as a feature of genre – is the assumption that the lecturer is telling the audience something they don't already know. People generally expect to get something 'new' from lectures (even if they often feel dissatisfied on this score). The presentation of 'new' information, however, depends on the existence of something already known or given, and a strategy common to many kinds of public speaking is to propose at the outset the existence of a commonly-held belief or assumption which the speaker then goes on to question. In this example the lecturer implicitly refers to beliefs about standard English (which mainly derive, interestingly enough, from schooling) which he feels are wrong-headed. In effect he holds a *dialogue* with imagined voices articulating the opposed position, and he assumes that some of his students at least some of the time may identify with those voices. Part of the lecture's structure, then, is this sense of a problem, or gap, involving widespread beliefs on the one hand and a more disciplined set of arguments on the other. In this respect this particular lecture is 'Rhetorical' in that it starts from the world of opinion (in contradistinction to 'logic', which starts from Truth in the fixed and absolute sense).

In Cicero's terms, this relationship between common belief and counter-argument is part of the process of *inventio*, of 'discovering what to say'. Lecturers themselves discover what to say, arrange it, work out appropriate phraseology (glossing technical words by more colloquial ones, for instance – which are then sometimes served back in student essays!), perhaps commit bits to memory, and deliver it. But this account gives a misleading impression of the actual sequence of Rhetorical operations. You discover something to say by having to 'perform', just as you tend to remember something if you know you will need to reproduce it on another occasion. Performance, then, means much more than merely delivery, or, in Goffman's term, 'animation'; here it also subsumes the entire process of 'authoring' as well.

There is one final point to make about the relationship between lecturer and script. We said above that the lecturer also performed the role of principal, in the sense that he or she 'stands by' the values embodied in the script. By its very nature, however, lecturing greatly complicates this relationship. Much of the time a lecturer has to reproduce the arguments that structure the very discipline itself, to which he or she is committed, perhaps, only as a practitioner of that discipline. In a sense, the discipline speaks through the lecturer. Often, however, a lecturer is challenged by students who assume a *personal* relationship between him or her and the arguments expressed. Thus, lecturers often feel the need to distance themselves from their scripts, and nowhere is this more true than when they have to summarize another scholar's argument or quote verbatim from a written source. Such quotation will generally be obvious to the listener since it will often be from material not written to be read aloud, and a sensitive lecturer might try to deliver such passages slowly, signalling to the audience that it is indeed a quotation, and perhaps summarizing its argument immediately afterwards. But in an extended sense the lecturer is 'quoting' most of the time, as we hope the rest of this book will make clear.

Preaching

'The book of the prophet Isaiah, thirtieth chapter; the fifteenth verse of the chapter – Isaiah, chapter thirty, verse fifteen: "in returning and rest ye shall be saved; in quietness and in confidence shall be your strength"; "in returning and rest ye shall be saved, in quietness and in confidence shall be your strength."

This is a story of a man who was in a hurry, and who travelled too fast. He was a white man trekking in a wild part of Africa, and he was having trouble with his African carriers. Every now and then they would insist on stopping and laying down their loads and sitting down by the side of the track. He was in a hurry to get on but no arguments, no threats, no promises of reward would induce them to move. They just sat there solidly. But at last, with great difficulty, he dragged out the reason for all this. The head man of the carriers explained that they'd travelled so far and walked so fast, they'd left their souls behind, and now they must sit down and wait for them to catch up. The pace had been too much for them.

Well, of course, one would not attempt to define the relationship which the untutored African conceived as existing between body and soul. But from this incident one thing is clear: that African head man, in his own graphic idiom, was depicting the condition of the people of the western world today: he was acting as unwitting interpreter to a whole generation; in that quaint explanation of his he laid his finger on the root of many of our present troubles and misgivings. This generation has travelled so fast that it's left its soul behind, and unless we pause and wait for our soul to catch up, who shall say what perils and disasters lie before us? The pace of life today is proving too much for us, and it's time we sat down for a while and laid aside our burden of care, took stock of our situation.

Somewhere Longfellow says that the sabbath is like a stile between the fields of toil where we can kneel and pray and sit and meditate. And here, this quiet sabbath morning, in this peaceful church, with a comforting sense that we are compassed about with a great cloud of witnesses, who through the ringing groves of change have steadfastly kept the faith; here we can sit and meditate, always with the words of our Lord Himself at the back of our mind: "What shall it profit a man if he gain the whole world and lose his own soul?" '

The relevance of the notion of quotation to the sermon above should be clear: it begins with a quotation, and also ends with one, in a paragraph bristling with 'quoted' Biblical words and phrases such as 'compassed about' and 'witnesses'. In fact, the whole sermon can be analysed as an elaboration of the initial quotation from the Book of Isaiah (itself said twice while the congregation settles). The elaboration can be further broken down: first into a narrative, then an argument, followed by a conclusion. The narrative opens with an abstract which contains a moral; it is not resolved by action so much as interpretation (which takes place in the 'argument' section). The argument offers an interpretation of the narrative but delays the central proposition until after a three-fold statement that the 'untutored' African in his 'own graphic idiom' had known something that western society has tended to forget. We are thus led up to the proposition, which itself is reinforced by the use of the Rhetorical question 'who shall say . . . ?' The proposition is then followed by an injunction that we, the congregation, sit down like the Africans in the narrative and find our souls. The sermon concludes by relating quotation, narrative, and argument to the here and now of the congregation in a particular church on a particular Sunday morning, sitting down, and therefore able to rediscover their own souls in the 'quietness' of the moment.

In many respects the sermon also recalls the language of the lecture. A proposition – 'This generation has travelled so fast that it's left its soul behind' – is held up for contemplation, and the congregation is implicitly being asked to draw on its own experience of modern life to test the validity of the proposition. 'Well, of course, one would not attempt to define the relationship . . .' is lecture-like in its affectation of detachment (the indefinite **pronoun** 'one' smacks of 'educated', perhaps also upper-middle-class usage; the modal verb 'would' distances the speaker from commitment to the task of definition). The language of argument, of metalingual discussion and referential statement has long had a place within the Christian religion, which for much of its history has struggled to accommodate the writings of the classical philosophers like Plato and Aristotle. But in many respects the sermon is quite unlike the lecture. First, many Christian denominations have traditions of lay preaching, so that the performer of a sermon does not have to be a professional. Second, the sermon has behind it the authority of a sacred text, the Bible, the source of most of its quotations (see Chapter 4). In the conclusion these quotations are set alongside the simple **deictic** (see glossary) forms 'this' and 'here', the meanings of which are entirely dependent on the context of utterance: a particular preacher to a particular congregation at a specific time. One effect of this is to gather up the whole history of the Church in both time (from the Biblical era to the present) and space ('the whole world', exemplified in this case by the transition from Africa to the place where the sermon is being performed), uniting both speech and writing as the Bible's written word is materialized through the preacher's spoken utterance.

By quoting from the Bible the sermon not only uses language familiar to many of the congregation, it draws on an authority that is ultimately beyond what is commonly considered argument, one based on faith and belief. Thus, the sermon is unlike the lecture in that the preacher does not tell the congregation anything new; he or she will be *reminding* it about what it is already supposed to know, and reactivating the thoughts and feelings appropriate to the faith. Exactly how this process of reactivation should work has been the source of much debate within the religion. At the centre of the debate is a clash of attitudes about language. As is well-known, the Biblical and liturgical texts dating from the sixteenth and seventeenth centuries have recently been 'translated' into 'modern' English, much to the dismay of many church-goers familiar with the traditional language from child-hood. (Here we have a case of an audience actively resisting the role offered them.) To them, the traditional language is as constitutive of worship as organ music and incense, and is to be defended precisely because of the way it works on congregations. It has recently been claimed that the traditional liturgy of Confession, for instance, exploits the *formal* properties of spoken language – rhythm, alliteration, various forms of repetition – in such a way that the congregation is made to feel humble and penitent. With 'we acknowledge and bewail our manifold sins and wicked-ness', with its doublets 'acknowledge' and 'bewail', 'sins' and 'wickedness', the congregation is actually confronted, it is claimed, whereas the modern version, 'we confess we have sinned against you' soothes and placates them. On this view, the writers of the modern version disavow, distrust, or fear the emotional effects certain kinds of language may have in a particular context. Traditionalists, on the other hand, conceive of the church service as a kind of drama, changing the congregation in its course by knocking them down and then picking them up again. Religious *feelings* are not assumed to exist prior to the service; they are kindled by the event itself.

Sermons, then, should be seen in the context of the other kinds of utterance deployed in church. Some preaching traditions, however, actually use the sermon as an entire service in itself.

The performance aspect of preaching is very clearly expressed in the Black sermon tradition of the southern states of the USA, in which the active role of the congregation is equally marked. The preacher consciously works to change the audience, who in turn 'complete' the act of worship by vocal and bodily participation. This *antiphonal* structure is organized largely through the use of rhythm. The sermon becomes increasingly rhythmical, so that by the end the rhythm has become the dominant feature of the language. As in the case of the sermon discussed above, the Black preacher makes extensive use of narratives, many of them Biblical (e.g. David and Goliath), to point a particular moral; on the whole, however, the Black sermon is less 'scripted' than those in our own tradition. What the Black preacher does is extemporize the sermon, drawing on a repertoire of stock phrases and patternings. An example is the 'stall formula' like 'Hark Hallelujah!' and 'God from Glory!' and 'Oh Lord!', so-called because it is used to fill a pause while the preacher thinks what to say next. Patterns of verbal repetition are particularly marked:

> Regardless of what anybody says or does
> Regardless of who turns against me
> Regardless of who's for me
> Let 'em mock let 'em scoff
> Let 'em make fun and make shame of me
> I'm gonna live for God.

This technique of extemporization should not be confused with spontaneity. The preacher uses patterns that he knows are likely to work (this, however, can never be predicted in advance). In fact, by inspecting these lines carefully, we can find at least three different kinds of repetition: of a word at the beginning of successive lines, of the same idea in different words, and of similar ideas by, more specifically, different verbs (e.g. 'mock', 'scoff'). The Rhetorical handbooks had names for all these types: *repetitio*, *interpretatio*, and *disjunctio*. Of course, it is not necessary to know the terms before you apply the techniques; moreover, there is a long tradition within Rhetoric, notably during the Renaissance, warning people of the sterility of merely sticking labels on to any piece of linguistic patterning they can find. What the terms do, however, is draw our attention to the forms and structures of language itself – as we hope to show, this is extremely important in developing a Rhetorical view of language. Needless to say, the preachers themselves are extremely reluctant to discuss these techniques with an outside observer. For them it is the 'message', not the form, that matters; the message, moreover, comes from God, who speaks 'through' the preacher. We shall discuss this disavowal of Rhetoric's role in religious utterance in greater detail in Chapter 4.

Political oratory

Political speeches, of course, are not made just by professional politicians. They are made by political activists in all parties and groupings in a wide variety of assemblies. There is in fact no clear definition of what constitutes a political speech, still less what is meant by the phrase 'the language of politics'. The sermon, for instance, makes reference to a colonial attitude in the phrase 'untutored Africans' which is nothing if not political. In British culture at the present time the definition of what is political has become the site of open and intense conflict. The Bishop of Durham is accused of making political speeches when he refers to the problems of the inner city; a trade union is prevented from referring to public expenditure cuts, which affect the jobs of its members, on the grounds that its campaign is political. One great advantage of a Rhetorical approach, in our view, is that it can call into question the categories of text and language that are dominant within a particular culture at a particular time. The reader may already have noticed that many of the arguments cited in relation to the issue of religious utterance are those more closely associated with the study of literary texts – an issue we discuss later in this book.

Our example of political oratory is a transcript of the opening of a speech, made by a man 'working in industry', at a Conservative Party conference. The debate concerns one of the central issues of our time: that of (Black and Asian) immigration. The speaker is in support of a motion calling for tougher restrictions on entry.

'Mr Chairman, in supporting this motion, I have to declare an interest. I am an Englishman. I am proud of being an Englishman. (Applause) It – it is no coincidence that today I am wearing a tie with the emblem of St George. But let me make it quite clear. In being proud of an Englishman [sic], I say I am proud of our traditions. That does not make me a racialist. It does not make me colour-prejudiced. (Applause) People like myself who are proud of their traditions do not want to see them changed . . . suddenly. They don't want to see large numbers of people of different cultures changing their culture. That is what is happening. And we all know it. (Applause) That's the emotional side of the argument.'

The speaker then goes on to present what he calls the 'logical' side: homes and jobs are already in short supply, so why exacerbate the situation by putting more pressure on scarce resources? He ends by saying that the government has a mandate to stop further immigration.

What should immediately be apparent from the transcript is the importance of audience applause, without which the oration could not be said to be complete. In this respect the role of the audience is every bit as significant as in the Black sermon (it is noteworthy here that Black political oratory in the USA is often similarly antiphonic). But the distribution of applause within the oration does not appear to be random and arbitrary. It comes directly after a rise in **pitch** and, in general, vocal energy on the part of the speaker: these usually occur on the final proposition of a three-part sequence. Thus declaring an interest, asserting Englishness, asserting pride ('proud', with it's 'confessional' quality, is uttered with strong stress) in that fact, are followed directly by applause. In the second instance both 'That does not make me a racialist' and 'It does not make me colour-prejudiced' are uttered in staccato delivery, with an extra strong stress on 'not'. The tone here is challenging: 'racialist' and 'colour-prejudiced' are implied quotations from some imagined voice asserting the contrary. Operating here also is an antithesis: pride in tradition is not the same as either of these. In the third instance, 'And we all know it' is delivered in similar fashion: as the assertion of (purported) common knowledge, it seems to cry out for confirmation.

The address of the speech is therefore complex. The speaker holds a dialogue not only with the audience, not only with opposing but absent voices, but also with the previous speaker at the conference, who has argued (without using the term 'racialist') that the motion would alienate Black and Asian people already settled in Britain. Thus while the speaker's script was not constructed as a reply to the previous speech, it is *heard*, in part, as exactly that. One mark of the speaker's deftness as a political orator is that in another part of the speech not reproduced here he actually refers to something that the previous speaker said. Improvisation to suit the interest of the moment is one skill of the successful orator.

In the act of performance, of course, the most obvious audience is the one facing the performer, and we need to ask not only *why* they applaud, but also why they do it in the particular places specified above. Here the analogy with Black preaching is useful. Clearly the audience at this conference *expects* to participate, like the Black congregation; unlike the congregation, however, it is divided on particular issues, and the orator has to try to win them over to a particular argument. But he doesn't do this by telling them anything new; like a preacher, he tries to cultivate a reassertion of values that he assumes many of them share. Since those values are in defiance of sections of the audience and certain voices outside the conference hall, the role of the audience in this particular speech is especially important. The speaker immediately appears to 'hook' his audience by his opening statement, in which he purports to bare his soul by affecting an unfitness to speak. The statement is a kind of disclaimer (cf. 'Unaccustomed as I am to public speaking'): the speaker at one level is saying that he does not have the quality of impartiality that the occasion needs, and that if he were speaking in another place, before another audience, he might be made to feel guilty. Interest, like bias, is something fair and reasonable people ought not to have; 'declare an interest', moreover, is a pun, meaning both 'announce an involvement with' and 'declare' (in the same sense of a Customs declaration) something in your possession ('interest' here puns on the use of the word to mean 'actual or potential financial gain'). When, however, we learn that this interest lies only in being English, we are supposed to warm to the humility, the assertion of ordinary humanity, something the speaker can do nothing about. But 'I am an Englishman' reveals nothing that is new or exciting; its power comes from its being the assertion of a sentiment the audience wants to hear asserted: the 'I' is the collective 'I' of all those who applaud, and potentially, of all those at the conference. Implicit here is a collusion with the audience against an absent 'them' who are purportedly opposed to such sentiments.

This analysis may strike many readers as over-elaborate and sophisticated: surely the puns, for instance, are neither intended by the speaker nor recognized by the audience? This brings us back to a point made earlier: utterances can exhibit patterns of rhythm and repetition over and above the meanings of individual words, and at the moment of performance their effects can go unnoticed, not least because of the feature of simultaneity referred to earlier. In accordance with a general principle informing the whole of this book, language has the capacity to generate meanings that are beyond the conscious control of either speakers (and writers) or listeners (and readers). We refer to this principle as 'play', and it is one of the elements that make the concept of address so complex. In relation to this particular example, we would claim that our analysis is far less insensitive than analyses that see such political oratory as a set of tricks to beguile an innocent audience. A recent study by Atkinson tends to treat audiences as automata, programmed to clap or cheer for a seven-second stretch every time a speaker uses a three-part pattern of statements or an antithesis. Lying behind such analysis, apparently, is an expectation, quite common among academics and sections of the political left, that political speeches should aspire to the condition of the lecture by presenting to the audience a structure of arguments for their rational contemplation.

This is not to say that political orators do not use techniques; *all* performance requires technique, and both non-professional and professional political orators make use of those we have tried to analyse. Professional politicians, of course, have to learn extra skills: convincing delivery of a speech authored not by themselves but by another, even one expressing ideas which may be party policy but which are not personally upheld by the particular politician. (Again we see the complexity of the role of principal.) They must also learn to address that most elusive and mysterious of audiences, the television viewer, with a performance repertoire suitable for the small screen rather than the large auditorium. Some professional politicians, like Margaret Thatcher, have taken great pains to eliminate certain vocal characteristics in order to win greater audience 'appeal'. As we shall see in the next chapter, both television and film screens tend to put the smallest facial, gestural, postural and vocal characteristics on display.

Storytelling

'My dad says – I said to my father one night, I said: "Dad I'm going out to a party." He said "If you're not home here at a certain time," he said, "I shall be after you." So I said, "Well, I'm – I – might be a bit late, Dad, d'you mind?" So he said, "Well, I've told you what time you've got to come in, I'm not going to have you out at d- late at night." So I was getting so . . . well away with this party that I got – I didn't think of looking at the clock. I overdone it. So I said to, er, one of these young women there, I said: "Oh, I'm supposed to be home at ten o'clock, I won't half get into trouble when I get home." So she said, "Come on then," she said, "Ann, I'll come with you." So I said, "All right, come with me." So I knocked on the door (she took me home, she went indoor, she lived down the same turning; she went indoor). And I knocked on the door and I couldn't get no answer. So I thought to myself, "Whatever am I going to do? I can't get in." So there was a low wall next door ('cause we lived at the last house). So there was a low wall next door so I climbed over the low wall and I got on to the lavatory door and soon as I got on to the lavatory door – years ago, we used to wear the old-fashioned lace drawers (audience laughter) – so I climbed over the lavatory door and as I got over I tore the lace off my drawers (laughs) and it hung on a nail (laughter) in – on the lavatory door. So course I creeps up to bed. So when I gets up in the morning my Dad said to me, "What time did you come home last night?" Oh," I said, "I wasn't late, Dad." He said, "You wasn't late?" He said, "What do you mean by that?" So I said, "Well, I wasn't late, Dad." He said, "I was abed." He said, "You must have come home after twelve o'clock." So I said, "I never," I said. So he said, "What's happened to this?" And he held the lace up (laughter) of the drawers. So I said, "I don't know, Dad." So he said, "You must have got over the bloody yard next door," he said, "and got on to the lavatory door, and you tore the lace off of your drawers." (Laughs) He said,

"You're found out now," he said. He said, "Don't let that happen no more," he said, "because you won't have the chance to go to another party in a hurry," he said. (Laughter; talk obscured) ". . . instead of you getting a good belting up." Oh dear oh Lord, very strict, the old people were them days. You couldn't do them of anything. If they said you've got to be in at a certain time, you did have to be in at a certain time, but I thought I'd go above the mark 'cause I didn't get in till 12 o'clock at night and I got found out in the morning. (Laughs)'

This is a narrative of personal experience, to many people a rather unlikely candidate, perhaps, for the term 'oratory'. Indeed, such stories seem so familiar and unremarkable that we hardly think of them as *performances*. Stories like this very often simply 'emerge' from the flow of informal conversation, often between pairs or groups of people of relatively equal status, and require no special settings. They are, however, very often 'framed' by an introductory utterance such as 'I never told you that I saw a ghost, did I?' or 'This amazing thing happened to me last night,' and a **coda** (see glossary) at the end, such as 'That was one of the most frightening experiences of my life,' or 'So that was that.' These act as signals to depart from, and return to, the turn-taking routine of conversation (see Chapter 4): a conversationalist becomes a temporary performer by 'holding the floor' for as long as the story lasts. To pay for the privilege, they are under some pressure to make their narrative interesting and relevant to the audience. In their turn, however, audiences can also become narrators: this happens, for instance, when a conversation between peers develops into a story-swapping session. Narrators vary, however, in the extent to which they see storytelling as an act of full performance. Some tend to 'step out' of the story to monitor their listeners' attention, check their understanding, or respond to questions which listeners put to them.

There are complex social and psychological reasons for telling stories. Age, gender, class, and ethnicity intersect in various ways to influence or shape characteristic storytelling events in different cultures. Black adolescents in inner-city areas of the USA tell fight narratives, it seems, to identify with their masculinist peer-group culture, one which rates verbal prowess as highly, perhaps, as the ability actually to perform the deeds recounted in the stories. In East European Jewish culture a high premium is placed on the use of narratives to serve as parables – it is felt that only low-status groups such as women and lower-class men tell stories 'for their own sake'. As we shall argue later, however, stories are never merely stories. There is always a 'point' to storytelling, even if the point may be lost on a particular audience at a particular time (and on the storyteller also). Sometimes a story may be told because the speaker feels they have something unusual or memorable to relate. This is often a chancy business, because what is unusual or memorable is usually difficult to define (and may be culture-, class-, age-, or gender-specific); a speaker may compensate for this by using all the resources of the performer in order to impress (if only temporarily) the audience. And an important component of much storytelling of this kind is probably self-aggrandizement. The role of storyteller allows us to project a version of ourselves to others (and also to ourselves).

Our example is a transcript (from tape) of a story told by a North London woman in her seventies to an audience of two: her daughter (in her forties, a costermonger like her mother), and a male researcher in his twenties, as part of a fieldwork project on speech and local history in London. As such the interaction had a quasi-interview status, except that this was mitigated by a tacit convention in contemporary British society that old people in general have stories, or even *a* story, to tell younger listeners, the point being that they have had access to experiences no longer available to succeeding generations. The story was prompted by the daughter, who clearly saw it as highly 'tellable'. For both her and her mother it was a valued story, one that had been told on numerous occasions, but to the researcher, sitting with them round the kitchen table, it was entirely new.

The story is framed by the prompt, 'Tell him the one about when you had to climb over the wall,' and by the coda beginning, 'Very strict they were, the old people, them days.' At first blush it might appear that the coda encapsulates the point of the story, a demonstration of how strict parents were at the time of the speaker's childhood. If this were so, it was not the point taken by the researcher, who interpreted it as being told for its humorous value (a response certainly aided by the gales of laughter that came from both storyteller and daughter at the detail of the lace drawers). To leave behind a piece of underwear as evidence of transgression is to tread the boundary between the acceptable and the taboo, something in itself quite likely to inspire laughter (the 'point' – or 'points' – of a story being always open to interpretation). The coda, then, should perhaps be analysed as a more conventionalized way of signalling to the audience that the story is over (as in the commonly-used coda, 'So that was that').

The story was fully performed, with no interruptions (apart from the laughter) from the audience, and no attempt by the speaker to step outside the story and explain motives, background, or circumstantial detail. In short, everything is embedded *within* the narrative: it could therefore be described as dramatized. The story is dramatic in the sense that there is a great deal of direct rather than indirect speech: it is useful to compare it in this respect with the narrative in the sermon discussed earlier. The use of direct speech allows for the full range of vocal, postural, facial, and gestural resources to be used: the speaker in effect acts out all the characters. This feature of the story, which should be immediately apparent when the transcript is compared with the other extracts analysed, is extremely widespread in oral narratives across the world (it could perhaps be called a universal: see Chapters 5 and 6). The story purports to show events which actually happened, but we are unlikely to feel that the direct speech is a report of what was really said: the teller invents it to recreate the sense of an encounter. The narrative is dramatic in other senses, too. It is constructed as a sequence of scenes: a dialogue with the father, another with a friend at the party, another which narrates the central action of climbing into the house, and finally the spoken confrontation with the father the next morning. The term 'scene' also refers to a relationship between the time it takes to narrate an event and the time it would have taken 'in real life'. Here we sense that the pace of the dialogue in the story matches that of the interactions themselves. But the story, or parts of it, is dramatic in other ways as well. At the point where the female protagonist realizes she can't get into her own home, the action is suspended by the representation of (free) thought, 'Whatever am I going to do?'; a similar suspension occurs where the father presses her on the question of what time she came home. In both instances there is the build-up of suspense often informally described as 'dramatic'. Finally, the narrative is dramatic in a deeper sense. The represented actions have been selected and sequenced so as to give a heightened sense of causality, giving us the impression that certain actions have consequences not only fitting but inevitable. In this respect the story is to a large extent fictionalized, despite its claim to be a narrative of real experience. A beginning, middle and end have been imposed on a flow of actions and processes that in life would have co-occurred within an infinite web of other relationships. (It is also noteworthy in this connection to point out that the opening scene may be analysed as a pair of actions corresponding to the *interdiction-violation* sequence of folk tales, to use the terminology of Vladimir Propp in his classic study of that genre.)

In contemporary British culture these and other characteristics of oral narrative (such as the tendency to keep **orientating** information about setting and protagonists to a minimum, and to distribute it at different points in the narrative as and when it is needed) tend to be taken for granted: we are usually content merely to describe someone as a good storyteller, or a particular instance of performed narrative as especially memorable. But it is equally important to remember that storytelling is also a matter of style and technique. Features of these are often recognized, itemized and evaluated in cultures which have no writing systems. In our own culture, paradoxically enough, it is only when we *transcribe* a performed narrative into written language that we begin to notice some of its stylistic devices. A well-known example is the use of the **historic present** tense, which in our example occurs in two instances at only one place in the narrative: 'so of course I *creeps* up to bed; so when I *gets* up in the morning . . .'. The use of this tense, apparently unconscious on the part of the narrator, has often been associated with the notion of 'immediacy', in that the narrator is supposed to re-create for the audience the sense that the narrated events are happening before their very eyes. It has recently been argued, however, that the meaning of this usage derives not from any inherent quality but from its *alternation* with the simple past tense (as in 'climbed' and 'got over'). In fact, it is a way of sub-dividing the narrative into shorter blocks or episodes: the tense is introduced at a specific point, and then we return to the simple past.

The act of transcription also tends to draw other aspects of speech to our attention. Since in our own culture writing is something consciously and explicitly taught in schools it tends to make us more aware than in our pre-school years of the formal characteristics of language. In the course of our school lives we become increasingly sensitive to the 'look' of a piece of writing on the page, the structure of the written sentence as distinct from the spoken, and the kinds of vocabulary and typographical conventions associated with different kinds of written texts. As a consequence, any piece of verbatim transcription of speech may strike us as formless and badly-expressed: its sentences will not conform to the patterns of the written language, and the hesitations, false starts and **fillers** such as 'um', 'er', 'you know' and 'sort of' will be seen as the hallmarks of inarticulacy and sloppiness. The transcriber quickly finds that the punctuation marks of writing – commas, dashes, brackets, for instance – cannot be used to indicate pauses and changes of direction while at the same time signalling relationships that are grammatical (the way they are used in writing). Moreover, we are taught to write in *standard* English, and it is from this perspective that we are likely to judge the obvious non-standardisms in our story such as 'them days', 'you wasn't,' 'I overdone it,' etc. Also, transcription tends to *defamiliarize* certain usages, such as the stereotyped **co-ordination** within the narrative: clauses and sentences tend to be conjoined with 'so' denoting not so much a causal connection as a temporal one. This tendency for the act of transcription to highlight the differences between speech and writing can be seen in one final respect. Once our narrative has been written down, we tend to judge it against the conventions of written prose fiction, particularly the short story. Seen against this background, our example might seem rather small beer, and it is for this reason that some scholars advocate a different transcription procedure, one that sets out the story to look more like a poem. Whatever advantages this might have, it should by now be clear that a Rhetorical approach to utterance must be aware of how our perception of performance events is influenced by the conventions of transcription.

Legal oratory

There is an obvious and ancient sense in which legal utterances are Rhetorical. As we have seen, one of the three branches of Rhetoric in ancient times was termed 'forensic', and was associated with the *agora* or legal assemblies. Here disputes about such matters as property rights were not resolved by recourse to a professionalized group such as lawyers but were debated openly in public. They were therefore political in the wider sense. It was only with the rise of a lawyer group that our modern sense of Law as a hieratic and reified concept began to emerge, and with it a repudiation of the Rhetorical foundations of dispute processing – a matter discussed in Chapter 4.

Central to legal procedure in numerous cultures across the world is the role of the audience, a group of people entrusted with the task of hearing and then judging the rights and wrongs of a particular case. It is significant that judgement is primarily made on the basis not of written evidence but of oral testimony: the witness has willy-nilly to 'perform' in front of those who stand in judgement. This tradition grants the accused the right to tell his or her own 'story'; the act of judgement is in effect the evaluation of different narratives. But it is not only witnesses who are asked to play this role. Lawyers are often cast in the role of orators who must persuade juries of the merits of a particular story. In the USA, for instance, the metaphors of drama and theatre pervade accounts of legal training: 'Time and again', as one handbook puts it, 'I have told apprentices in my office that the moment they enter the courtroom they are on stage . . . I like to refer them to Act 1, scene ii of *Hamlet* . . .'. In an adversarial system of dispute processing such as that of the USA, trials are often reported in the press as 'duels' between famous lawyers. This tends to encourage a polarization of issues and attitudes around the strategies and techniques of opposing lawyers, sometimes with drastic consequences for an unfortunate defendant. A recent account of a rape trial in Israel shows how the woman involved suffered a total loss of 'face' as she was caught between opposing narratives: the prosecuting lawyer cast her in the role of a Madonna, the defending one in the role of a whore. The performance techniques of the lawyers concerned will be discussed in Chapter 4.

In some cultures the face of disputants is preserved by allowing an element of 'play'. Here the term 'performance' takes on its more limited meaning, which has become conventional in contemporary British culture. One example from the Tiv of Nigeria shows this quite clearly. A man involved in a dispute with another composed a song portraying his adversary as a skunk. He sang and drummed it every night until his opponent was provoked to hire his own song-maker. After three weeks of competitive singing the disputants were summoned to the compound of a tribal leader, who conducted a hearing of both the evidence in the dispute and the songs. In the end one party won the dispute while the other won the song contest. To western eyes this outcome has the advantage of maintaining the face of both disputants.

In other African cultures this performance aspect of dispute processing is expressed not through song but through eloquence – a notion cultivated in many parts of the continent, notably amongst people with no tradition of writing. (This makes non-sense, incidentally, of the notion of the 'untutored' African mentioned in the sermon.) For the Anang of south-east Nigeria – their very name means 'ability to speak wittily yet meaningfully on any occasion' – eloquence is not only something to take great pride in, it is necessary in the conduct of disputes. In Anang traditional 'courts' there are no lawyers, and disputants are each given a turn to represent themselves for as long as they see fit. Trials are valued as performances, with people in attendance listening with concentrated attention and sometimes applauding the contributions of disputants. In presenting their own stories, each disputant makes great use of quotation: not from statute, but from a corpus of utterances which appear to serve a similar function, proverbs. (Proverbs – for Aristotle an 'ancient witness' – were also extensively used in the legal assemblies of ancient Greece.) Audiences at proceedings are particularly appreciative of the introduction of a little-known – even original – proverb at a crucial point in the litigation. Their use is very persuasive: a chronic thief accused of robbery became the object of considerable antagonism when his opponent attacked with: 'If a dog plucks palm fruits from a cluster, he doesn't fear the porcupine.' Oil palm clusters, like porcupines, contain numerous sharp needles; the implication of the proverb is that the thief is so used to stealing that he would think nothing of robbing his neighbour who lived close by. Often such a proverb would be enough to clinch the argument, but in these particular proceedings the defendant parried with the following proverb after the submission of further evidence: 'A single partridge flying through the bush leaves no path.' Partridges usually fly close to the ground in coveys, leaving behind them a trail of bent and broken grass. In using this proverb the defendant compared himself to a lone bird who had no supporters to lend him sympathy. This proverb enabled the accused to construct a narrative in which he, as the central character, was placed in a more favourable light. Although the Anang themselves tend, like us, to claim that their legal system is objective, it is difficult not to conclude that the skilful use of proverbs is very persuasive. In the dispute described above, the accused eventually won the case.

Notes and further reading

Substantial parts of this and the subsequent chapter are based on recent American folklore scholarship, much of which is heavily oriented towards the notion of performance. The St Vincent example is taken from Roger Abrahams in R. Bauman (ed. 1984); the example of Nigerian legal oratory is from Messenger (see A. Dundes ed. 1965). Other valuable collections of articles in this field are Paredes and Bauman (1972) and Ben-Amos and Goldstein (1975). The quotation from Cicero is taken from *De Oratore* (1948, I., p. 142).

American folkloristics has been heavily influenced by perspectives from anthropology, which in turn have underpinned much recent work in the ethnography of communication and sociolinguistics. Saville-Troike (1982) is a useful survey of this work, Bauman and Sherzer (1974) a pioneering collection of articles. Within sociolinguistics Labov's work on oral narrative in Black American culture has been seminal (1972). Subsequent articles by Polanyi (1979, 1982a and b), Robinson (1981) and Wolfson (1982) have enabled us to take a more Rhetorical approach to stories of personal experience. Research on 'speech events' in different cultures has also fed into the study of legal discourse; for an overview see Danet (1980). The Israeli rape-trial example is taken from Liebes-Plesner (1984). For further references to legal discourse see notes to Chapter 4.

The English sermon is reproduced from Crystal and Davy's *Investigating English Style* (1968), one of the first attempts at a linguistic description of spoken as well as written texts. For a 'literary' appreciation of traditional liturgy, on which much of our discussion is based, see Doody (1980). The Black preaching example is taken from Rosenberg (1975), whose study, included in a collection of articles on folklore, argues that Black preaching, like so many so-called oral genres, is 'formulaic' – see notes to Chapter 2. The problem of transcribing a spoken 'text' into writing has been illuminatingly discussed by Ochs (1979). Detailed and sophisticated analyses of the speech/writing relationship are contained in two volumes edited by Tannen (1982,

1984). For discussion of the 'performance text' in folklore see Fine (1984) and Tedlock (1983).

The analysis of the lecture was greatly helped by the work of the American sociologist Goffman (1981). For Goffman and his followers 'society' is something constituted largely by people talking to one another: their work on conversation has become increasingly influential in the branch of linguistics known as discourse analysis (for a useful overview see Coulthard 1985). A more formalistic approach to the lecture is that of Coulthard and Montgomery (1981).

The political speech is an extract taken from the BBC's coverage of the 1979 Conservative Party conference. Our analysis is in large measure a 'reply' to the work of J. M. Atkinson (1984).

Chapter two

Performance II: popular pleasures

FOUR-YEAR-OLD BOY: Dad, when is a bus not a bus?
FATHER: I don't know, when is a bus not a bus?
BOY: When it turns into a street.
FATHER (*and other adults present*): Ha ha.
BOY (*five minutes later, taking his father aside*): Dad, why is that funny?

Certain kinds of utterances, like jokes, are at least *associated* with particular effects on audiences, even if the effect in this case (laughter) could hardly be described as uncontrollable. What the little boy has learned, even before he understands the word-play involved, is the role of joke-teller. The more thoroughly he sees himself as a performer of this role, the more he is likely to seek out jokes and store them in his memory. In this chapter we consider examples of performance – childlore, popular songs, and drama – which, like jokes, are associated with memory, verbal play, pleasure, and the popular: issues which we shall need to examine in turn as the chapter proceeds. The material to be analysed is often classified as being *aesthetic* in function, suggesting the precedence of form over content, delight rather than instruction, feeling rather than cognition, fiction rather than fact. In our view, however, a classification based on this term is misleading. We have already seen the role of aesthetic considerations in our discussion of both sermons and oral narratives; and *all* scripts and texts, moreover, can be viewed as fictions, since they can all be said to be constructed from prior *interpretations* of the universe. Ultimately, the distinctions conventionally drawn between different kinds of 'texts' are not given but are the product of history.

For this reason we have tried to put more emphasis on historical considerations in analysing the examples in this second chapter.

One thing our examples do have in common is the strong emphasis on memory as a condition of performance. We expect actors and singers to 'remember their words', and the idea of delivering a joke with the aid of a written script seems absurd. Memory, you will recall, was one of Cicero's five categories in the training of orators, and it has long been thought that an oration is more effective if delivered from memory. The ancient Rhetoricians accordingly paid much attention to techniques of memorization, and it is arguable that modern psychology, with its distinctions between short- and long-term, conscious versus unconscious memory, has not contributed much more to our understanding of this enigmatic operation of the mind. What seems a certain, and powerful, spur to memory, however, is performance. People who complain about their inability to remember jokes have probably lost sight of this: successful and effective joke-tellers, on the other hand, perceive a potential audience in the material at their command, and try jokes out whenever the opportunity arises. The actual process of memorization, however, can vary according to the kind of material concerned and the context of learning. Childlore and popular songs can be learned almost effortlessly, as can the script of a play if actors absorb it in the course of rehearsal rather than consciously memorize it before rehearsals begin. And the *form* of what is remembered can also vary. In the case of proverbs, for instance, this is usually a fixed sequence of words, permitting no variation; it has often been argued that such formal features as extra regularity and grammatical conciseness are an aid to memory. 'Feed a cold and starve a fever', for instance, has a regular trochaic (stressed followed by unstressed syllable) rhythm, while 'Waste not, want not' combines alliteration of /w/ with condition – if you waste nothing, you'll lack nothing – that is implied rather than foregrounded by the highly economical and patterned syntax. Other proverbs, such as 'A rolling stone gathers no moss' may be memorable for their capacity, through sheer metaphorical concreteness, to suggest a visual image. But very often it is a pattern that we remember, a pattern that consists of relationships rather than specific items. The joking riddle performed by the small boy hinges on the pun on 'turn into'; it still works, however, if 'bus' and 'street' are substituted by other items such as 'car', 'lorry', 'garage', and 'road', etc. Memory, then, is often re-creative, as we saw in the case of the oral narrative: remembered events are shaped and understood by the imposition on them of the patterns of story.

For the joke-teller there is pleasure to be gained from the power to delight an audience, but the patterns of language itself can be a source of pleasure from the earliest stages of our lives. The babbling babies do at around six months may be prompted by the pleasure derived from the sheer exercising of the organs of speech, which, like the muscles of the arms and legs, are there to be wriggled and stretched. This pleasure may in turn be part of a wider pleasure in repetition. It has been argued that the unborn child's perception of the (regular) heartbeat of its mother sets up an expectation of repetition which, when experienced outside the womb, is pleasurable because it is comforting and reassuring. The repetitions of consonant + vowel + consonant sequence – not necessarily those found in the language(s) the child eventually learns to speak – may afford it pleasures that are both auditory and kinaesthetic.

Once the child has learned to speak it does not take long before it finds enjoyment in the patterns of the language(s) it knows. A two-year-old, for instance, is capable of appreciating the rhythmical and phonological repetition of 'oopsy-daisy' (trochaic rhythm, repetition of unstressed final /i/). By about the age of five children are transmitting their own forms which, like 'oopsy-daisy', manipulate the properties of the English sound system without possessing any referential meaning. 'Eeny-meeny-macker-acker-rare-raw-dominacker-shicker-lacker-lolly-popper-om-pom-push' suggests that the child 'knows' that a finite number of sounds can be combined with a much larger number of rules of combination allowing some sequences and not others (even those forms which are not actually English *could* be).

But lore of this kind, which can be called 'gibberish,' is not to be seen merely as evidence of linguistic knowledge. It is also a challenge of performability – of delivery (getting your tongue round the syllables) and memory. And there is also the defiant pleasure derived from transgressing ordinary 'sense', of delivering meaningless sound sequences in such an extended and deliberate fashion.

As suggested in the preceding paragraph, there is a clear

relationship between such lore – anonymous material animated by and for children and probably also authored by them – and the knowledge children have of different levels of linguistic structure. Since children acquire grammatical, phonological, and semantic rules in stages according to age, it is reasonable to assume that the different kinds of childlore are themselves age-graded. A recent study in the USA suggests this to be so. After about the age of seven children's taste is for 'tangle-talk' such as:

> One fine day in the middle of the night
> Two dead men got up to fight.
> Back to back they faced each other
> Drew out swords and shot each other

which suggests the sense of triumph and delight afforded by the recognition that semantically incompatible phrases can be perfectly acceptably joined by means of syntax. By the ages of 11–14 the fashion is for parodies (often lewd) such as

> Tragedy
> When your knickers fall down
> In the middle of town it's
> Tragedy

(based on a Bee Gees' song of the 1970s) and for risqué tongue-twisters like 'I chased a bug around a tree' – to be uttered as speedily as possible. And by this age, too, pre-adolescents are capable of generating lore which exploits the kind of 'perfect pun' found in our 'When is a bus not a bus?' example, in which the syntax works perfectly whatever meaning of 'turn into' is selected. Before this age children generally prefer looser puns of the 'My heart beets for you/With your turnip nose' variety (in which 'beet' is used eccentrically as a verb, and where 'turnip' is only partly homophonous with 'turned up'). Thus our four-year-old joke-teller was delivering a pun well beyond his full linguistic and Rhetorical competence.

We cannot fully understand these Rhetorical skills unless we examine the social functions such lore serves in the life of the child. Childlore is characteristically learned by word-of-mouth from other children, and accordingly offers a role defined not by adults but by the child's own peer group. In this respect it might be more apt to speak not of the child's acquisition of such lore but of childlore actually acquiring him or her. It already exists prior to the child, who plays the roles it offers: she or he may make a contribution, but most of the time is in fact quoting given material (though not necessarily verbatim). At one level, childlore can be seen as a 'reply' to the power that adults wield over children. Thus one of its functions is to explore the boundaries between what adults define as permissible and proscribed behaviour. Saying 'I chased a bug around a tree' as quickly as possible tests the adult taboo on swearing; if reprehended, the child can always blame the utterance. But as is so often the case, such utterances are not only pleasurable but they are also profoundly educative: they allow the child to test out adult roles and norms. Thus if they are defined as 'play', that word is to be understood not in the contemporary 'adult' sense of 'non-serious activity opposed to work' but as conventional and predictable routines, moves, and patterns – a sense we shall need to bear in mind throughout this chapter (cf. also the use of the term 'game').

Childlore is much more, however, than the creation of a world in opposition to that of adults. Children themselves could be said to reproduce the hierarchies and boundaries of social power by operating their own norms and taboos which marginalize cowards, sneaks, children who wear glasses, and so on. Another source of distinction is age. Children are aware that certain kinds of lore are enjoyed by those younger than themselves, and have their own snobbish hierarchies of taste. An item of childlore is therefore never 'merely' verbal play (just as stories are never merely stories): it carries the connotation of a particular age-group. It is instructive to compare how 'fashionable' society in eighteenth-century England attached a social stigma to proverbs: they smacked of sententiousness, preliterate, pre-packaged 'wisdom', obscurity, and perhaps even of popular rather than educated taste.

The final aspect of childlore to be considered here is the patterns involved in their formation. As in the case of the Black sermon discussed in Chapter 1, we can find in childlore the unselfconscious use of a range of devices, known as 'figures', that would be familiar to anyone who has studied the Rhetorical manuals of either the classical or Renaissance worlds. Puns, for instance, can be subsumed under the general figure of *adnominatio*, tangle-talk under *contentio* (the juxtaposition of opposite ideas). In addition we can find examples of *gradatio* (linking repetition of words leading to a climax) as in a rhyme about going downtown to see Mrs Brown:

> She gave me a nickel
> to buy a *pickle*
> The *pickle* was sour
> She gave me a *flower*
> The *flower* was dead
> She gave me a thread

(and so on), *conversio* (repetition of the last word(s) in successive phrases), as in

> I scream
> you scream
> we all scream
> For ice cream,

homoioteleuton (repetition of the last element of a word), as in

> Lift the nozzle
> To your muzzle
> And let it swizzle
> Down your guzzle

and finally *complexio* (repetition of both first and final words in successive phrases) as in

> Are you the guy
> That told the guy
> That I'm the guy
> That gave the guy
> The black eye?

The pleasures to be found in playing with the formal structures of language are not of course confined to childhood. They can persist well into adult life. Certain kinds of slang offer the pleasure of transgressing 'polite' norms by exploiting dysphemism (the opposite of euphemism). To refer to a mouth as a 'cake-hole', for instance, is to draw attention to the physical and functional properties of the mouth as the site of eating. Rhyming slang, such as 'one and t'other' for 'brother', is often used self-consciously as a display of verbal ingenuity. And nicknaming sometimes exploits a delight both in word-play and in interactional competition.

Liverpool dockers traditionally coin nicknames for each other such as 'The Lazy Solicitor' (someone who always sleeps on a case), 'The Destroyer' (someone who's always looking for a sub-(sidy), and 'The Bishop' (someone who always works on Sunday) in this spirit of friendly contest.

The pleasures of form are also a prerequisite for the enjoyment of verse. It is a curious irony that children who display such enthusiasm for their own lore often leave school with a keen dislike of 'poetry'. This may be because schools have tended to downgrade in general what we might call the **ludic** function of language and to treat poems as the highly serious 'messages' (often hidden) of uniquely talented individuals – something we discuss at further length below and in the next chapter.

Songs and singing

The orientation towards poetry referred to in the last paragraph can be described as an orientation towards 'expressive' language. The notion of expressivity, which is often linked to the term 'lyric', assumes that the individual has feelings, imaginings, and drives that can, and perhaps ought to, be externalized through language. It is easy to see how this emphasis tends to overlook, or even repudiate, the notion of audience; writing poems is conceived as an activity for the benefit of the composer rather than the reader or listener, and the address (if indeed the concept arises) is thought of as wholly internal. In literary criticism during the last two hundred years this notion of expressivity has gained ascendancy and it is still dominant in the practice of English teaching in schools. But the notion has been generalized beyond the compositions of poets (and other so-called 'imaginative' writers). In the twentieth century an influential linguistic approach adapted it to specify a particular function of language (for which the term 'emotive' was used). In utterances such as 'What a nice car!' it is alleged that the focus is on the feelings and attitudes of the speaker rather than the referential content: you learn less about the car than about what the speaker thinks of it (see Theoretical postscript).

The notion of expressivity is also often invoked in relation to songs and singing. We all sing to ourselves, and it is widely felt that such singing has a clear therapeutic function. Thus even if (as is likely) we have not ourselves authored the song we sing, we can still animate it as a vehicle for the expression of whatever it is inside us that is struggling to get out. It is the melodic component of song that has often been seen as facilitating this release. Music, it has often been argued, is pure form: its sounds refer to nothing outside themselves. On this view, the words of songs are there to carry the tune, and the appeal of songs is that of sound, in and for itself: something innocent and timeless. It is easy to see how songs learned effortlessly in early childhood, as in childlore, can function in this way. As in childlore again, the referential meaning of the lyrics is less important than the properties of sound; indeed, song lyrics are frequently heard only imperfectly, and the listener reanalyses them, a process often resulting in nonsense. The final two words in 'We three kings of Orient are' might become 'Orientar', as though that were the name of a place. No one seems to bother about such reanalysis because song lyrics, unlike poems in school, are only rarely contemplated and analysed. They appear to be learned and stored beneath the threshold of full consciousness, which is why advertising jingles are so readily and thoroughly assimilated by the (often unwilling) listener. Songs learned so early in life preserve for adults the values they like to project on to childhood, and are often thought to be expressive of innocence, vitality, and sheer *joie de vivre*.

But to make generalizations about songs is both difficult and misleading. Many other kinds of songs actually seem to assert the values of shared rather than personal feeling, the communal and collective experience rather than the individual or unique. This is reflected in the fact that hymns, anthems, and work songs such as sea-shanties are most usually performed not by one singer but by the whole group in unison, and the function of each type is clearly related to the institution of which they form part. The appeal of hymn-singing in church, for instance, is heavily **phatic** (see glossary): it reinforces the sense of belonging to a whole congregation. In fact, it has recently been argued by Booth that the appeal of song in general lies precisely in its capacity to dissolve boundaries, and therefore heal divisions, between an individual and other people, on the one hand, and, on the other, between an individual and the world of 'outer reality' itself. On this rather utopian view, songs, like music, and 'Art' in general for that matter, have the capacity to evoke a world of unity, harmony and timelessness, a world which, like childhood, can only be experienced fleetingly. Songs accordingly have the potential for being popular in the sense derived from the eighteenth-century meaning of 'widely-favoured' – they transcend divisions based on age, gender, and class.

Of course, many of us ascribe to song values that are utopian, particularly to those called 'old songs', which may remain favourites for generations. But the values are not so much in the songs themselves as the contexts in which they are heard and learned. Certain nursery songs, for instance, have been learned in childhood for hundreds of years, allowing us to create around them an idealized past, made more poignant by the feeling – usually mistaken – that like proverbs (and indeed much childlore) they may be on the verge of disappearance. Other songs, particularly pop songs heard in our teens, have the capacity to remind us of highly specific – though in retrospect greatly idealized – moments in our lives. And some songs, in common with certain types of music, may give us the illusion of recalling memories we have never actually possessed. The reasons for such meanings are, however, cultural and historical. It is part of the argument of this book that there are never any 'pure' forms, even though in a given instance the characteristics of particular forms cannot be ignored. The meaning of particular songs in any case has a great deal to do with the traditions from which they stem, and the relationships they hold with other representations of experience, knowledge, and feeling in the culture at a particular time.

Our discussion so far suggests that there is no general principle of address to be associated with song. In singing 'Daisy, Daisy, give me your answer, do' in the bath one part of me appears to be addressing another part; if I sing 'O Jesus I have promised/To serve you to the end' as part of a church service I *appear* to be addressing Jesus (as in the case of many prayers) but my words are better interpreted, perhaps, as a demonstration of solidarity with my co-worshippers. When we turn to more conventional examples of singing as performance, where a singer stands facing an audience, the issue is no more straightforward. The singer does not so much sing *to* an audience as *for* them. This can be illustrated if we turn to our first extended example of a specific singing tradition, that of rock.

Today the term 'popular song' is most likely to evoke that

song tradition historically associated with the rise of the sound-recording industry and generically related to rock and roll. In this context the term 'popular' derives its meaning from its opposition to other terms denoting different musical traditions. Its most obvious **antonym** is 'classical,' a word denoting a canon of 'serious' musical works by named composers which, as part of the general corpus of 'Art', are considered to be worthy of, even demanding, sustained study, and which are thought to be of permanent value. Against this, rock is seen as ephemeral and therefore trivial – in some ways the exact opposite of a meaning of 'popular' noted earlier in this chapter. 'Popular' has now become a term of disapproval, in much the same way as popular literature – science fiction, historical romance, detective stories, and thrillers – is seen as the opposite of the kinds of texts studied in the formal education system. The disapproval is ultimately directed at the audience allegedly interested in such material, one that is assumed to be lazy and susceptible to reassurance and even flattery rather than responding to the discipline of more 'demanding' works. The intended audience of rock is ostensibly 'youth', although its appeal is considerably wider (including people born in the 1940s). But it is youth addressed in the role of consumer. Rock is there to be purchased: its emphemerality is not incidental but constitutive, in that the record industry depends for its commercial survival on the constant production of new material. In some quarters the 'commercial' aspect of such popular forms is held to be a sign of their worthlessness. Work of real value cannot be produced when the aims of the record industry are to make a fast buck: commerce and value are therefore opposed and mutually exclusive.

There is, however, no homogeneous social category of 'youth', and those consumers who are potential candidates for inclusion in this category cannot be lightly dismissed as the passive dupes of a commercialized culture. One effect of rock's ephemerality is that it leaves individual consumers the space to invest a new song with their own personal contextual meanings. We can often remember exactly when and where we first heard a song, and we are likely to attach to it a good deal of nostalgic sentiment. Similarly, the marks of address within the lyrics themselves allow audiences considerable freedom for interpretation. The performance convention in rock and some other genres of pop song is for the singer to utter the second person pronoun 'you' in the course of singing, while facing the audience, as though addressing them directly; but the audience has the scope to interpret that 'you' in at least four different ways. It can refer to an individual specified in the song itself; any singular listener; an individual listener as a member of the larger group who are also addressed; or, fourth, an individual addressee determined by the listeners themselves (where listeners identify with the 'I' of the lyric). In songs sung by women, there is an additional convention that 'you' tends to refer to the first category, although the individual is not specifically *named* in the song. According to Alan Durant, on whose work this account is based, 'the density of second-person pronouns . . . [in rock] . . . appears virtually without parallel in song-forms of any earlier periods . . .' and he goes on to suggest that this helps to account for the effect of immediacy often ascribed to the address of rock.

Another performance convention in rock (and many other genres of song) concerns an aspect of vocal delivery. Falsetto and crooning are two well-known examples, but it has also often been observed that singers generally affect a particular pronunciation in the course of performance. During the 1950s and 1960s, for instance, it was common for British pop singers to adopt American pronunciations from both northern and southern states in a mixture that never occurs in any actual spoken variety. It might be thought that this was an attempt to identify with Americans. In our view, however, an Americanized pop pronunciation is better seen as an assertion of the performer's role, by distancing the singers linguistically from their audience. But it is also a sign that the singer is in effect *quoting*, playing a performance role in accordance with certain traditions of genre. Thus, the singers separate themselves not only from their audiences but also from other traditions of singing dominant at that particular time. Finally, such an accent advertises itself within British culture as in a sense classless. As noted earlier, the 'culture of the voice' within Britain is highly marked, especially within England, and notably within the acting profession, as we shall see.

Our examination of rock has been limited entirely to the verbal aspect of performance, an aspect experienced auditorily and readily available from listening to radio, records, and tapes. Live rock, of course, is as multi-coded as theatrical performances: lighting; dress; make-up; dance; the gesture, movement, and posture of the singer; the instrumental accompaniment and breaks, all contribute to the meaning of the total event. Somewhat paradoxically, technological developments such as television and video, by capturing many of the components of live performance, have restored to audiences the *visual* aspect of singing that used to be a common experience before the invention of sound-recording. A full analysis of rock must of course take account of all those different codes, many of which work simultaneously (and in rather mysterious ways!).

Singing: from 'popular' to 'folk'

Since the Second World War there have been tendencies within popular music to resist what is seen as its commercialized aspect in favour of forms which are 'popular' in a different sense: they are created and disseminated by and for 'the people' themselves. Skiffle in the 1950s and punk in the 1970s have both been seen as reactions against the 'alienating' effects of the recording industry in favour of a more intimate, face-to-face engagement between performer and audience, one that emphasizes not the skill and charisma of the performer but the potential in everyone to make music themselves. Here we begin to see a three-way distinction emerging: 'popular' in this new sense is opposed not to 'classical' but to 'commercial' (professionalized, big business, 'high-tech'). This meaning of 'popular' overlaps with that of another key term, 'folk'. The term 'folk' is often used to denote songs (and other forms such as legends and childlore) created, and above all transmitted, by 'ordinary' people with no interest in personal profit or self-advancement. Indeed, a prerequisite of folk genres is that they are anonymous. Another important ingredient of the definition is that folk materials derive from and are circulated by oral rather than written means. The official, dominant culture is seen as based on literacy; folk culture, by contrast, has often been seen as operating in isolation from (and, by some, in opposition to) the dominant one.

The issue of orality is both highly significant with respect to Rhetoric and extremely problematic. What many discussions of folk song seem to have done is invert the speech/writing hierarchy discussed in the last chapter. Orality has been seen as the guarantee of a song's 'authenticity' as folk culture. Writing, especially print, has been seen as a source of contamination because of its stabilizing and fixing influence on the ever-changing forms of folk. These are never fixed, and are supposed to change with every performance (even in that of an individual singer). Discussions of folk song traditionally use the metaphor of the biological organism to explain its characteristics: like a healthy plant, folk song grows, flowers, and reseeds itself through time and space, and the guarantor of the whole process is orality.

In part this attitude to the oral versus the written can be traced back to debates among the early Greek philosophers like Plato. At that time the invention of literacy was still recent enough for people to argue about its possible advantages and disadvantages. While some claimed that writing was a useful *aide-mémoire* others feared that it would eventually replace memory altogether. It is this latter argument that appears, consciously or unconsciously, to have influenced the attitude of many folklorists towards folk songs. One claim often made about 'authentic' singers of folk song is that they have such prodigious memories that a song can be learned and reproduced after only one hearing. Such feats are explained by the claim that the speakers' memory is re-creative: he or she does not memorize words verbatim, but stores patterns and structures that allow the song to be changed in the course of a performance. One example of such a pattern is the formula, a stereotyped sequence of words, fixed to a certain extent, which is used regularly and predictably in performance. Careful examination of contemporary Yugoslav oral epics shows that their length varies enormously from one performance to the next; what remains constant, however, is the use of the same formulas. This observation was used to explain the characteristics of Homer's epics *The Odyssey* and *The Iliad*. Both are of great length (and therefore, according to the theory, incapable of being memorized verbatim) and are packed with formulas (where the sea is mentioned, for instance, it is regularly referred to as 'wine-coloured').

A major problem with the opposition of orality versus literacy is that it is so often seen as timeless and universal. We have only to look at the history of the words 'popular' and 'folk' to see how their meanings are part of debates held in specific historical circumstances. A key concept in the history of both has been tradition, in turn linked in various ways with the impulses of nationalism. 'Folk' is a nineteenth-century term imbued with the mystical notion that the 'essence' of a nation lies in the traditions of its 'common people'. 'Traditions' are practices that link us to the past; those of the common people are preserved in unbroken continuity not in books but in memory and custom, and are therefore key elements in the history of a nation. In the nineteenth century such traditions were known as 'folklore'; before then, as 'popular antiquities', a term suggesting that they, like ancient earth-works, were in danger of crumbling away and being lost forever under the tide of economic change, literacy, education, and fashion. But it is precisely those people identified with such forces who constructed the notion of folklore in the first place; attitudes towards it are accordingly complex and even contradictory. Most usually associated with the common people not of the city but of the countryside (often inappropriately termed 'peasants'), folklore is sometimes seen as innocent in relation to the 'corrupt' world of urban fashion, and in certain historical periods this innocence is conflated with childhood, a world which adults have lost but are always struggling to relive. But wherever, on the other hand, folklore is considered irrelevant or even pernicious, it tends to be associated with women. An explanation or remedy felt to be ineffective came to be known as an 'old wives' tale'; a practice felt to be threatening to established order could be seen as witchcraft (the image of a witch is invariably female).

Many of these points may be usefully explored by examining the concept of popular song during the Tudor period. At this time the cultivation of nationalist sentiment was a political necessity, since the monarchy needed to justify religious autonomy and its aggressive policies towards peoples such as the Irish. The observations of antiquarians could therefore be used as evidence for the distinctiveness of England's past. In this period also the meaning of popular song had its own particular inflection. The distinction made today between poetry and song was not drawn so sharply; many songs, moreover, were composed in response to religious or dynastic controversies and could therefore be used, as in many African cultures today, to censure groups and individuals. In their turn the songs themselves were often censored. We can also see that writing, far from being the guarantor of permanence, was at this time the facilitator of ephemera. In cities like London the early printing presses, like the record industry today, depended on the constant production of ephemera for their commercial survival. One example of such ephemera was song-texts, printed on a single sheet of paper and known as broadsides, which were sold cheaply in hundreds of thousands. Presumably the people who bought them could read, but they could also be enjoyed by those who couldn't, since the purchaser could always sing them to family, friends, and workmates (usually the name of a well-known tune was included on the broadside). In the ceaseless demand for songs to print, known writers came to write 'novel' songs about such things as sensational monster whales, giving the purchasers a brief moment of glory as the temporary 'authors' of a song with which to entertain and amaze their peers. But the broadside press did not deal only with 'the latest'. It managed to fuse the 'new' with the familiar by printing fresh words to tunes already known. An immediately singable text was shrewd marketing before the advent of mass sound-production. And the presses also published songs of unknown authorship, many of which may already have been favourites in the countryside as well as the towns. Again this was good commerce, since it may have provided buyers with a sense of stability and continuity in the increasingly competitive and individualistic environment of the city.

The 'popular', then, like 'youth', cannot be seen as a given category, a taste already existing, but rather as the product of a relationship between composers, disseminators, and recipients at a particular time and place. The term takes on additional meanings when, during the course of the eighteenth century in particular, there was a trend towards publishing collections of songs in book form. Such collections were in many cases made by men from provincial artisan or lower-middle-class backgrounds who wanted recognition from influential sections of London society. They often contributed to nationalist sentiment: already in Charles I's reign a book of English songs had been used to counter that monarch's predilection for Italian music. By the eighteenth century, however, it was in Scotland that the clearest association between songs and nationhood was being made. The Act of Union (with England) in 1707 stimulated the collection of Scottish songs which in turn became fashionable in London 'society'.

In what was effectively an appropriation of the notion of popular song to serve particular cultural interests the eighteenth-century collectors often republished the anonymous broadside texts of their own and earlier periods. In doing so they paid scant regard to the integrity of the texts (as we would put it today). This was not because they saw them as oral (and therefore fluid in form) but because they were not regarded as anybody's property: they were not the products of Great Authors. In fact, one writer of the Jacobean period, Ben Jonson, maintained that to be great an author had to avoid 'popularity' at all costs, and strive to be read by academics and gentry alone. In his view Shakespeare was a hack, since he wrote for the popular stage, a process that did not include producing a fixed text for publication (in fact publication of Shakespeare's plays was eschewed in order to prevent rival companies from performing them). Increasingly, the 'market' for the authored and published text was the practitioners of the gradually crystallizing institutions of literary criticism, the origins of which lay with the coffee-house culture of the early eighteenth-century bourgeoisie. One of its central tenets was the cultivation of 'correct' literary taste; the compilers of song-books therefore felt under pressure not to offend this precious commodity, and accordingly often rewrote the song lyrics. In effect, the lyrics increasingly came to be regarded as a kind of literature, to be judged by literary standards.

These standards were generous enough, however, to welcome the publication in 1765 of Thomas Percy's *Reliques of Ancient English Poetry*, a collection of old broadsides and other sundry material. The appeal of this to both literary and antiquarian interests (the two often overlapped) was such that by 1794 it had run to its fourth edition and was to inspire a whole generation of poets who came to be called the Romantics. The *Reliques* contained verse of the kind increasingly termed 'ballads' in the course of the eighteenth century. Although the term had before this time, and continues to have, a wider meaning, the poet Shenstone's distinction between 'ballad' as a term denoting action, and 'song' as the expression of sentiment became increasingly influential. Ballads, according to this literary definition, were versified narratives, capable of being sung, possibly aristocratic in origin, transmitted in the Middle Ages by 'minstrels', but by the eighteenth century preserved largely by the 'common people'. Percy's *Reliques* inspired a number of other song collections, notably in Scotland; and by the end of the nineteenth century ballads had become the object of academic study. The American scholar F. J. Child produced what came to be regarded as the sacred text of ballad scholarship, *The English and Scottish Popular Ballads*, and in the USA at least ballads could be included in the study of literature (whereas in England their position relative to other literary genres remains less secure).

The appropriation of ballads by the institutions of literary criticism has generated some rather sterile quests for the origins of particular versions, for evidence of their 'authenticity' (Child distinguished between the ballad of tradition and that of the broadside 'hack') or of oral rather than literate transmission. Other studies have sought to establish the status of the ballad relative to other genres (is it narrative, dramatic, or lyric?) and to decide whether ballads have a distinctive 'poetic' language. Many of these concerns were shared by early folklorists and collectors whose primary concern was the rescuing of 'texts' before they died out. Modern folklorists in the USA, however, have reacted against these concerns by shifting the emphasis towards the singers themselves rather than the songs. Increasingly the emphasis has been on performance rather than text. Studying the repertoires and singing styles of particular singers reveals the inadequacy of previous characterizations of 'folk'. Modern singers often keep scrapbooks with the words of their songs, their repertoires are much more varied than folklorists might wish, their song categories are not necessarily those of the scholar, and delivery features are highly variable, suggesting that there is no single singing style that can be called traditional. In short, 'folk' turns out to be as problematic a category as 'youth' and 'popular'.

Certain regional, social, and cultural groupings, however, may have distinctive singing styles. The non-verbal aspects of delivery – posture, gesture, face – are often noteworthy. The tinkers (or, as they prefer to be called, the travellers) of different parts of the British Isles adopt a stiff posture while singing, with their heads thrown back. In fact, an impassive, static bearing with eyes closed and a hand cupped behind the ear became something of a stereotype of the 'traditional' singer during the folk song revival of the late 1950s and 1960s. In England, however, this model seems never to have been universally adopted, many local singers preferring a far more 'kinetic' delivery with what might be called a button-holing stance towards the audience. At the verbal level there are some interesting **phonological** features to note. In parts of Ireland, for instance, singers often intrude a **nasal consonant** /n/ before the final **plosive** in words like 'red'. A general feature of singing pronunciation that has often been observed is that singers whose customary speech is dialectal tend to adopt a more **RP** (received pronunciation)-influenced accent when singing. On the other hand, younger aficionados of the folk revival, often from middle-class backgrounds, affect a kind of 'mummerset' accent – nasalized, **rhotic** (see glossary), with a general tendency towards the rounding of vowels – when singing. Like the Americanized accents of some British pop singers this is not localizable but appears to be based on a selection of features associated perhaps with a non-metropolitan or rural environment.

The emphasis on singers rather than texts enables us to contextualize the learning of songs and the meanings they might have for individual singers. For Jeannie Robertson, a traveller from the north-east of Scotland, the ballads were the 'auld songs' sung among the travellers at night on the road (in contradistinction to the songs preferred by the younger generation). They were moreover the songs she learned as a child, listening to her mother singing her to sleep as she worried about her husband and two sons fighting in the First World War. They had appealing stories and fine tunes, and many referred to places she actually knew as a traveller along the byways of Aberdeenshire and Perthshire. All these considerations contributed to the meanings the songs had for her. But those meanings were not static. As her audience widened beyond the circle of travellers to the audience at university folk clubs, and, eventually, the international audience for 'serious' traditional singing, her perception of herself as a singer began to change. As in some sense a 'star' performer she came to identify herself more and more with particular songs, such as 'My Son David', a version of the ballad most commonly known as 'Edward'. Her delivery of that song changed accordingly: with the winning of international acclaim her delivery slowed, and the tune became more decorated.

The shift in focus from song to singer is the reverse of a movement in literary criticism that occurred in the course of the present century, when the post-Romantic emphasis on the artist was challenged by attempts to concentrate on 'the text' as something in its own right. Whereas in literary criticism there has since been a resurrection of interest in the role of readers, the emphasis on performance in folklore study tends to remain expressivist rather than audience-centred. The singers may be animators rather than authors, but the focus is on the relationship between them and their songs rather than their negotiation with audiences. But the neglect of the audience was also an inevitable corollary of the early collectors' supreme indifference towards the singers. What mattered was getting the song down on paper: in effect the audience was the actual collector who either hurriedly tried to write down words (and tunes, if he or she was interested), sometimes stopping the singer in mid-song to allow this, or who sat beside a microphone. Many versions of songs in the collections must therefore be transcriptions of semi- rather than full performance. In some cultures, however, it has been possible to study the immediate effects on a performance brought about by a change in audience. The performance in Turkey, in the 1960s, of a *hikaye* – a narrative in both verse and prose animated by a professional accompanying himself on a stringed instrument called a *saz* – was considerably longer, more formulaic, more obscene, and more self-referential before the customary audience in the local coffee bar than before a professional middle-class audience at the Teachers Union Hall. At the latter venue the singer's introductory formula, which contained the words 'I smoke the best cigarettes. Of course I can smoke them only if you provide them. However, I don't mind if you don't; I'll just give them up' brought no response, whereas the audience in the coffee bar – farmers, woodcutters, small shop-owners and their apprentices – immediately offered cigarettes. In general, coffee bar performances are much more interactive, partly because the minstrel gets to know his audience (who come there also just to drink with their friends and listen to the radio news). He varies his performances accordingly: songs celebrating religious and moral conduct are included for the benefit of older listeners, love songs for the young; he even shifts to songs of sorrow specifically for the benefit of one listener – whose unfortunate circumstances were known to all – as soon as the latter entered the coffee bar.

We lack the evidence for a similar approach to an example of British song, but what we can try to do is contextualize one performance and suggest a Rhetorical analysis centring on the notion of the song's address. The example we shall analyse is a song conventionally known as a ballad called *Lord Gregory*.

Below is a transcript of a taped performance by an elderly woman, Elizabeth Cronin, a country farm housewife of County Cork, Ireland, in 1952. The recording, widely regarded as one of the finest contemporary examples available, was undertaken by a professional folklorist who was himself also a piper, singer, and storyteller of great virtuosity. As has so often been the case, the 'audience' for the singer in this instance was someone primarily interested in *preserving* the particular variant of the ballad being performed; in this case, however, the singer seems not to have been adversely affected by this constraint. For Elizabeth Cronin was an informant not untypical of contemporary 'bearers of tradition', the kind of amateur antiquarian so much at odds with the traditional notion of the unlettered peasant. As the widow of a schoolmaster and locally regarded as an expert on the Gaelic dialect of her area, with an extensive repertoire of songs in both English and Gaelic, Elizabeth Cronin clearly shared the folkloristic expectations brought to the recording session by the collector: she self-consciously played the role of tradition-bearer as well as performer.

The ballad, which is of the kind often described as traditional, has been circulating since at least the middle of the eighteenth century, and variants have been recorded in Scotland and North America, as well as Ireland, as recently as the 1950s. Two famous versions associated with the eighteenth-century Scotswoman Anna Brown – the daughter of a professor – have recently been used as evidence in support of the oral-formulaic theory of ballad composition. What is more likely, however, is that certain versions of the ballad crystallized into more or less fixed form and were memorized by singers loosely rather than verbatim. Cronin's version is very close to one collected in the same year from a singer in Glasgow and to one collected from an anonymous labourer in Meath, Ireland, during the 1840s. Behind all three is perhaps a broadside version of the mid-eighteenth century called *The Lass of Aughrim*, which seems to be the oldest version in existence. Whether or not the broadsides were in turn based on orally-created and transmitted versions can only be speculated on: what cannot be denied is the role of printed versions in the circulation of this particular ballad (a process probably very common in the transmission of songs generally). The role of broadsides in Irish tradition is at any rate very well established; Irish travellers were hawking them in towns as late as the 1950s. Thus it seems in general rather fruitless to try to pursue the notion of the ballad's 'authenticity', the extent to which it is the product of either tradition or commerce.

Lord Gregory

1 I am a king's daughter
That strayed from Cappoquin
In search of Lord Gregory
May God I'll find him

2 The rain beats at my yellow locks
And the dew wets me still
The babe is cold in my arms
Lord Gregory let me in

3 Lord Gregory is not here
And as full can be seen
He is gone to bonny Scotland
To bring home his new queen

4 Leave now those windows
And likewise this hall
For it's deep in the sea
You should hide your downfall

5 Who'll shoe my babe's little feet
Who'll put gloves on her hand
And who'll tie my babe's middle
With a long and green band?

6 Who'll comb my babe's yellow locks
With an ivory comb
And who'll be my babe's father
Till Lord Gregory comes home?

7 I'll shoe your babe's little feet
I'll put gloves on her hand
And I'll tie your babe's middle
With a long and green band

8 I'll comb your babe's yellow locks
With an ivory comb

And I'll be your babe's father
Till Lord Gregory comes home

9   Leave now those windows . . . etc.

10 Do you remember Lord Gregory
That night in Cappoquin
When we both 'changed pocket handkerchiefs
And that against my will?

11 For yours was pure linen, love
And mine was coarse cloth
Yours cost one guinea, love
And mine but one groat

12 Leave now . . . etc.

13 Do you remember Lord Gregory
That night in Cappoquin
We both 'changed rings off our fingers
And that against my will?

14 For yours was pure silver, love
And mine was black tin
Yours cost twelve guineas, love
And mine but one cent

15 Leave now . . . etc.

16 Do you remember Lord Gregory
That night in my father's hall
When you stole away my fond heart
And that was worse than all?

17 Leave now . . . etc.

18 My curse on you, mother,
And my curse it be sore
I dreamt the Lass of Orms
Came rapping to my door

19 Lie down, you foolish son
Ah, lie down and sleep
For 'tis long ago her weary locks
Are waving on the deep

20 Come saddle me the black horse
    The brown or the bay
    Come saddle me the best horse
    In my stable this day

21 I'll range over valleys
    And o'er mountains alway
    Till I find the Lass of Orms
    And I lie by her side.

The pronouns in the song suggest relationships between singer, audience, and song that are different from those discussed above in relation to rock lyrics. The question in stanza five, 'Who'll shoe my babe's little feet . . . ?' appears to be answered in stanza seven by a different voice: yet another voice seems to be heard in stanza 18, since it is referred to in the next stanza as a male one. All the stanzas in fact are speech, and appear to be split between three characters: a woman made pregnant by Lord Gregory, Gregory himself, and the latter's mother (who in stanzas seven and eight appears to be masquerading as a man – perhaps Lord Gregory himself). We say 'appear' because the speeches are untagged – unlike those in the narrative of personal experience, not attributed to particular speakers – and there is no attempt to differentiate utterances to suit the different protagonists. Nor does the singer attempt to 'act out' the different parts: each stanza is sung in much the same impassive delivery, the melody repeated, in canonical ballad style, from stanza to stanza.

The identity of the protagonists does however seem to be sig-nalled by the stanzaic groupings. Throughout the first seventeen stanzas there is a clear pattern of alternation based first on paired stanzas, then (after stanza 8) paired stanzas followed by the single 'Leave now those windows . . .' stanza which acts as a kind of refrain. At many points the action performed by the utterances seems clear: the lass pleads to be let in (presumably she is shut outside Gregory's dwelling), she is rebuffed by – presumably – Gregory's mother, Gregory curses his mother for not telling him what has been happening, and vows to find his love. As such the ballad consists of a succession of **speech acts**, at the centre of which is a sequence of plea/refusal. The 'Do you remember' stanzas suggest that the lass has decided that Gregory is actually at home, despite the assurance in stanza three that he is not, and that she thinks she is addressing him – perhaps challenging him to remember her and come to her aid. The ritualistic response 'Leave now those windows . . .' lends the situation the quality of a nightmare. Equally nightmarish is the sense that the lass may not be able to *see* her addressee: she can only reveal her plight by speaking.

So far, however, we have made two assumptions about our example. First, we have assumed that the 'voices' do actually belong to people conversing with each other. Stanzas 10 to 16 however could be said to test this assumption: the lass could be speaking in a kind of despairing apostrophe, flinging her words at the intractable home of her lover, and receiving in reply the changeless, echoing 'Leave now those windows . . .'. One of the interesting characteristics of ballad dialogue in general is its flexibility: the same words can be used by different protagonists to accomplish different ends. The second assumption is that the utterances actually *narrate* something. We do appear to see a shift in time involving two scenes: the first where the lass addresses someone, the second where the son addresses his mother, vowing to do something as a result of what has happened in the first scene. The ballad narrates much as drama does: rather than positing a beginning, middle and end, it presents a succession of speech acts which in themselves constitute a scenic development. But there is a kind of pattern to the events, minimal as they are, which Rhetoricians call 'chiasmus'. The ballad starts with the king's daughter hoping to find Lord Gregory; it ends with Gregory himself vowing to find her. In between, first the lass, then Gregory are rebuffed by a woman who we can now infer is Gregory's mother. She acts as a pivot to the narrative, keeping the two lovers apart.

It can now be appreciated that as far as this particular version is concerned, the attempt to fit it into just one of the categories narrative, dramatic or lyric seems mistaken. The fact that the ballad is sung, and that much of it seems to be the expression of the lass's feelings, might incline us towards lyric; but the emphasis on a small number of scenes, together with the absence of a narrating voice, might incline us towards drama. Particularly relevant in this respect is the fact that although the twenty-odd recorded versions of the ballad vary considerably, almost all contain a stanza in which the lass begs to be let into Gregory's house (often a castle). Stanza 2 of Cronin's version, verbally very close to the corresponding one in at least three other versions, provides the pattern. Even where the precise wording may vary, the essential structure – a plea, often accompanied by a justification (it is wet and cold, and the baby is exposed) – is usually preserved. This suggests that the *idea* in the stanza is particularly memorable. What matters is the situational meaning rather than a precise form of words. That situation is affecting, and part of its power may be that it enables both singer and audience to visualize it.

A great deal of ballad scholarship has concentrated on the issue of memory and the means of ballad transmission. Central to much of it has been the rather deterministic notion that ballads are structured the way they are to enable singers to remember them. Thus in our particular example the patterns of repetition, opposition, parallelism and question-and-answer sequences would be seen as mnemonic devices. Examples are the reiterated 'Who will . . . ?' and 'Do you remember . . . ?', 'For yours was . . .' and 'For mine was . . . ', and so on. A similar view would be taken of the formulaic diction: in ballads, the female's hair is invariably yellow, for instance, and the use of a whole stanza such as 'Come saddle me the black horse . . .' (often used in ballads where a protagonist has to make a swift journey of rescue or revenge) would be seen as easing the singer's burden by effectively composing the ballad for her. But such patterns – which would be called 'schemes' by a Rhetorician – can also be analysed as constituting a distinctive mode of address. Like the repetitions in the Black sermon discussed in Chapter 1, the schemes enable the audience to participate by allowing them to predict the completion of a pattern. If, moreover, these devices are familiar to them, an audience may derive pleasure from that process of recognition. Against this, however, may be set the stringent demands placed on the audience's ability to comprehend the ballad as a narrative: there are an enormous number of gaps to be filled in. Thus, the ballad may be said to activate two different kinds of pleasure: that of familiarity and reassurance (what Barthes calls *plaisir*) and that of crisis – the audience has to struggle to make connections between voices and events (what Barthes calls *jouissance*).

Real audiences at different times and in different places will of course bring varying sets of expectations to their experience of the ballad. Audiences in Ireland during the last two hundred or so years may have been familiar, or half-familiar, with the story of the ballad and may therefore have been able to draw on knowledge no longer widely available. Modern *readers* of the ballad, on the other hand, may be likely to speculate on the significance of Cappoquin and the identity of Orms, since once the ballad has been transcribed and arranged in stanzas we tend to see it as a poem, and judge it in accordance with the dominant assertion of poetry criticism that every word counts. Thus there is no single meaning of the ballad, nor is there any court of appeal to which we can turn if we want to find one. Part of the ballad's interest, however, may have remained constant throughout its history: the image of the excluded, rejected woman will always evoke powerful feelings as long as social relations continue to be based on patriarchy.

Acting and the playscript

With the opportunities afforded by the pop music industry, success, even stardom, for the singer is more likely to occur without training than is the case for the actor. Training for acting, however, tends to be geared more towards the theatre than towards cinema or television, where many of the job opportunities lie. And within that training it is the verbal and vocal components of delivery, rather than the gestural or facial, that tend to be highlighted. 'Actor-like' signifies a cultivation of the voice, a legacy of performance in large auditoria where projection was vital, but which today is more of a mannerism than a necessity. Accent is an important aspect of the actor's voice: the norm for 'serious' roles, particularly in Shakespeare, has traditionally been RP, stamping the British acting tradition with the inevitable imprint of social class. But actors will also have distinctive variants of RP, such as the open, 'north-country' pronunciation of /æ/ as [a] in words like 'hat' and 'man', and a **palatalized** form of /s/ in e.g. 'sing' and 'sip', where the sound approximates to the /ʃ/ of 'ship'.

Another aspect of the dominant tradition in theatre is the emphasis on what can loosely, and somewhat problematically, be called naturalism. At one level naturalistic theatre will use scenery and costume appropriate to the setting of the play being performed: thus a play set in a late nineteenth-century, middle-class London home will have scenery painted to look like one, and use costumes like those worn in that period. Naturalistic language, generally speaking, will strive to represent some of the character-istics of conversation, presenting the illusion that the play's charac-ters are talking to each other and the audience is merely 'overhear-ing' them. The language of individual characters will also be delivered, and perhaps marked by the playwright, in such a way that it seems appropriate to the social backgrounds of the charac-ters (e.g. the use of regional and class accents) and their personal histories. It should be clear from this that underlying these conven-tions is a view of character that has already been discussed in Chapter 1. Naturalistic drama tends to be character-centred, pre-senting character as the source of action: we do what we do, in other words, because of what we are. And the essence of natural-istic acting is to present the illusion of not really acting at all. We assimilate the actor totally to the character; we lose sight of technique, and see all the aspects of acting as properties of the character rather than of the performer.

Naturalistic conventions in effect try to persuade audiences that they are watching a slice of 'real life'. Our exposure to these conventions will be very extensive if we regularly watch certain types of television serial, in particular police series like *Z Cars*, *The Sweeney* and *Hill Street Blues*, and 'soap operas' such as *Coronation Street*, *Eastenders* and *Brookside*. But the considerable differences between these examples should alert us to the diffi-culty, and ultimately the absurdity, of judging artistic represen-tations as accurate reflections of reality. For one thing, scripted dialogue is always *triadic* in nature, whereas conversation need not be: the words characters utter to each other are also addressed to a third party, the audience. Scripted dialogue has to make explicit a variety of information that need never be expressed in conversation. Second, there is a contradiction in practice between the artistic demands of naturalism and the convention of using well-known 'stars' to perform naturalistic roles. Stars are, by defi-nition, highly visible when they are away from the screen, by means of such agencies of display as chat-shows, feature articles in magazines, presentation galas, and the like. Their mannerisms, voices and gestures will be known to us, making it difficult for us to identify them completely with the character they play. Finally, our view of what constitutes an accurate reflection of reality tends to change with every new programme that we feel makes this claim. Any representation has to make a selection of features attributed to reality: thus, during the early 1960s, *Z Cars* seemed more real than its predecessors like *Dixon of Dock Green* partly because it selected different and less flattering aspects of the policeman's role. Beside *Hill Street Blues*, however, with its over-lapping dialogues, inaudible speech, and moving camera, *Z Cars* might seem stylized and unconvincing, with its carefully scripted talk. In the final analysis we tend to judge representations of reality, and even reality itself, against other representations rather than against our own personal encounter with the 'real'. Neither the camera eye nor the human eye can see the world innocently 'as it is'; both see from within a frame, one that is physical, psychological, linguistic, social and historical.

There are, of course, theatrical conventions which do not share, or are actively opposed to, the canons of naturalism outlined above. The Brechtian tradition, for instance, doesn't seek to con-vince audiences of the credibility of characters so much as make the concept of character itself problematic. Rather than attempt to play characters naturalistically the Brechtian performer draws attention to the act of performance by means of clearly stylized gestures and detached delivery: the audience is asked not to admire the spectacle or lose themselves in it, but actively to con-sider it. Other traditions emphasize posture, gesture, and move-ment at the expense of words; some dispense with the verbal element altogether. Thus, at any one historical moment there may be competing traditions, each of which is based on a series of assumptions about character, language, and the relation of both to reality and to the audience. Sometimes changes in tradition are brought about by developments in technology: film and television, for instance, require that the face signify more than the voice, and actors need not only to develop technique in this area but to learn how to act in front of an imaginary audience, all of whom will see exactly the same camera image (for this reason many prefer to work in the theatre in front of a real audience when they can). But changes also stem from developments in scriptwrit-ing. The so-called 'Method' style of acting was a response to the demands made on actors by the plays of Chekhov: once hailed as the epitome of naturalism, it has since become, particularly in the performances of Marlon Brando, something of a cliché.

Shakespeare's plays provide us with a well-known and instruc-tive example of a change in theatrical conventions. So grounded are we in the naturalistic tradition, however, that we often tend to 'explain' certain of Shakespeare's conventions in inappropriate ways. Thus, the fact that Shakespeare's theatre functioned largely without the use of costume and scenery (as we think of them today) we are apt to see as a terrible disadvantage, and 'explain' the 'wordiness' of his plays by arguing that the playwright had to find some way of compensating for this lack. But Shakespeare's theatre was in general a highly verbal one, including a complex range of utterance types, such as the aside, the soliloquy and the apostrophe, which pose problems for those with naturalistic expectations. In all probability it was also a theatre of gesture. Renaissance training manuals suggest that gestures, particularly those of the hands, were highly codified, so that emotions like anger, despair, and scorn could be depicted in ways that were clearly externalized: a turn of the hand, a stamp of the foot, beating the breast, frowning, staring eyes. Thus the multi-codedness of dramatic performance was exemplified through the use of a different combination of theatrical codes than those activated in the naturalistic tradition. And, as is well known, it was also a male tradition; female parts were played by boys, partly because the social position of the actor was held to be dubious, at least in some influential quarters.

Playing Shakespeare obviously presents a number of challenges to contemporary performers and their audiences. One of the most important of these is that over the last two hundred or so years the plays have become texts, objects to be analysed, contemplated, interpreted, and argued about. Large sections of the modern audience will therefore have studied them, and some speeches – notably soliloquies, which have often been anthologized as though they were poems – will have been memorized as thoroughly by them as by the actor. The modern performer must therefore strive to 'coin' a speech – present it almost as though it were being heard for the first time by Shakespeare's own audience. Such an act of re-creation is of course in practice impossible, since the various kinds of audiences that packed performances in Elizabethan England would have had different knowledges, assumptions and probably interests from those of today. One aspect of this would have been their experience of theatrical traditions – associated with mystery, morality and mumming plays – which were different from the 'classical' models of tragedy and comedy known to Shakespearean scholarship. In a study by Weimann these traditions are termed 'popular', a word which has thus a particular inflection in relation to Shakespeare's plays. In the popular tradition it is not the fictive setting of the play but the actual theatrical event – the act of performance – that constitutes the drama. One of its most salient features is the manipulation of space so that few barriers exist between actors and audience. A key role is that of the Clown or Fool, who occupies a downstage position close to the audience and shares with them a common language – full of proverbs and word play. He acts as a bridge between the world of the play and that of the audience by commenting directly on both, and in so doing he often invokes the principle of inversion, turning the given world upside-down by decrying the high-born and lauding the low. The most famous Elizabethan clown, Dick Tarlton, was renowned for his ability to sing extempore on any themes given to him by the audience, and for his love of parodying legal and religious ceremonies. It was Tarlton's pupils who were to play the role of Fool in Shakespeare's own plays.

The Elizabethan audience, however, has often been disparaged by subsequent scholarship: assumed too fidgety to sit through three hours of *Hamlet* (the play must therefore have been cut in performance, so the argument goes) and to be in constant need of bawdry (any puzzling feature in a play can be explained away as a titbit for the 'groundlings' whose point is now lost on us). For some, Shakespeare has always been too good for his audiences, the plays always sullied by the transition from page to stage.

Shakespeare's plays continue to generate inexhaustible layers of meaning for different audiences (including readerships), not least because they have achieved the status of the quasi-sacred text: see Chapter 4. For the performer, however, the play is pre-eminently still a script; something to be worked from, a point of departure. Today he or she cannot ignore the weight of Shakespearean scholarship, but will also be guided by a director whose job it is to choose from the available possibilities of interpretation. In Shakespeare's own time however, players did not have directors in the modern sense, and actors worked from a script much more provisional than the edited and amended text we know today. It is arguable that in Shakespeare's own time the playscript itself contained implicit directions to actors. The switches between verse and prose, and between the two forms of second-person pronoun 'thou' and 'you', may be interpreted as signals for a change in delivery (for instance, in degree of emotional intensity); a high density of monosyllables may have suggested slower delivery, rhythmic departure from the dominant iambic metre, perhaps extra assertiveness. These signals alert actors to possible sources of meaning within the plays, but are also useful as aids to memory by helping to break up the script into manageable units.

We can illustrate some of the difficulties encountered by the modern actor by considering just the two famous opening lines of *Richard III* (a play which, incidentally, is noted for the self-conscious Rhetoric of its speeches). As in so many of the so-called history plays, the opening is 'prospective' in that it points forward to the ensuing events. Its overt address to the audience and the sheer weight of linguistic patterning make a 'naturalistic' rendition extremely difficult: in fact, the lines could be described as 'unsayable' within this perspective:

> Now is the winter of our discontent
> Made glorious summer by this son of York.

Underlying these lines are a series of propositions: we have been discontented; our discontentment is now over; the Yorkists are ascendant. Linking them is the (implicit) proposition that the speaker is himself a Yorkist. The lines themselves generate a rich range of meaning beyond this by means of deixis, metaphor, and verbal parallelism. 'Now' and 'this' are deictic, firmly rooting the words to the act of utterance ('now' refers to the particular moment of Yorkist ascendancy in the triumphant figure of Edward IV; 'this', referring to the king, suggests some pointing gesture to accompany it). The speaker is therefore both part of the play's action and also (temporarily) outside it, sharing directly with the audience his perception and interpretation of the events: both 'now' and 'this' accordingly need to be highlighted in the course of delivery. The speaker's voice must also use **intonation** to foreground some units of information rather than others, such as information that is new to the audience as distinct from information that is assumed or already given. On the face of it the choice seems automatic: it is the 'son of York' that is bringing about the change, so this phrase must carry the **nucleus**. But 'the winter of our discontent', which is closely parallel in structure, cannot be uttered as though it were merely given. The actor cannot assume the audience to know it already: moreover, the metaphor 'winter' needs highlighting to point the connection with 'summer' in the next line. (There is extra danger for the modern actor here: 'winter of discontent' has become since Shakespeare's time a semi-proverbial quotation, requiring that the actor take care to 'coin' it as if it were an inventive metaphor). 'Son' also needs highlighting to point the pun on 'sun' (which in turn connects with summer; Edward IV also used the sun as an emblem). But 'York' is also important information, since it is opposed to Lancaster, the rival dynasty. Virtually every word, therefore, deserves to be 'played with' by the actor, not only because he is informing the audience of something, but also because of the relationships between the words themselves. In short the actor must draw attention to the language itself, and in so doing create a particular *role* for Richard – that of the self-conscious manipulator of words (and, by extension, of people).

Such verbal display constructs Richard not so much as a character as a *dramatis persona*, in this case that of Vice, a role consciously adopted. It is in many of the comedies that we find a similar perspective on language and character especially rewarding. In one sense the comedies seem to be more about language itself than about either (non-verbal) deeds or character. They abound in the kinds of verbal games common in childlore and in the ludic displays of language discussed elsewhere in this book. In *The Taming of the Shrew*, for instance, Katharina and Petruchio vilify each other in sequences like this:

KATHARINA: Let him that mov'd you hither
Remove you hence. I knew you at the first
You were a movable.
PETRUCHIO: Why, what's a movable?
KATHARINA: A joint-stool.
PETRUCHIO: Thou hast hit it. Come, sit on me.
KATHARINA: Asses are made to bear, and so are you.
PETRUCHIO: Women are made to bear, and so are you.
KATHARINA: No such jade as you, if me you mean. (II. i, 195ff)

What this game recalls strongly is the session of ritual insults indulged in by black American teenagers, where what matters is the *display* of inventiveness rather than the aptness or seriousness of the insults themselves. In fact such games tread a very narrow line between 'serious' and 'playful' insult: that is part of the fun. But of paramount importance is the fact that such games follow very well-defined rules. In fact there is a strong tradition within English drama of exploiting 'flyting' games of this kind, stretching back to the Wakefield mystery plays. Our example contains not only puns (e.g. 'bear') but in general what we have called 'schemes', as in the virtually verbatim repetition of the '/Asses . . . /Women . . .' pair of lines. Various types of Rhetorical scheme are foregrounded in the comedies. An example of chiasmus, for instance, can be found in *Love's Labours Lost:*

> ARMADO: I love not to be crossed.
> MOTH (*aside*): He speaks the mere contrary: crosses love not
>   him. (I. ii, 32–3)

in which A ('I' – a pronoun) is followed by B ('crossed'), by B ('crosses') by A ('him' – also a pronoun).

The response of scholars and critics to this aspect of the comedies has often been negative. Shakespeare is accused of self-indulgent games with language 'for their own sake'. There are a number of assumptions underlying this response, some of them probably held quite unconsciously. First, there is a notion, derived from Aristotle, that the language of drama is in some way subordinate to the action; therefore any play which seems to foreground language is bad drama. If, however, we see language itself as a kind of action (as in the ballad) this distinction tends to crumble. Second, there is a notion of artistic development linking quality with maturity; since many of the comedies were written earlier than the tragedies, they therefore do not belong to the pinnacle of the artist's achievement. Third, there has been a preference for certain classes of Rhetorical device over others – although today many of us would not recognize the issue as being one of Rhetoric at all. To put it simply, the comedies tend to foreground *schemes*, whereas the Romantic and Post-Romantic taste is for *tropes* – such as metaphor, irony, and so on. In 'A'-levels today students are directed to look for 'images' – a loose term covering a number of tropes, the interest in which derives partly from the habit of treating Shakespeare as a poet rather than as a playwright. It is, however, characteristic of much modern discourse on language that such preferences are seen not as an issue of Rhetoric but of 'authentic expression' – something often projected onto poems such as the Wordsworth sonnet discussed in the next chapter. To put it bluntly, schemes are identified as being part of Rhetoric, and consequently rejected on that score because of the modern prejudice against Rhetoric.

One obvious objection to this critical position is an argument that will by now be familiar: verbal games are never 'merely' verbal games, they are always part of a dialogue with other aspects of a culture at a given moment. Thus the verbal games in the comedies can be seen in the context of Renaissance predilections and debates about language and its relationship with culture and reality. It is difficult not to see the comedies as, in places, parodying Renaissance obsessions with courtly linguistic etiquette and the Rhetorical naming of conversational turns. The clown Touchstone in *As You Like It*, on letting it be known that he disliked the cut of a certain courtier's beard, received a reply from the courtier that it was in fact well cut, a reply Touchstone names the 'Retort Courteous'. He goes on:

> If I sent him word again, it was not well cut, he would send me word he cut it to please himself: This is called the Quip Modest. If, again, it was not well cut, he disabled my judgement: This is call'd the Reply Churlish. (V. iv, 74–77)

And so on, through the Reproof Valiant, the Countercheck Quarrelsome, the Lie Circumstantial and the Lie Direct. In part, Touchstone's fantasy is directed against the Renaissance obsession with naming – something with an important philosophical issue behind it. It has been argued that during the Renaissance the relationship between words and their referents was seen as non-arbitrary: there was an inherent 'rightness' in the names given to things. This 'magical' attitude to language is contrasted with that of modern linguistics, which argues that there is no essential link between signs and what they stand for. Costard's response on being given a tip of three farthings in *Love's Labours Lost* (III. i) could be said to exemplify the naive view: on hearing it referred to as 'remuneration', he assumes that this unfamiliar word is Latin for three farthings. But here, as in so many instances in the play, we can interpret Costard either as a dimwit, or as someone playing the *role* of one, in which case the joke is on his 'betters' (and also, in a sense, on the audience). Elsewhere in the comedies we find what is in effect an opposing attitude towards words: the relationship between word and meaning is so arbitrary that words can be made to mean whatever suits your argument. In *Much Ado About Nothing*, Beatrice asks Benedick what has passed between him and Claudio:

BENEDICK: Only foul words – and thereupon I will kiss thee.
BEATRICE: Foul words is but foul wind, and foul wind is but foul breath, and foul breath is noisome – therefore I will part unkissed.
BENEDICK: Thou hast frighted the word out of its right sense, so forcible is thy wit. (V. ii, 48–52)

In fact, this verbal game between Beatrice and Benedick might seem to illustrate the error of trying to postulate the existence of a single Renaissance attitude to language (or anything else for that matter). Just as in our own time, there was argument in Renaissance times about such matters: what the comedies do in part is dramatize it.

The arbitrariness or otherwise of the sign was an issue not just in the Renaissance period but also in classical Greece; some would maintain that it is not yet dead, even today. Another issue of perennial interest related to the principle of expressivity referred to earlier is the relationship between language and intention. There is a long rationalist tradition, again stretching back to classical Greece, that sees language as the image of the human mind, which in turn distinguishes people from animals. On this view the contents of a speaker's mind can be 'transferred' directly to the mind of a listener through language: indeed, the intentions of the speaker may be directly 'read off' from their language. A related view is that language is the direct reflection of something called 'character' or personality. In this case the part of the body that stands for character is not the mind but the heart. The heart is the site of integrity and, above all, what is called sincerity.

Quite apart from the dubious opposition between mind and body underlying this distinction, there are a host of problems with these views of the speaker-language relationship. It should already be apparent from Chapter 1 that the issue of meaning cannot be tied down merely to the conscious intentions of the speaker. Utterances, moreover, have the habit of playing games, even tricks, with both speakers and listeners. If I say 'I'll give you your book back tomorrow', my utterance is likely to be interpreted as a promise, even though my intentions may have been quite different. A teacher who says to a pupil 'Can I see you for a moment after the class' is likely to be interpreted as intending some kind of reprimand, even though the teacher may be seeking some perfectly innocuous information. And from the view that utterances are capable of conveying the 'heart's message' it is easy to see a related, prescriptive view emerging, that such *ought* to be the case. In fact, this is one of the most strongly contested issues within Rhetoric itself. According to the Roman orators Cato and Quintilian, if language is the direct image of ourselves, then the more perfect our language, the greater our goodness. Eloquence, defined in Rhetorical terms, is accordingly equated with morality. This view had already been promulgated among the Greeks, with Plato one of its severest critics; not surprisingly, the debate continued well into the Renaissance period. It was the puritans in England who argued most strongly in favour of the prescriptive view; for them, of course, acting itself was fundamentally immoral, because in plays, especially comedies, actors pretended to be other than they were. But for the puritans sincerity needed expression in 'plain language' rather than eloquence. An extreme version of this view - one that is still widely held – is that 'true sincerity' is actually inarticulate. For Theseus in *A Midsummer Night's Dream*, the simplicity of the labouring men is the sign of their honesty. And there has long been a view that eloquence, even speech itself, and the protestation of true love are actually incompatible.

These issues are at the centre of the opening scene of Shakespeare's *King Lear*. The ageing king, feeling too old to rule, asks his three daughters which of them loves him most, intending to apportion his kingdom in accordance with their replies. What the critical consensus sees at stake in the scene today is the issue of sincerity; Cordelia alone is sincere, Goneril and Regan are held to be devious, and the king unimaginative and foolish. It is sometimes claimed that these judgements are based not on how the events of the play turn out (Goneril and Regan epitomize wickedness) but on the actual utterances made by the three daughters. In short, Cordelia's sincerity is 'read off' from her reply to Lear's question; and it is sometimes claimed that this quality can be revealed through close linguistic analysis.

In responding to this claim it's necessary to say that just as there are different views of the relationship between speaker and utterance, so there are many, often conflicting, views of the nature of language itself. Throughout this book we examine language as a kind of action, always involved in a context of dialogue: as Bakhtin, the Russian scholar, put it, 'verbal interaction is the ultimate reality' in language. This approach, which sees language as part of the social world, is opposed to one which has been dominant in modern linguistics, in which language is seen primarily as a system, in itself and for itself: this latter view, which in turn is a 'reply' to the nineteenth-century view of language as an ever-changing, living organism, has a very narrow concept of meaning, often seeing it as wholly the property of relationships among the different parts of the system. What we are proposing as a Rhetorical view of language will focus in this opening scene on the 'actions' of asking and replying. Questions, in general, are powerful and heavily loaded kinds of utterances, sensitive to varying and often conflicting interpretations. They are often also culturally relative. In British child-rearing practice, parents usually ask questions in order to elicit a response rather than seek information; by about the age of three children have learned to retaliate by bombarding parents with questions of their own. Questions in job interviews are often invitations to the interviewee to talk about what interests them; unfortunately, many candidates fail to sense this. And occasionally there may be a clear clash of expectations about questioning behaviour. Black schoolchildren in the USA have been found to reject quite forcefully what to them are the pointless questions of their teachers, which are seen as requests for information of people who don't know from people who do.

But questions and replies are also actions in another sense. As we saw in the case of the ballad, they also have a narrative function. This is particularly salient in relation to *King Lear*, whose plot is based on a folk tale that pivots, as is very common with this genre, on the asking of a question. Within the conventions of storytelling the question and its reply prompt in the audience a further question: what happens next? In short, the old man asks his question because the narrative depends on it. Modern, character-centred analysis of drama, however, tends to ask different questions: what sort of man is it who asks such a question? Both questions are valid in their own terms, and indicate that new layers of meaning can always be found in the play. These layers are not necessarily to be seen as reconcilable. Similarly, different voices within the play can be seen as representing positions that cannot be accommodated to each other. Throughout the first three acts the Fool – who cannot be considered a 'character' in any naturalistic sense – threatens to subvert the convention that in tragedy, unlike comedy, speaking rights are generally invested in the powerful and noble *dramatis personae*. The Fool colludes with the audience against the king, using proverbs and traditional sayings as a means of censuring him.

Lear's kingliness in Act I, scene i can be seen in his power to initiate events by making utterances. He has the power to decide when to abdicate, to stage question-and-answer sessions, to pronounce on his daughters' futures and to banish a devoted courtier, Kent. To use the terminology of speech act theory, he can make **declarations**, utterances that actually bring about a state of affairs: his 'sentence' is his 'power'. The central sections of the scene, in which Lear divides his kingdom, involve the whole of his court: whatever is said between Lear and the three sisters will be overheard in public. Thus, within the play itself, the utterances of the sisters will be *triadic*, addressed not only to the king but the whole court. The sisters therefore have to take on the role of public speaker, something they – and of course the actors playing their parts – will need to bear in mind. Lear's question can therefore be seen as functioning as the first move in a language-game which tests his daughters' ability to speak in public. Lear is handing power over to his daughters and since the exercise of power is based in part on the use of a certain kind of language, Lear's question can be seen as a test of their fitness to take the reins. In such a public domain, the daughters have no choice but to respond to the question, knowing that what they say will be heard – and judged – by the assembled courtiers, as well as by the king himself.

But Lear is not only a king, he is also a father addressing his daughters. Our interpretation of this scene depends very much on our perception of the kind of question that Lear is asking, and the role that the king is playing in asking it. In this respect, the audience is placed in much the same position as Lear's daughters. There is a modern tendency to assume that a question is a request for information by someone who does not know the answer and who expects the addressee to be able to help. The addressee is expected to be *co-operative* in their reply, that is, to say what they believe is true, and to say it in an economical, unambiguous and relevant way. Seen from this perspective, Lear's question is preposterous and cannot be adequately answered. Cordelia's response fits the modern predisposition: a daughter cannot tell her father in public how much she loves him, since love is not a commodity that can be adequately measured. Sincerity, therefore, would seem to demand inarticulate expression. But it is important to remember that the interaction is not just that of father and daughter. Lear is also king, and he is addressing those who will succeed to his kingdom. Lear's question, then, can also be seen as the opening move in a Rhetorical game, in which each daughter is invited to speak on the theme of love. The question can therefore be seen as an eliciting device, and the responses of Goneril and Regan suggest that this is how they themselves see it. Goneril's offering is suitably conventional: she starts with the paradoxical proposition that language itself is unfit for the purpose in hand, and goes on to seek other commonplaces of value with which love can be compared. Regan's move is bound by Goneril's, in a sense replies to it: thinking on her feet, she finds an absence, or weakness, in Goneril's case and speaks to that. This is a game, however, that Cordelia cannot play, or, perhaps more fittingly, refuses to play. Her response, moreover, draws attention to the game *as a game;* and since this action is comparable with a defendant exposing the routines of a court of law for the games they in fact are, her behaviour is subversive.

What we are arguing is that Lear's game is not a test of sincerity, and Goneril and Regan cannot be said to be insincere on the evidence of their responses alone. Above all, it is inadmissible for some critics to suggest that their insincerity can be demonstrated by analysing their language. Similarly there is nothing in Cordelia's 'Good my lord / you have begot me, bred me, loved me' that can be used to argue her simplicity and honesty; these are prior interpretations that are being projected on to the language. This speech of Cordelia's is every bit as patterned as those of her sisters; her words, to recall Bakhtin, are already more than 'half someone else's', they are the *borrowed* language of the marriage vow. But because Cordelia's characterization of her sisters' speeches as 'glib and oily' chimes with the modern dislike of Rhetoric, many modern critics have chosen to 'centre' the play on her alleged sincerity and to thematize it as a struggle between this quality and its opposite, which is seen as Rhetoric. These views are also shared by many modern actors and theatre directors. In a recent book, *Playing Shakespeare*, members of the Royal Shakespeare Company dismiss Brutus' speech in *Julius Caesar* justifying the assassination of the dictator on the grounds that it is not 'spontaneous' and is therefore insincere. This assumption that planned speech is somewhat suspect is widespread and powerful and, in our view, quite untenable.

If Act I, scene i, of *King Lear* is seen as a straightforward clash between Lear's foolishness and Cordelia's honesty, then it is drained of a great deal of its drama. If, however, we see its two chief protagonists as getting involved in a verbal game which in a sense catches both of them out, it becomes more complex and interesting. It becomes less easy to apportion guilt or innocence, praise or blame. Of course Lear's game is potentially dangerous, since it depends on all its participants recognizing what it is and agreeing to play by the rules. Part of the tension in the opening scene is between Lear's role as king and his role as father: the actor playing him must bear this in mind. But there is also a third source of tension. Lear is also a man with human needs – for warmth, shelter, sustenance, and companionship – which he feels should be satisfied because he is, or has been, king; unlike Goneril, Regan, and the Fool, he believes that he is entitled to be treated as a king even after he has given away his kingship. The play does not necessarily resolve these issues. A major impulse in literary criticism, particularly marked over the last hundred years, has been to demonstrate the 'unity' of literary works. Our analysis, on the other hand, tends to see *King Lear* as generating questions rather than providing us with a single, unifying 'message' which we need to uncover.

Since *King Lear* is a play, its utterances are triadic in another sense. They are addressed primarily to the audience, even though they maintain the illusion of being directed to other *dramatis personae* within the play. Part of that address is a convention of tragedy, as described by Aristotle, that audiences may be moved to the emotions of pity and terror. But audiences also enjoy certain privileges of interpretation. The utterance of a *dramatis persona* can be seen not only as part of conversational exchange but as a voice raised as part of a dialogue with other voices elsewhere in the play. The use of proverbs and sententiae, first by the Fool, and then by Edgar, invites the audience to judge the play's action against those protagonists' perception of it. Another very important aspect of the play's address is the scope for ironical interpretation. The Rhetorical figure of irony, which – partly because of its many meanings – is the cause of frequent confusion, concerns the relationship between intention on the one hand and, on the other, outcome or interpretation. Its most usual and obvious application is to utterances which can be said to mean exactly the opposite of what they appear to say. Thus when, in replying to Brutus' justification for killing Caesar, Mark Antony says 'Brutus is an honourable man' we are inclined to interpret him as intending us to believe the proposition; this inclination is gradually undermined as Antony's oration proceeds. Thus an important aspect of irony is the realization that the intentions of a speaker are always open to interpretation. Mark Antony's strategy is effective partly because it allows the audience to draw their own conclusion about his commitment to the validity of the proposition. But there is always room for argument about whether the irony in an utterance is consciously intended by the speaker. When Regan asserts that she is of the same 'mettle' as her sister Goneril, we might ask whether she knows that this can be interpreted as meaning that she loves her father as *little* as Goneril does. And when Cordelia announces that she has nothing to say in answer to Lear's question, how far is she aware that 'nothing' *sounds* as if she doesn't love her father, and that her 'I love you according to my bond' sounds like not very much (when for her, apparently, it means a great deal)?

Further possibilities for irony are generated by the processes of narrative. An action may be described as ironic if its outcome is the reverse of that intended by its agent. Audiences are often in the position of knowing what some of the *dramatis personae* themselves don't know (we know, for instance, unlike Gloucester, that it is not his son Edgar who is plotting against him). This kind of irony, usually termed 'dramatic irony', may be extended to other cases in which the audience knows the outcome of an action and is able to judge it against the words used by a protagonist in proposing it. Such instances are therefore a challenge to the audience's own powers of memory. When in Act I the king talks of his 'darker purpose', we appreciate the ambiguity in 'darker' once we know where the king's actions lead: 'darker' for him means secret; for the audience it can also mean terrible, wrongheaded, even evil. And Lear's expressed desire to crawl 'unburthened' to his grave is painfully ironical when we see him die weighed down by the dead body of Cordelia that he has been carrying in his arms.

Notes and further reading

Notions of the 'popular' are addressed in the work of Bakhtin (1968), the Italian marxist Gramsci (1985), and Raymond Williams; see, for example, Williams's entries under *popular* and *aesthetic* in *Keywords* (1983) and for a more extended discussion see also *Marxism and Literature* (1977), where there is a seminal essay on language. *The Politics and Poetics of Transgression* by Stallybrass and White (1986) has also been a great stimulus. See also Límon (1983). Pleasure – a concept far from innocent! – has been extensively theorized in recent years: for pioneering discussions see Barthes (1977), who distinguishes between the *plaisir* of the familiar and reassuring and the *jouissance* associated with the perception or experience of rupture or crisis.

Childlore is discussed by the Opies (1959), but the framework adopted here is that of Sanches and Kirshenblatt-Gimblett in the latter's invaluable collection *Speech Play* (1976). See also Bascom (1965). For other key studies addressing the relationship between language and childhood see Rose (1984) and Steedman (1982).

The discussion of song in general is to some extent based on Booth (1981). The so-called expressive fallacy is succinctly discussed by Belsey (1980). For 'reanalysed' song lyrics see Fox (1984). The discussion of rock is based on Durant (1984a); that of the 'folk voice' is to some extent a reply to Trudgill (1982). See also P. Kennedy (1975). The notion of orality is discussed by Ong (1982), and applied to Homer by Kirk (1976); see Finnegan (1977) for a comprehensive and convincing reply. The history of popular song publishing owes a great deal to Harker (1985); see also Shepard (1962) and Boyes (1986). Jeannie Robertson is discussed by Gower (1968) and Porter (1976). See Başgöz (1975) for the material on Turkish *hikaye*. The version of *Lord Gregory* analysed is taken from the *Journal of the English Folk Dance and Song Society* (1956); other versions are discussed by Fowler (1968) and Andersen and Pettitt (1979). General studies of the ballad include Bronson (1969, 1976), Buchan (1972) and Andersen (1984); for ballads in Ireland see Shields (1972) and Carroll (1986).

The discussion of acting owes a great deal to all the contributors to a volume of the theoretical journal *Screen* (26:5, 1985). The approach to Shakespeare's language is based on two works by Elam (1980, 1984); see also Williams (1982). For Shakespearean acting and stagecraft see

Weimann (1978) and Barton (1984). The analysis of *Lear* was prompted in part by a collection of essays entitled *Questions and Politeness*, edited by Goody (1978); for a similar view of Act I, scene i, see Valesio (1977). A recent attempt to use linguistic analysis to demonstrate Cordelia's 'sincerity' is by Aers and Kress (1981); see also Hoey and Winter's linguistically-based analysis of Brutus's address to the crowd in *Julius Caesar* (1981). And for an account of how a British linguist found herself in a Cordelia-type situation in the Soviet Union, see Thomas (1985).

Act, scene and line references to Shakespeare's plays are to the Arden editions.

Chapter three

Argument

all . . . endeavour to criticize or uphold an argument, to
defend themselves or to accuse . . .

Aristotle's *Rhetoric*: that sounds forbidding. Surely the work is
rigid, schematic, and remote? On the contrary: the book begins
by discussing something that concerns 'all' people – arguing. Arguing is where Rhetoric starts – and arguing is an ordinary activity,
a universal activity, according to Aristotle. Rhetoric is no arcane
rigmarole, and Aristotle does not focus on 'figures of speech' or
on special kinds of discourse.

Aristotle gives only one way of presenting Rhetoric, a way that
has been more interesting recently than for a long time. George
Kennedy's *The Art of Persuasion* makes Aristotle's work central
to the early history of Rhetoric; Kathy Eden's *Poetic and Legal
Fiction in the Aristotelian Tradition* insists that *Rhetoric* be added
to the more famous *Poetics*. Gerard Genette draws attention to
Aristotle's concern with a Rhetoric other than figures of speech,
the focus of modern studies. As Ernst Curtius has shown, Aristotle's *Rhetoric* has not been a standard work for much of the history
of European thought about language and literature; reviving it –
and this is what critics and commentators have been doing – is
important to our approach.

Aristotle begins with human activity: people interacting with
one another. Kennedy shows that Aristotle is rejecting the idea
that Rhetoric is about something specialized, about the arcane
tricks of lawyers, for instance. Instead, in Kennedy's words, Aristotle asserts 'the need to deal with all kinds of oratory. The
early handbooks were concerned only with the oratory of the law

courts.' Aristotle also rejects categories that are rigid, contrary to his usual reputation. He condemns 'all those who definitely lay down, for instance, what should be the contents . . . of the parts of the discourse.' They 'are bringing under the rules of art what is outside the subject.' Aristotle wants Rhetoric to be about something people do: how do people argue, what do they argue about, why arguing is important, where must argument stop. He begins by exploring the way argument occurs in different contexts, such as law, politics, and general debate.

Our first two chapters are, therefore, in this Aristotelian spirit, because they focus on people speaking in concrete situations and for specific purposes. Chapter 1 is Aristotelian in considering law among other varieties of oratory. Chapter 2 links oratory with other performances, including drama. That again is in line with Aristotle's linking of Rhetoric with *Poetics*, where he considers drama. More generally, our approach has tried to keep an Aristotelian openness and flexibility. We are resisting the idea that academic study should lay down definitive rules of speaking and writing, whether prescriptive or normative. The approach is to look for ways of analysing human activity without imposing rules.

So it is very much in the Aristotelian spirit to have begun with types of performance. We have not followed Aristotle's own typology, which is specific to his culture and moment. But we have followed his questions, and continue to do so now, by concentrating on argument itself. The sequence is important: first, performances, and then argument, a more abstract problem.

In *Rhetoric*, Aristotle explores argument practically. He considers how people use language to argue, and stays close to familiar experience. The Rhetorician tries to organize experiences that are familiar; he does not resort to elaborate schemes or abstract rules. Two points are central. First, argument is about the relations between one voice and others, one view and others. Arguing happens when voices oppose each other, when views conflict. Rhetoric seeks to understand how and why voices conflict; for Aristotle this is a problem that is practical:

the orator should be able to prove opposites . . .

That sounds strange. Why should Rhetoric help the orator to 'prove opposites'? The purpose is not cynical nor flashy. It is so that the real state of the case may not escape us . . .

To argue is to engage with other views and voices, either explicitly (dialogue) or implicitly, anticipating how others may react to what one says. A second point is that argument is about address, about people addressing other people and other views. The aim is 'to counteract' arguments which seem 'false' and to 'defend (themselves) or accuse'.

For Aristotle argument is rich and creative; it is also central to the understanding of language. To argue is to be human:

> . . . it would be absurd if it were considered disgraceful not to be able to defend oneself with the help of the body, but not disgraceful as far as speech is concerned, whose use is more characteristic of man than that of the body.

Yet argument, like Rhetoric, often has a bad name. Argument is often seen in a negative way. Among the most dismissive assumptions about the nature of argument are those which are associated with 'rows' or 'disputes'. These terms tell stories in which conflicting positions may be held rigidly or angrily and occur in distinct succession to each other or in isolation. In this kind of story, which frequently figures in news reports, 'rows' create trouble, or exacerbate trouble, or are symptoms of crisis. It is natural to assume, given this view, that there would be less antagonism in the world if people did not contradict each other, and that when contradiction ceases, antagonism is lessening. Typical instances are the staples of political, industrial, and international news, involving 'bitter disputes' and 'heated argument'. These 'incidents' arise when normal processes have 'broken down'; the 'way out' involves a 'backing down', or 'concessions' being made. The metaphors are those of retreat; nothing creative results. Reaching agreement is likely to follow 'demands' and an 'ultimatum' may have to be met. Strong patterns of verbal association give these recurring stories great force. They seem to be natural in personal as well as public life. To be 'argumentative' means to look for trouble, or even to pick fights. An unhappy relationship is one in which the parties are 'always arguing' – and the arguing only makes matters worse. It is a sign that the relationship has failed. How *easy* it is to absorb this kind of story: it is pervasive in the public culture.

A second kind of assumption about argument concerns the making of a case. Terms such as 'bias', 'pressure', and 'manipulation' are used. This assumption contrasts biased comment unfavourably with an ideal of objective reporting or scientific analysis. The most spectacular villain in this scenario is called 'propaganda'. On the other hand, it is right to be 'objective', 'impartial' and 'sincere' (in so far as it implies honest expression with no ulterior motives). The great thing about a 'frank exchange', according to these valuations, is that no one is being manipulative, everyone is just airing their opinions, getting things 'out in the open'. These distinctions seem natural and inevitable. Third, in another view of argument, it is often assumed that time is wasted by formal procedures of debate. Many ready phrases illustrate this attitude: 'to make a debatable point', to be 'contentious'. The phrase 'for argument's sake' can mean that something is not meant 'seriously'.

A philosophy can develop to justify the distrust of argument. Here is Descartes' view:

> Whenever two men come to opposite decisions about the same
> matter, one of them at least must be certainly be in the
> wrong, and apparently there is not one of them who knows;
> for if the reasoning of the one was sound and clear he would
> be able to lay it before the other as finally to succeed in
> convincing *his* understanding also.

Ideally, debate is ended by pure reasoning. When argument persists, something is wrong: Descartes does not think of argument as *becoming* creative. The longer debate continues or the attempt at persuasion lasts, the *less* it achieves.

This chapter presents another view of argument, a very different view from those commonly held, which find argument to be negative or destructive. This is a Rhetorical view of argument which is being put forward, a view centred on address. To begin with, two literary examples are studied: they are recognizably argumentative situations, and they yield a great richness when explored from a Rhetorical point of view, a richness far greater than the notion of argument might commonly imply.

Literature, Rhetoric, and argument

Why begin with examples from literature? We are not applying Rhetoric to literature; instead, we are connecting Rhetorical with literary understanding of argument. Classical Rhetoric frequently turns to literature for an understanding comparable to, and richer than, its own; and we are following that tradition. In doing this, we are inspired by some modern examples. D. Russell and M. Winterbottom have shown how closely Rhetoric is bound up with literature in their collection *Ancient Literary Criticism*. Kenneth Burke has re-created the practice of thinking through Rhetorical problems by attending to literature, especially in his neglected book *Attitudes toward History*. M. M. Bakhtin's work gives an exemplary model for the understanding of general problems through the reading of literature, an understanding that is not available in any other way. That is, reading literature is not a way of confirming what is already known, but a way of extending our understanding. One can say this while being aware that 'literature' is a category full of its own problems and difficulties, in any given case.

First, then, we turn for understanding to Jane Austen's *Emma*, and to one particular scene of two characters arguing. The context can be given briefly; what matters here is not so much the plot as the novel's texture of dispute. At the start, Emma loses her companion, Miss Taylor, who has replaced her dead mother. Miss Taylor has not died, she has only married. Trying to be brave, Emma claims that

'I planned the match from that hour; and when such success has blessed me in this instance, dear papa, you can't think I shall leave off matchmaking.'

So the story is launched – Emma tries to make a match between young Harriet Smith and the eligible Mr Elton. Significantly, though she addresses her claim to 'dear papa', it is Mr Knightley who responds, Mr Knightley who is to marry Emma at the end of the novel:

'I do not understand what you mean by "success",' said Mr Knightley . . . 'Why do you talk of success? Where is your merit – what are you proud of? You made a lucky guess; and *that* is all that can be said.'

Emma reacts:

> 'And have you never known the pleasure and triumph of a lucky guess?'

Reply and counter, a pattern is set: as Aristotle has it, so it is in *Emma*:

> all . . . endeavour to criticize or uphold an argument, to defend themselves or to accuse.

The point is to connect Rhetoric and literature, so that our approach can draw on both for understanding of argument. Literature contributes through diverse readings, of course, and especially when read closely. Consider, now, an exchange between Emma and Mr Knightley once the plot has advanced. Emma has decided that Harriet should definitely marry Mr Elton; Mr Knightley has encouraged Robert Martin, a young farmer, to propose to Harriet. Emma has made sure that Harriet has refused, but Mr Knightley is not yet aware of that when he arrives and announces cheerfully:

> 'I have reason to think . . . that Harriet Smith will soon have an offer of marriage, and from a most unexceptionable quarter . . .'

He adds, proudly:

> 'Robert Martin is the man . . . He is desperately in love . . .'

Mr Knightley is amazed when Emma tells him Harriet has refused, and he suspects that Emma has used her influence to prevent the marriage. He tackles Emma over what happened. He objects to the fact that Harriet rejected Robert Martin:

> 'Then she is greater simpleton than I ever believed her. What is the foolish girl about?'
> 'Oh! to be sure,' cried Emma, 'it is always incomprehensible to a man that a woman should ever refuse an offer of marriage.'

And Mr Knightley replies:

> 'Nonsense! . . . He [Robert Martin] has too much real feeling to address any woman on the hap-hazard of selfish passion . . . He had encouragement.'

It is perfectly in keeping with ordinary usage to say that here a man and a woman are arguing. But if *this* is argument, what precisely does it involve? Can the whole richness of the passage be included in the concept of argument? Why does the reader feel such a strong sense of encounter between the characters, a sense of the two characters engaging with each other? The ancient Rhetorical idea of argument helps here: to argue is not merely to put forward a view, but also to speak, or write, *in the awareness of a differing or opposing view*. That idea of argument puts an emphasis on address, the crucial point being that *many different kinds of address* may result from an awareness of the other position, and all are likely to be complex. In this episode from *Emma*, the idea of argument is not simply in the conflict between characters: instead, the utterance given to (and by) each character is saturated with a sense of opposing positions. When Mr Knightley says '*then* she is a greater simpleton . . .' his use of the word 'then' hooks his view onto Emma's version of what has happened and 'than *I* ever believed her' (our italics) continues to engage with the idea of different interpretations. His *own* view is that though Harriet may be a simpleton, she is not so simple as to have turned down Robert Martin spontaneously. Indeed, he modifies 'greater simpleton' by adopting the phrase 'foolish girl'. In his view, Harriet is foolish and inexperienced, but there are limits to her folly which make nonsense of Emma's story. Emma appears to ignore his question ('What is the foolish girl about?') But what she answers ('Oh! to be sure!') only makes sense in the light of the (rather comic) fact that he claims only to be asking a question. What she picks up is that he is only pretending to be baffled in order to put the question, and that such male pleas of confusion are really a way of contrasting masculine reason with female irrationality! The relation between what he says and what, on the other hand, is said by her, gives an insight into the way the *other* position is present throughout what somebody says, without in any way being directly reproduced. What Emma says makes sense only in relation to her idea of what Mr Knightley believes, even though she appears to be dodging sideways to avoid what he *actually* says. The narration's use of 'cried' ('cried Emma') points up the fact that Emma takes up a position which represents her gender against a male voice. The whole performance, including the way she accentuates the unmasculine quality of her voice, can be seen as part of an argument, if argument includes the whole of the address which results from engaging with an 'other' position. There is much to be gained in the understanding of what people are *doing* with words by employing such an open idea of argument, and by recognizing the essential contributions under this heading to what are, historically, literary writings. This comic scene – whose comedy is integral to its insight – explores the situation which we recognize as argument with a precision and depth that extend to the philosophy of disagreement. One of the major preoccupations of Rhetoric has always been the philosophy of disagreement.

Mr Knightley's exclamation 'nonsense' is, of course, self-evidently saturated by a sense of another position, but just how subtly saturated! At several levels, the conflict is about rationality. Mr Knightley confronts Emma's story of a proposal rejected, as an action ridiculous in itself which has also been recounted in an absurd way. His 'nonsense' also applies itself to what is outwardly her general view of men and women. Indeed, in one sense, the word even engages against the novel itself: Emma may be on weak grounds in so far as she *has* influenced Harriet, but it turns out in the novel that other men do seem to hold the same view of women as Emma accuses Mr Knightley of holding. And even if Mr Knightley is substantively 'in the right' about Harriet when he implies that Emma influenced her, he himself made a misjudgement concerning the proposal. In context he does seem rather bland about the relations between the sexes which make for a marriage. Emma has identified a certain facility about his assumptions. Her expression, 'to be sure', reacts against his complacency. To be *sure* is indeed a problem in the novel's world.

All kinds of competing judgements about the world saturate further Mr Knightley's assertion that Robert Martin 'has too much real feeling to address any woman on the hap-hazard'. He is most directly countering the idea that Robert Martin may not have 'real feeling' because he is insufficiently genteel or educated, which is what he imagines Emma thinks. But even as he counters the notion of Robert's deficiencies, what he says contains the idea of them. Simultaneously the reader gets what Mr Knightley believes about the proposal, and what he thinks Emma believes. At the same time, we as readers form our own judgements about what happened, and judge for ourselves what Emma believes. His words engage still further, with an opposing idea about 'feeling', which he contrasts with 'selfish passion'. He makes this distinction between authentic feeling and 'selfish passion' on the basis that others, including Emma, may not have the necessary powers of discrimination. (His use of the word 'address' in the statement 'he has too much real feeling to address any woman' is felicitously, if perhaps fortuitously, pertinent to the case about Rhetoric since he recognizes 'address' to involve a whole performance centred on an audience.)

In these passages the concept of argument is more precise and richer than is implied in the familiar use of the word 'argument'. The idea that this richer sense of argument is *Rhetorical* may be surprising if Rhetoric is still understood in a pejorative sense (as bombast, manipulation and so on). That negative sense of what Rhetoric is could not apply to the behaviour of the individual characters nor to the writing of the whole passage. But the alternative idea of Rhetoric, which emphasizes the *understanding* achieved *through the concept of address*, does apply to the way the whole passage presents a man and woman arguing. The idea of what can take place when people disagree is a profoundly Rhetorical one. When an argument takes place between characters, what each says is full of a sense of opposing positions. The possibility of creating a scene like this depends on such an idea of argument. The idea does not have to be seen as the intentional subject of the passage. Rather it is a precondition for the scene. One of the central points about address is that it is often affected by an engagement with other views. The passage shows that when another view is encountered, a response is made not only *to* that view, but also *at* the source of that view, which here is another character. The two characters seem to be talking to each other so intensely because what they say (in words) is saturated by the views of the person to whom they are addressed and also by the presence of that person. To such an extent is this true that the words make no sense outside of the context. To be comprehensible these words demand to speak towards *someone* as well as against an opposing position.

There are several ways in which the address is more complicated than a table-tennis pattern of argument would imply. This is partly because someone else's point of view enters into what each character says so profoundly, partly because that other point of view is also held by other people. So Emma addresses her 'to be sure' to Knightley, and *also* to all those others who hold the same beliefs as he does about men and women. Conversely, Knightley's 'non-sense' addresses itself to everyone who does not share the view which he considers sensible. In a sense, those are partisan positions, which each speaker addresses in arguing against the other. More generally, the argument is overheard by *an audience of readers*: there are two ways in which that audience is involved. The whole passage addresses itself to someone who has read the earlier part of the novel and is going to continue reading it. Second, all the issues are about *what is probable*. What is probable at a personal level concerning Harriet's behaviour to Robert Martin? What probably happens in general when men address women (and propose marriage to them)? These issues continue to be argued in the mind of the reader as other events occur in the novel and other proposals are made. It is obvious that episodes in novels have an audience, but not obvious how deeply that audience enters into the *process* of the fiction. Even arguments between people outside of novels presuppose witnesses. Even if a witness is not present on the spot, argument of this kind (one to one) is a performance, a competitive performance, which always implies the possibility of an adjudicator. What makes the passage Rhetorical is the richness of what is here involved in addressing the opposing view.

Here 'Rhetorical' refers to an attitude towards what people do with language and what language does for people. That attitude is characterized by an emphasis on the 'to-ness' of utterance – the extent to which speaking *to* or writing *to* is a central idea in making sense of speech and writing. Utterance to an audience is obviously the basis, historically, of certain kinds of performance, and these are often the starting-point for Rhetoric's enquiries. Another starting-point is the effect on address of encountering other positions, an enquiry which can be presented under the broad heading of argument. Such encounters between differing positions are implicit in several types of performances and therefore the two lines of Rhetorical enquiry are closely linked. However, here attention focuses on the process of engaging with the other position and upon the wider implications of understanding that process more richly. The episode from the Jane Austen novel depends upon a profound understanding of such engagements. The whole tradition of writing and reading such episodes is imbued with such understanding of argument and address, a tradition which is centred on Rhetoric in the terms of the present study. We draw on the understanding shown in fiction to explore the full range of sources for the project of Rhetoric, not to stake out a territory as Rhetoric. It is not a case of saying fiction is in fact Rhetoric but of saying that the essential questions of Rhetoric can be more fully explored in the context of fiction, amongst other contexts. Take the question of play. Rhetorical thinkers have explored how arguing overlaps with play – various kinds of play. For instance, people may play with words even while arguing. The Greek orator Demosthenes is an example of this. Demosthenes put his Rhetoric into practice: he wrote speeches which demonstrate his principles. Kennedy describes how Demosthenes composes a speech: 'He carries along simultaneously a number of different themes, all of which are repeatedly illustrated . . . A symmetry is observable . . .'. Demosthenes puts a case; but he also makes patterns out of words and themes. Or there is play in a different sense, play meaning 'free play'. Here is Cicero on how orators need to indulge the free play of ideas and of words: 'In fact, the poet is next door to the orator . . . virtually the same, indeed, in one thing, at least, that he sets no bounds to his prerogatives, to his freedom to wander where he likes . . .'. Or there is play in the sense of a certain excess, the play of language itself. Mikhail Bakhtin suggested that argument is the play of language: 'The word plunges into the inexhaustible wealth and contradictory multiplicity . . .'. These senses of play overlap too much for them to be distinct, even theoretically. The vital point is that arguing includes playing, in many senses.

But we still need the way Jane Austen illuminates how play enters into an argument, variously and profoundly. In the case of Emma and Mr Knightley, they can be understood to be at play in the sense of relishing the process even while they genuinely compete against each other to win, and what they say only makes full sense if we realize this. Mr Knightley refers to Harriet as 'the foolish girl' and already there is that slight excess in the slide from 'simpleton' to 'foolish', the excess without which persuasion is impossible and yet which goes beyond the persuasive. At this point, where words displace each other so precisely and yet so decisively, it makes sense to enquire: 'who is at play?'. There is no single or easy answer. Mr Knightley, the novel, the language, and the reader are all, in different senses, at play, although to say that the language is enjoying itself must remain metaphorical. None the less it is a metaphor which corresponds with a kind of will or wilfulness in words. When Emma says 'it is always incomprehensible to a man' she plays with the vocabulary of gender. If Knightley makes 'girl' impact with the word 'foolish', Emma makes 'a man' sound absurdly weighted with claims that lie behind the word 'man'. Certainly they are trying to persuade each other, but the forces at play in this exchange are larger than those required by persuasion. This kind of disproportion is a central fact about address, and is all the more striking in the context of argument.

Play goes deeper than vocabulary or content, or even Emma's half-teasing attitude. The process of disagreeing displays patterns and rhythms which have the pleasurable connotations of play. For instance, there is the rhythm of syntax: Knightley's half-exclamatory question 'what is the foolish girl about?' continues into Emma's 'Oh', which in turn passes on to Knightley's 'nonsense!'. There is a single curve of increasing exclamation which passes from voice to voice so that one rhythm is established throughout the whole exchange. That rhythm is very pleasurable. In that pleasure it is impossible to separate reader from characters, characters from each other, or any of these from the language and the novel. But without that pleasurable rhythm there is no argument.

Rhetoric has also concerned itself with the issues on which people are most likely to find themselves engaging with other views. Classical Rhetoric even went so far as to compile lists of the most contentious issues in terms of the most obviously opposing views. These issues are sometimes referred to as 'topics'. The term 'topics' is tricky, because it has had so many meanings. Ernst Curtius shows how 'topics' may identify key subjects and their appropriate images – a usage central in medieval theories of literature. In Aristotle, however, 'topics' are sites of controversy. It seems reasonable to employ the term in that sense, while acknowledging others. But the term is not what matters, really. It is the idea that is important: the idea that there are issues which give rise to conflicting views or voices.

Kenneth Burke gives this idea a modern twist, in his great work

Rhetoric of Motives. He discusses conflicting views and suggests that it is helpful to place these views in the context of an issue which contains both sides:

> The battlefield, for instance, which permits rival contestants to join in battle, itself 'transcends' their factionalism, being superior to it and 'neutral' to their motives, though the conditions of the terrain may happen to favour one faction.

Hayden White has extended this thinking, bringing back some of Aristotle's topics specifically, such as 'the topoi of natural size and place' – the idea is that particular arguments spring from the issue of 'natural size' (is this state, say, too large or too small?).

Generally, this sense of topics, of issues, being defined by the possibility of opposing positions is worth noting. It does not mean that all views and their opposites are equal – but that they are available to utterance. For Aristotle, and in a different sense for Jane Austen, the important point is to be aware of the possibilities inherent in an issue. It is not a question, either for the Rhetorician or the novelist, of mechanically charting oppositions, but of being aware how certain issues give rise to vistas of contention.

Aristotle does identify two topics as universal, as present in all others. These universal topics are: the greater and the lesser, and the possible and impossible. The argument between Emma and Mr Knightley can be seen as involving these universal topics. At its simplest, is one gender greater than the other? But also, the argument raises the question of what is possible (and impossible): can a woman such as Harriet reject a proposal freely? What matters for the theorist, for the novelist and for the reader of both is to explore the scope of argument. Feminist criticism has deepened our sense of how and where issues of gender are arguable – and so connects Emma and Mr Knightley with the theory of argument in another way. No modern Rhetoric can be alive without a sense of what feminist criticism has contributed to our sense of argument.

At the start of the chapter, it appeared that there were two kinds of argument: that in which two sides dispute a case, and that in which one side presents an argument. The whole of Virginia Woolf's book *A Room of One's Own* can be seen as argument, where argument includes the idea of one side putting a case, as well as the idea of two sides disputing directly with each other. *A Room of One's Own* puts several cases concerning women and fiction. The phrase 'women and fiction' turns out to contain many issues which need arguing about. How much have women contributed to literature? How should women contribute to literature? How far are ideas about women themselves fictional? How far, indeed, are ideas of gender, more generally, fictional? Cases are put from what the book identifies as a woman's point of view on these questions. As Toril Moi has suggested, the book may in this way have contributed to the agenda of the women's movement. In the context of the questions she raises, Virginia Woolf puts the case for rewriting literature and redefining culture from the point of view of women. That rewriting involves both the past and the future.

The book explicitly presents a lecture to an audience at an 'Oxbridge' women's college. The reader is continually reminded that a lecture is involved by the way the writing addresses itself to the audience:

> Have *you* any notion of how many books are written about women in the course of one year? Have *you* any notion how many are written by men? Are *you* aware that *you* are, perhaps, the most discussed animal in the universe? (Our italics)

The first 'you', in 'have *you* any notion of how many books?' may address readers in general. The second 'you' may still address readers generally, but comes after 'written about women' and just before 'by men', and that raises the question of gender. In the sentence 'Are you aware that you are . . . ?' the 'you's' address the women who are an 'Oxbridge' audience of women students, and the reader-as-woman. The issues are all about women (and fiction); the address is often *towards* women. The views are, broadly, in defence of women. Yet when, on the central issues, a case is put, the effect on address is still complicated.

One aspect of 'women and fiction' is fictions of gender. Here the case is that women have possessed the power of creating fictions of man, and that they have been possessed by the power of that fiction:

> Women have served all these centuries as looking-glasses

possessing the magic and delicious power of reflecting the figure of man at twice its natural size.

The address is still towards the 'women' who 'have served as looking-glasses', taking their side, talking to them, talking for them. But what about 'magic and delicious'? To whom has that power of 'reflecting the figure of man at twice its natural size' been most delicious if not to man whose figure has been magnified thus? The word 'delicious' and also the metaphor of the looking-glass, in which what is seen is always seen from the other side, turn the sentence *towards* those who have seen the image reflected back to them and who have tasted that delicious flavour (men?). The phrase 'twice its natural size' then takes aim critically at those who believe that the 'figure of man', particularly in the sense of the male figure, is naturally grand. (At the same time the sentence addresses sympathetically those 'women' who 'have served as looking-glasses'.) The word 'natural' is wrested from those who believe that men are 'naturally' more imposing, and spun back to them with the opposing emphasis: that nothing could be less natural. Despite the fact that one side is being put, the other is palpably present and even addressed, to such an extent that it is possible to construct *topics* here, that is, foci of opposing views and voices. One topic that is possible, among several others, is 'the magnitude of the male', itself a sub-topic of two larger issues, opposition within gender, and the Aristotelian universal of the greater and the lesser.

The passage continues to argue about 'the magic and delicious power of reflecting the figure of man': 'Without that power probably the earth would still be swamp and jungle.' There is a palpable sense of address towards the view that men alone have created civilization. The case is that civilization occurred – progress seemed possible – because 'the figure of man' was created on such a huge scale by women. That fiction-making power is being half celebrated and half lamented, in so far as, for all its effectiveness, that power has been used for purposes beyond its own control – the passage goes on to refer to 'the glories of all our wars' which would also be 'unknown' were it not for 'that power'. Without the power of women to reflect the figure of man, civilization would not be possible and so 'the earth would still be swamp and jungle'. The force of the argument is obtained by denial, not by assertion, denial that civilization would have been possible in any other way. The effect is that of speaking *to* as well as *against* another belief about how civilization becomes possible. No particular source needs to be ascribed to that belief, but the impact of denial, the denial that anything else were possible, suggests that the view could be said by others and argued by them. Addressing the 'Oxbridge' audience, and the reader-as-woman, the sentences about that power are sympathetic, if sad. Addressing the established culture and the reader-as-man, the sentence is admonitory. The phrase 'swamp and jungle' engages forcefully with the view that man (without woman) has done the civilizing, insisting that in the absence of the power possessed by women there would have been no progress at all. The wit addresses itself intensely *to* the 'other' history, which says that man (in the sense of men) has naturally conquered nature and built civilization. Not merely would the earth remain 'swamp', but 'swamp and jungle' – not a shred of culture, not a brick or a fire in sight. Every word, the whole rhythm, *denies* that anything at all would have happened. Therefore the view being rejected is almost audible, certainly possible, even if not being expressed by anyone else in the room, not just now. *A Room of One's Own* makes the *other* view almost audible by addressing it. But recognizing that another view is possible is very different from suggesting that both views are equal.

The address of that individual passage is complex, being put to different people, different genders, different groups among them, individuals among them, such as the reader, as well as addressing divergent views of civilization and history. The address and argument are related to each other in complicated ways. Perhaps in the wider context of the whole work, the complex address becomes part of another case, a case being put about androgyny. The case is that each individual and certainly every writer is potentially androgynous, that is to say, he or she contains both genders. A phrase such as 'magic and delicious power' addresses both a male position and a female position, so each reader can feel addressed in both ways and readers discover something inside themselves which is capable of conceiving of both forms of experience. The word 'man' in 'figure of man' may in this enlarged context be reclaimed for both genders. The 'other' view then becomes the belief that both genders are entirely distinct.

The point is to connect Rhetoric with reading literature, connecting, for instance, address or topics with the passage by Woolf. Problems of argument are then explored, being illuminated by Rhetorical theory and by reading Woolf. So there are opposing positions to be found in this passage, and these positions spring from issues which overlap and metamorphose into each other. In Rhetorical theory, too, topics overlap and cannot be regarded as separate entities. Aristotle shows that topics form subtle chains, complicated patterns in which one issue links onto another, each issue being defined by opposing voices. We gain one kind of understanding from reading Aristotle, and another from reading Woolf: a living Rhetoric of topics will need both kinds of understanding.

Classical theory connects with theories that are modern, as well as with the reading of literature. Indeed reading literature can be a way to explore how classical ideas compare with modern ideas. Sometimes there is a link that is direct, as from Aristotle to Burke and White. But other links are more oblique. For instance, Mikhail Bakhtin proposes a theory centring on 'dialogism', a theory in which opposing views are very important. This theory is touched on earlier in a passage about play, where 'the word . . . plunges into . . . contradictory multiplicity'. Here it may be helpful to introduce more generally Bakhtin's idea of 'dialogism'.

Bakhtin proposes a theory of language, a theory which asserts 'the internal dialogism of the word'. What this says is that 'every word is directed towards an answer'. Words mean by answering each other: meaning is essentially argumentive. This idea clearly connects with the thinking already presented in the work of Aristotle and also in the art of Jane Austen. However, it is important to recognize what Bakhtin does with his idea of 'dialogism'.

Bakhtin formulates laws, laws of language:

every word is directed towards an answer . . .

and

The phenomenon of internal dialogization . . . is present to a greater or lesser extent in all realms of the life of the word.

Bakhtin develops rules of genre:

> In genres that are poetic in their narrow sense, the natural dialogization of the word is not put to artistic use . . .

(We will be challenging this particular rule later in the chapter.) Bakhtin's laws of language are essentially Rhetorical, and should be understood not as a sudden breakthrough, but as one part of a tradition. Bakhtin turns that tradition against other kinds of linguistic theory – a move which is important to this chapter. But Bakhtin's laws are part of a discussion about the Grand Theory of Language. We are not operating in those terms, and would resist the obligation to produce such a general system, while acknowledging Bakhtin's influence. At the same time, we are interested in how Rhetoric can speculate generally, if not in how it can establish grand laws. The next section explores the way Rhetoric has speculated about arguments – about argument and society.

Rhetoric, argument, and society

So far two essential types of argument have been defined and explored: the one-to-one process, as in the example of Emma and Mr Knightley, and the concerted putting of the case, as in *A Room of One's Own*. These types of argument have been defined through the process of close analysis in an essentially literary way. Two main Rhetorical principles were used in this exploration: that of engaging (persuasively, yet also in play) with the other view of the issue, and the principle of address. However, instead of thinking out the meaning of such principles in relation to reading, say, *Emma*, there is a more speculative way of examining such principles by applying them not to the analysis of literary contexts, but to questions of society and politics.

What follows is not a 'history' of Rhetorical approaches to 'argument and society' and 'argument and politics'. These are examples taken from different periods, all of which show that it is possible to generate ideas about society or politics when address and argument are connected. First, there are classical examples from Greece about Athenian democracy. Democracy in Athens was not the same as British democracy: the key idea was the assembly of citizens, so that the democracy was participatory rather than representative. In classical Athens, several views of democracy arose from thinking about address and 'other' views. Indeed Kennedy has argued that the democratic institution is an essential context *for* Rhetoric and related thinking. Questions about persuading audiences and arguing cases are raised by the political process, where issues are debated and speeches made. The *result*, Kennedy suggests, is much thought about addressing arguments, including thought about democracy and society.

By thinking Rhetorically about argument, some Greek theorists reached conclusions supporting 'democracy'. The sophists of the fifth century BC, Protagoras and Gorgias, have been perceived as supporting democracy with a Rhetorical theory of argument. They thought about why argument is *necessary* and this led them to defend political institutions which favoured the widest play of arguments. For instance, Protagoras held the principle that 'man is the measure and the measurer of all things'. There is no absolute truth. Therefore, to quote Kennedy, 'truth must be approximated in each time and place'. As regards politics, all the cases must then be put to the people. Hence it could be said that such a theory is 'democratic', regarding 'democracy' as the institution of arguing. Gorgias' politics was also based on the need for each side to be put to the people. Protagoras and Gorgias were opposed by Plato in the dialogues given their names. He criticized them, as we shall see, because his idea of argument is different, not because he is against arguing.

Isocrates, like Plato a disciple of Socrates, set up a school to train pupils for political activity. As Kennedy says, Socrates 'showed a loyalty to, but decided lack of enthusiasm for, Athenian democracy as it existed in the fifth century BC'. Isocrates increasingly, wanted 'a return to a much more restricted democracy'. This was *not* because Isocrates was against argument but because he wanted a 'moral synthesis of arguments', that is, a more elaborate kind of arguing, less 'punchy' than that required when addressing the people. But, more generally, Isocrates had an idea that society is based on argument rather than on force. Indeed, the classical theory of argument often emphasizes the importance of arguing as the central alternative to violence. For Isocrates, without addressed argument there would be no society of any kind:

> Because there is born in us the power to persuade each other
> and to show ourselves whatever we wish we not only have

escaped from living as brutes, but also by coming together have founded cities . . .

People, so the argument goes, do not naturally 'come together'; they need persuading to 'found cities', rather than to continue 'living as brutes'. There is nothing natural about society: arguments *for* living in a society must have been addressed to people at some stage, encountering and answering the 'other' view, which would be that people should continue 'living as brutes', each alone, each for himself or herself. The social order depends on that arguing, and on its continued efficacy in countering and over-coming the 'other' view. Even when a Rhetorician such as Iso-crates is primarily talking about language and persuasion, there is usually a reminder that persuasion is not the whole function of language. Isocrates describes the more-than-persuasive function as being to show ourselves whatever we wish. He implies a playful power of representing the world according to our desires.

Other Greek thinkers reached 'anti-democratic' conclusions. Here an essential idea is that addressing the popular audience corrupts. They contrast flattery with real argument. In his dialogue called *Gorgias*, Plato composes a debate between Socrates and the sophist Gorgias. It is thought that the dialogue reveals Plato's bitterness towards the Athenian political institutions which had condemned Socrates to death. One thrust is against arguments being addressed to an ignorant audience. According to Plato's Socrates, there are certain kinds of Rhetorician and orator who relish being able to convince the ordinary, the popular audience. Plato's Socrates rejects that kind of power of address; the case of medicine is used as an example. Gorgias has claimed that he can defeat doctors in an argument about medicine:

SOCRATES: You said just now that even on matters of health the orator will be more convincing than the doctor.

GORGIAS: Before a popular audience – yes, I did.

SOCRATES: A popular audience means an ignorant audience, doesn't it? He won't be more convincing than the doctor before experts, I presume.

Gorgias is forced to concede defeat in Plato's dialogue. The prin-ciple is that the popular audience encourages Rhetorical skill without knowledge of the truth, or even *against* knowledge of the truth. But that idea does not reject argument itself. On the contrary, argument is valued so highly that it should be protected from having to convince the popular audience. (Here Plato is 'against Rhetoric' only in the sense of being against a narrow version of Rhetoric as popular appeal.)

Plato gives another example of the same kind in a later work, *The Laws*: the judging of competitions between poets. He warns that it is dangerous to appeal to the wrong constituency:

> The present Italian and Sicilian practice of handing over to the mass of spectators and deciding the winner by a show of hands has corrupted the poets.

Judgement must be in the right hands. To say that is not to be against argument, against the weighing of cases for and against policies and poems. Plato criticizes the idea of depending on the 'ignorant audience'.

Like Isocrates, Plato has a general view of language which is integral to his theories of society. In *Phaedrus*, Plato asserts that the function of speech is 'to influence the soul'. In this passage, speech does refer to spoken language, but the *criterion* applies to written language as well. The point here is that in Plato's view of language, address is as central as it is for Isocrates. Indeed in *Phaedrus* there may be a slightly different emphasis on audiences. The arguer

> must arrange and organise his speech accordingly, addressing a simple speech to a simple soul, but to those which are more complex something of greater complexity which embraces the whole range of tones.

Overall, Plato's case is perhaps against adapting argument too narrowly to the popular audience as he sees it: there is a need to address *all* audiences, and not to bring argument down to a low level. For Plato, arguing must always proceed from knowledge and towards truth. He recognizes that opposing views are always possible. In *Phaedrus* he extends the idea of opposing views from law and politics to ordinary speech. But he emphasizes that it is necessary to work through opposing positions in pursuit of truth.

Discussion of argument and society continues after classical Greece in many forms which include Rhetorical contributions. For instance, the classical theory of argument takes a democratic turn in the thought of John Stuart Mill, the nineteenth century English philosopher. In *On Liberty*, a major essay from 1859, Mill makes an exemplary enquiry into address engaging with other views and suggests that in most subjects different views are possible (excepting mathematics and some science). He emphasizes that arguing is all about encountering the 'reasons on the opposite side' as fully as possible. To think about a subject means to consider other views, not merely to develop one's own views. Further he says that it is not enough to be aware of other views apart from one's own, a serious thinker must bring other views 'into real contact with his own mind'. To recognize an opposing position means experiencing that other position as real. Mill suggests that people do not work out what they believe as comprehensively as they would if they felt they had to address their beliefs directly to others with opposing ideas, 'and, consequently, they do not in any proper sense of the words know the doctrine which they themselves profess. They do not know those parts of it which explain and justify the remainder'. A whole society can cease to think if there is no consciousness of the need to address opposing positions. For Mill, the only way to understand one's own beliefs is to address them to people who hold other views, both in imagination and in action. Therefore, Mill continues, 'if opponents of all-important truths do not exist, it is indispensable to imagine them and supply them with the strongest arguments'. *Unless it is possible to imagine addressing a view to an opponent, that view ceases to have any meaning.* This is so even with well-founded beliefs.

This emphasis on imagination connects persuasion with play: to be truly persuasive one has to *imagine* the other view, and be able to 'play at' addressing it. Such an act of playful imagination continues to be necessary even in the act of addressing someone with another view. These ideas come from a work concerned with liberty of thought and discussion: Mill regards such liberty as essential for social progress. He defines liberty in several ways: you should be free to do what you like so long as it is not hurting anyone else. According to Mill, many things can prevent the full play of opposing views, such as censorship and unequal education.

For him democracy is about the widest possible diffusion of free discussion. This brings him into conflict with a different definition which is that the opinion of the majority must prevail. All of these views are clearly political and at the same time are connected directly to classical Rhetoric. Cicero stands for the true understanding of argument:

> The greatest orator, save one, of antiquity, has left it on record that he always studied his adversary's case with as great, if not still greater, intensity than even his own. What Cicero practised as the means of forensic success requires to be imitated by all who study any subject in order to arrive at the truth.

Paul Feyerabend is a contempory philosopher of science who currently exploits ideas of argument that are Rhetorical. He has been concerned to defend 'diversity': diverse views and diverse cultures especially. He suggests that the modern West threatens to impose 'increasing uniformity in the world'. Included in this uniformity is the suppression of argument – by dogmatic reason which knows all the answers. Feyerabend insists that

> Argument, like language, or art, or ritual, is universal; but, again like language or art or ritual, it has many forms.

Feyerabend adopts an approach like that in Aristotle's *Rhetoric*: 'all . . . endeavour to criticize or uphold an argument', and argument is infinitely rich and diverse in detail.

Feyerabend develops many ideas about individuals and societies, ideas that come from using a Rhetorical sense of argument. For instance, he asserts that there is a need for what he calls 'democratic relativism'. The ideal 'city' (society)

> needs *all* the agencies that made it grow

and so

> It makes sense to preserve faulty points of view for possible future use.

A society needs voices to differ from each other – that is how growth takes place. Ideal discussion is what promotes growth:

> The participants get immersed into each others' ways of

thinking, feeling, perceiving to such an extent that their ideas, perceptions, world views may be entirely changed – they become different people participating in a different view and different tradition.

Ideally, argument is creative: that is the central idea of Feyerabend's democratic relativism.

Such democratic relativism is only one modern outcome of thinking about argument Rhetorically, about addressing the 'other' view, the 'other' voice. Hans-Georg Gadamer, for instance, reintroduces a topic theory in terms of questions. For Gadamer, questions are like Aristotle's topics:

questions include the antitheses of yes and no, of being like this and being like that . . .

Gadamer asserts that the greatest need is

to prevent the suppression of questions by the dominant opinion.

Questions belong to elites.

Or there is Hayden White's sense of Rhetoric's mission. For White, Rhetoric's understanding

might permit us to mediate between contending ideologues, each of whom regards his own position as scientific and that of his opponent as mere ideology . . .

Many modern thinkers include address and argument more obliquely in formulating ideas of society. One is Hannah Arendt, whose theory covers politics and philosophy. She was born in Germany, and educated there, but left in the 1930s because she was Jewish; after the war, she settled in America. Her political position is difficult to define on a 'Left-to-Right' spectrum. Arendt's major works include *The Origins of Totalitarianism* and *On Revolution*. The first analyses the Nazi and Soviet systems in the same terms, and has been influential in establishing an idea of what totalitarianism is. *On Revolution* defends the *idea* of revolution, although opposing its dominant forms in the twentieth century. Arendt idealizes the American Revolution of 1776, although she is critical of its outcome. She sees politics as the source of freedom, where many people assume the reverse. For

Arendt, freedom does not exist outside public life. She discusses the Greek example and generalizes from it:

> The life of a free man needed the presence of others.

To be free is to be *with* others, and includes speaking with them. Indeed political action is free action only when it is witnessed, or addressed to a group of witnesses. Arendt emphasizes that arguing in an assembly is the epitome of politics:

> Freedom itself needed therefore a place where people could come together . . . the political space proper.

If people cannot gather to debate, there is no freedom. She envisages a new revolution:

> . . . a new form of government that would permit every member of the modern egalitarian society to become a 'participator' in public affairs.

People would participate as audiences, as speakers, and as actors whose acts are witnessed.

These examples from Greek and from modern writings may appear to concern public matters about which it is inevitable that arguments will involve more than one side. Such public contests also have associations with rowdiness and noise: it is indeed one of the dismissive views of arguing that arguing obstructs thought. Both in the sense of reasoning and of imagining, the noise and the conflict of arguing seems alien to thinking. But Rhetorical matters, to which address is central, involve the most private functions, and are even basic to thought itself.

Rhetoric, argument, and thinking

At first sight, it may appear incongruous to connect the process of thinking to address, since thinking goes on 'in the mind' and appears to be an example of language which is not being addressed. Thought could be a refuge from the exchange of views, which is assumed to be noisy. This refuge from opposing views would be a haven for the imagination of the poet as well as the logic of the scientist. One of the damaging effects of being 'contentious' is that it conceals lack of thought and prevents an audience from thinking. These ideas are based upon distinctions between talking and thinking, between the outward act of talking and the inward act of thinking. Such distinctions have been questioned. Billig presents a passage from Plato's *The Sophist* which questions this distinction:

> Thought and speech are the same: only the former, which is a silent conversation of the soul with itself, has been given the special name of thought.

Another example, from Cicero's *On Invention*, challenges the distinction between thinking and arguing. His first sentence is:

> I have often seriously *debated with myself* whether men and communities have received more good or evil from oratory . . . (My italics)

The original Latin is

> . . . hoc mecum cogitavi . . .

Cogitavi would usually be translated as 'I have thought', and *mecum* as 'with me'. In context the verb suggests both thinking and debating.

Here is a view of thinking which could be termed a 'model'. By 'model' is meant a general construct, a 'diagram' representing the essentials of thinking. This model presents thinking as *inner dialogue*: 'silent conversation' and debating 'with myself'. These are concepts which suggest some kind of address, or a speaking *to*. . . . As the ideas of conversation and debate imply, such address is itself a response to an 'other' position. This model could be said to define thinking as *reciprocal address*: a to-ing and fro-ing of responses in the mind. This is most obvious in the quotation from Cicero, which suggests sides engaged in dialogue. If you say 'I have often debated with myself . . .', as Cicero says, you imply that one side is trying to persuade another. Others make the point more explicitly: thinking should be defined in terms of persuasion. For Isocrates, thought consists of one side making a case convincing, to another, which is implied:

> . . . the same arguments which we use in persuading others when we speak in public, we employ also when we deliberate in our thoughts.

Billig gives as an example Francis Bacon, the Renaissance philosopher, who

> drew attention to the similarity between what we say 'in argumentation, when we are disputing with another', as 'in meditations when we are considering and resolving anything with ourselves'.

Such a model of thinking implies a psychology, a view of the self. If thinking involves address, then the self cannot be a simple entity, a unity distinct from everything which is 'not self'. This model corresponds to a quality of experience. We appear to experience our own thought both from within (as agent or speaker) and from outside (as witness or audience or interlocutor). It is a model used in philosophy, psychology, literary criticism and literature. M. M. Bakhtin, the Russian literary critic, presents this view by exploring thinking in the novels of Dostoevsky. According to Bakhtin,

> Every thought of Dostoevsky's heroes . . . senses itself to be from the beginning a *rejoinder* in an unfinalised dialogue.

Bakhtin is identifying the way in which Dostoevsky's characters *think*: in terms of rejoinder. On the one hand, Bakhtin sees this mode of thought as 'specific' to Dostoevsky in the history of the novel, on the other hand, it makes Dostoevsky's fiction universal. This type of ambiguity between what is Dostoevsky and what is general is inevitable in both literary criticism and literature. It is a particular way of looking.

Literature is an influential source of ideas about thinking. Some of these ideas correspond to the model of thinking as reciprocal address, the to-ing and fro-ing of responses. When they occur in literature, models of thinking are both distinctive and generalized so that, if we consider a Wordsworth poem, what we are getting is a unique experience with universal implications. But haven't we chosen *just* the wrong example? Can there be any dialogue between traditions of argument and a poem by the writer who has often been felt to epitomize the aesthetic of expressivity discussed in the previous chapter?

'Upon Westminster Bridge'
Composed upon Westminster Bridge
September 3, 1802

Earth has not anything to show more fair:
Dull would he be of soul who could pass by
A sight so touching in its majesty:
This City now doth, like a garment, wear
The beauty of the morning; silent, bare,
Ships, towers, domes, theatres and temples lie
Open unto the fields, and to the sky;
All bright and glittering in the smokeless air.
Never did sun more beautifully steep
In his first splendour, valley, rock, or hill;
Ne'er saw I, never felt, a calm so deep!
The river glideth at his own sweet will:
Dear God! the very houses seem asleep;
And all that mighty heart is lying still!

Is this language 'free' of address? Does it escape from the condition of debate about issues? There *is* a feeling of being independent from others:

silent, bare,
Ships, towers, domes, theatres and temples lie
Open unto the fields, and to the sky . . .

Seeing becomes pure experience which seems to be registered for its own sake. The poem also *expresses emotions*. The poet sees

A sight so *touching* . . .

Sight and emotion interpenetrate:

Ne'er saw I, never felt, a calm so deep!

Is the utterance of true feeling happening *without* any sense of responsive address? The poem would seem to represent the possibility that literature resists Rhetorical impulses and acquires its values in that way. But *do* the words of the poem transcend persuasive address? Does Wordsworth avoid those engagements of a voice with other voices which characterize the Rhetorical sense of arguing and thinking? How does the poem work?

The poem opens with the words:

Earth has not anything to show more fair . . .

This is a form of negation. Other negations follow:

Never did sun more beautifully steep . . .
Ne'er saw I, never felt, a calm so deep!

Because these words are negative, they emphasize other kinds of rejection within the poem:

Dull would he be . . . *who could pass by* . . .

In this way, by adopting negative forms, the opening establishes the essential character of the poem. The *effect* is affirmative, but the process is full of negatives. These negatives coincide with strategic points in the poem's sonnet form. A sonnet divides after eight lines. The first eight lines, or octave, began with a negative; the sestet, or six lines that follow, recommences with another negative:

Never did sun more beautifully steep . . .

There follows the negative sequence:

Never . . .
Ne'er . . . Never . . .

The play of word forms adds to the negative effect, because in the word 'ne'er' the 'ever' part is hidden.

Why should a poem affirm such impressions as 'beauty of the morning' and 'calm so deep' with speech phrased in negative terms? Is this a way of 'undermining' the emotions of the poem? On the contrary, it appears that there is no simple parallel between grammatical form and emotional content. A negative grammar need *not* imply a negative state of mind. What then is the effect of the negations? The answer is that to say

Earth has not anything to show more fair

is a way of making a reply. The quality of *responding* is intrinsic: the line comes into being as a *rejoinder*. This sonnet senses itself to be a rejoinder from the beginning and continues in the same way. Issue is taken with an opposing position, and in this case the opposing position would be that 'earth' *has* many scenes to show 'more fair' than 'this City'. The poem is *responding* in several ways: to *these* sights here, seen from Westminster Bridge, and to *other* voices with different views about these sights. It is all about responsiveness, visual, and emotional, but is also *Rhetorical*. The poem presents itself as a 'spontaneous' expression, composed on the instant and on the spot. Such an effect of spontaneity need not be anti-Rhetorical; on the contrary, the effect heightens the sense of engaging with other positions. The poem offers itself as an authentic experience ('Composed upon Westminster Bridge, September 3, 1802') *and* is Rhetorical in the sense of being addressed to other positions. Negative turns of phrase allow for other voices, voices which could contest the judgements which are being made. Indeed the order of events within the text of the poem is such that the sense of replying in the negative comes before we know what the experience is which is being affirmed. Putting affirmations negatively is risky and to do so requires courage because the 'other' possibility is raised into view.

So far the poem does seem to involve argument as Rhetoric understands it. The question which arises next is the way in which the poem presents thinking. The words insist that no one else is present (on the bridge). No one else is imagined. The lines surround themselves with a world which, above all, is bare of people. It is as if no other *consciousness* is awake or conceivable:

> . . . the very houses seem asleep . . .

No other minds inhabit this moment. The poem disengages from other people and also from the life of a society ('all that mighty heart is lying still!'). The experience occurs in a pause, a pause in which the whole culture is 'silent', 'asleep', 'still'. The sense of pause leads from silence through sleep to a kind of temporary death; from people not being visible, to 'houses' being asleep, to a collective body at rest. Even the exclamation, 'Dear God!' does not simply that God is present: it is a formula which actually *prevents* the poem becoming a prayer. The point about such formulaic exclamations is that they are *not* addressed to God. The poem insists upon being a reply; it also insists that no one else is physically present, and that no other consciousness is accessible. How then is the dialogue happening? The writing explores what it means for experience to be in the mind, and what happens 'in the mind' becomes apparent to us. This process confronts us with the model of thinking in a particular way – in the form of a poem

– just as Bakhtin finds it in the form of Dostoevsky's novels. To *think* is to *respond*, partly to sights and feelings but also to other voices. *Reply* involves *address*, to a differing view, or anticipating a different view. The poem lets us place this address nowhere except within the poet's mind. In this model, 'mind' is not simple, or a simply entity in which one voice speaks. Thoughts are *addressed* within the mind, and addressed in a persuasive form. There is nowhere in the mind outside such contending address. The key to this coherence would be Rhetorical. The poem creates a dialogue in which different voices engage each other.

The relation between voices heard in the poem can vary. This depends on how the words in the line are stressed. When the stress falls as follows:

Earth has *not* anything to show *more* fair . . .

a strong sense of an opposing voice occurs, an insistent, forceful voice. On the other hand, the stresses may shift:

Earth has not *anything* to show more *fair* . . .

and here there is a sense of superlative affirmation, and the 'other' voice is more restrained. As the stress plays over the words we can feel the process in which voices engage with each other. The relation between the voices is *negotiable*. Different degrees of domination are possible. The voices are *not* valued equally, but the emotional force of the process depends upon the encounter between unequally valued voices. Indeed that is the coherence which the poem explores: the coherence of an unequally weighted dialogue. Affirmation triumphs but the point is not in the triumph – it is in the whole process of engagement. Arguing enters into the rhythmic body of the language. A contention that

This City . . . *doth* . . .

meets another qualifying emphasis:

This City *now* . . .

The emphasis on 'now' suggests that this is a special moment, uncharacteristic of London in general. There is a real sense in which these positions address each other. The weighting of the different views is difficult to decide – rhythmically and in terms of which is winning the argument. This is the most direct of all reciprocal exchanges, fully internal to the mind and to the rhythms of speech.

It is possible to formulate a different Rhetorical account of Wordsworth and consciousness. Paul de Man emphasizes the splitting of consciousness which is effected by different voices. In that case, it is easier to talk about the 'subject' being divided up, where 'subject' is derived from subjectivity. It seems more appropriate to use the word 'mind' if the emphasis is on the process of thinking. In that process of thinking, different voices engage *with* each other rather than splitting apart.

A process of address has been revealed within the poem: phrases conjure up opposing views. But the address extends further – to the reader. How does the process of address within the poem address itself to the reader? Consider the lines:

> Dull would he be of soul who could pass by
> A sight so touching . . .

The reader can *identify* with the poet as not the 'he' who would be so dull of soul as to pass by this sight unmoved. The poet is not that person. The reader is not that person. Yet how easily both poet and reader might have been that person who *could* pass by – the movement of the lines leaves a pause before the sight, a pause in which we recognize that the sight might not have been seen. That recognition makes us identify all the more strongly with the poet rather than with the one who would pass by. Kenneth Burke, the American Rhetorician, shows that giving audiences the opportunity to identify with the speaker or writer is an important form of address. One of the ways of doing this is to enable the audience to identify with the speaker against somebody else. In the poem we as readers identify with the writer on the bridge by denying that we could be so dull of soul. Because the process is one of denial, it links with the process of arguing as it occurs throughout the poem, in which negative forms have been so explicit. We enter into the process and we feel addressed.

The reading of the poem as argument raises the question of topics. Topics, as has been noted, can be issues defined by oppositions or opposing voices. One topic is that of City and Country: which is better? This is an established topic, already present in Roman poetry such as that of Horace, for instance, and in Dryden.

The fact that it is already established makes certain things possible for the poem, things which can still be done because the topic remains recognizable, although in a different form. Familiarity with the topic makes possible the economy of words, which makes the sonnet form conceivable. Another thing which is possible because of this familiarity with the topic is that the poem can begin abruptly, without explaining, as it were, what is at issue. A familiar topic is being replayed for different emphases. The usual handling of the topic in poetry suggests that the Country is more beautiful than the City. Indeed, Wordsworth's own poetry has handled the topic in this way before. The poem introduces a recognizable topic, although here the voices that defend the City are more forceful than usual. The topic of City and Country overlaps with another topic – that of London. Views for and against London are also familiar. Strong supporting voices have been heard, for instance, in the poem 'London thou art of Cities a per se . . . of Cities sovereign'. Contrary voices dominate Samuel Johnson's poem *London*. This topic is interwoven with the first topic in an elusive way, which is part of its appeal. The poem can be seen in terms of a process which brings these topics to new life. That process is one of arguing and thinking. The classical term for such a process would be 'invention'. Reading the poem makes us aware that invention is not mechanical. There is no recipe for bringing to life the topics of City and Country and of London in the way that this poem does. There is something fundamentally mysterious about the way in which invention works. Play has been an important concept throughout the reading of the poem in the sense that the process of argument cannot be reduced to the opposition of positions in the abstract. When a topic comes to life it interweaves with other topics; voices test out other voices in an engagement. The topic is teased out. The result is a feeling of pleasure, almost suspenseful pleasure: what will happen next? As the topic is elaborated, what goes on is also persuasive in the sense that different voices try to persuade each other and also the reader. One of the particular contributions of poetry to the understanding of invention is the experience it offers when play and persuasion are so obviously inseparable. This affords an insight into thinking and arguing generally. As Cicero says:

There are in my opinion three things that oratory should bring about: the instruction of the hearer, his being given pleasure, his being strongly moved.

Notes and further reading

One of the chapter's own arguments is that classical Rhetoric is important for the understanding of argument. The main sources are Aristotle, *The 'Art' of Rhetoric* in the Loeb edition and translation by J. H. Freese – references for argument generally are to Book I, i and those for topics are to I, ii, I, iii and I, vii, and Plato, *Gorgias*, in the Penguin translation by W. Hamilton (1971), the central passage being on p. 37. Plato's *Phaedrus* is also discussed, references being to the Penguin translation by W. Hamilton (1973), particularly p. 100. The passage from Plato's *Laws* is in Russell and Winterbottom (1972). Cicero, *De Inventione*, I, i is quoted from the Loeb edition of M. Hubbell.

G. Kennedy (1963) is a major account: Chapter 1, 'The nature of Rhetoric' includes Isocrates on society (pp. 8–9); Chapter 2, 'Techniques of persuasion in Greek literature before 400 B.C.' discusses democracy and Rhetoric; Chapter 3, 'Early Rhetorical theory, Corax to Aristotle' is illuminating on Aristotle's *Rhetoric*; Chapter 4, 'The Attic orators', explores Isocrates and Demosthenes among others. This is a work at once informative and accessible.

D. Russell and M. Winterbottom (1972) is an essential collection of translations from classical Rhetoric and criticism. Our chapter quotes briefly from the extracts of Cicero's *De Oratore* on the poet and the orator, and from Cicero's *Brutus* on the effects of oratory. There are also helpful selections from Plato and Aristotle.

Michael Billig's 'Thinking and arguing' (Inaugural Lecture, University of Loughborough, 14 May, 1986) is a brilliant analysis of why classical Rhetoric matters to modern psychology, and includes Isocrates and Bacon on thinking. Billig (1987) develops these ideas more fully.

Descartes on arguing is from Perelman and Olbrechts-Tyteca (1969 translation). John Stuart Mill is cited in the Penguin edition. We recommend Chapter II 'Of the liberty of thought and discussion', pp. 98–105, which is the source of the Mill passages. Hannah Arendt's *On Revolution* is quoted from the Penguin edition (1973), p. 31 and pp. 264–5. H.-G. Gadamer (1979 translation) is important on questions and differences, especially Part 2 (The extension of the question of truth to understanding in the human sciences'), quotations being from Part 2, II, 3, pp. 228–30. Feyerabend (1987) explores argument and diversity, and references are made to the 'Introduction' (p. 8) and to 'Notes on relativism' (pp. 60, 33, 29). Hayden White on 'History and Rhetoric' in White and Manuel (1978), is cited on topics, and White (1978b) on ideology: together these works are fundamental to modern thinking about Rhetoric.

M. M. Bakhtin (1981 translation) is one literary approach, especially Chapter 4 on 'Discourse in the novel', from which pp. 278–86 are especially relevant and helpful. Bakhtin (1984 translation) is important on literature and thinking, particularly Chapter 1 on 'Dostoevsky's polyphonic novel'. Kenneth Burke (1969) is a major rethinking of topic theory in a modern context, and we have quoted p. 11 and referred more generally.

Jane Austen's *Emma* is quoted in the Penguin edition (1966). The main reference is to Chapter 8, with Chapter 1. Virginia Woolf's *A Room of One's Own* is quoted in the Granada/Panther edition, with particular references to Chapter 2, especially p. 27 and p. 35. Wordsworth's sonnet is widely available.

On Rhetoric and argument generally, we also recommend Booth (1974a), a lively polemic on the subject in a contemporary context; Genette (1982 translation), especially the essay on 'Rhetoric restrained'; and Curtius (1953 translation) for a classic account, especially Chapter 4, 'Rhetoric', and Chapter 5, 'Topics'. On feminism and argument, Showalter has a fine essay entitled 'Feminist criticism in the wilderness' in E. Abel (1982) and Furman has a pertinent argument on 'The politics of language' in Greene and Kahn (1985). Kristeva has an essay on 'A new type of intellectual: the dissident' in Moi (ed.) *The Kristeva Reader* (1985). P. M. Spacks (1975) is illuminating on Austen, Woolf and other novelists. On Wordsworth and thinking, Kerrigan (1985) is a stimulating essay from another perspective; P. de Man (1983) includes the influential account of 'The rhetoric of temporality', a particular version of Wordsworth and Rhetoric with which our reading implicitly takes issue. B. Johnson (1980) is stimulating on Rhetoric and the reading of poetry, particularly Chapter 3 'Poetry and its double'. Kritzman (*Yale French Studies* 66) gives a helpful account of ideas of play in the thinking of Barthes and others.

Chapter four

The prison-house of Rhetoric

So far in this book we may have given the impression that all utterances and any texts are amenable to Rhetorical analysis. Does it follow, therefore, that any utterance is an example of Rhetoric, thereby robbing the term of all specificity? On the face of it this does seem to be the case, judging by the titles of such recently-published books as McCloskey's *The Rhetoric of Economics*. And we have already seen how Rhetorical terms can be applied in the most unlikely-looking places, and how it sometimes seems that even positions in an argument have not only been anticipated, but actually *named*, by the Rhetoricians. At times Rhetoric seems to be a map of the entire universe, future as well as past, hypothetical as well as real. While it is not necessary to adopt this posture we would like to suggest that all examples of language in use are Rhetorical in so far as they must carry the trace of argument, play, and address. And it is necessary to assert this because the counter view, which would try to restrict Rhetoric to only a few cases, is still very much in evidence. Northrop Frye, for instance, speaks of 'advertising and propaganda [which] are designed deliberately to create an illusion, hence they constitute for us a kind of anti-language, especially in the speeches of so-called charismatic leaders that set up a form of mass hypnosis.' Advertising and propaganda are seen here as a departure from the 'normal' use of language, which, of course, is seen as 'plain speaking'. It is because we reject this opposition that we have eschewed consideration of either of these uses of language as they are conventionally understood and have concentrated instead on instances that seem much less promising, and are therefore more challenging, with respect to our project.

In this chapter we discuss kinds of utterances that are widely felt to be either below, or above, the concerns of Rhetoric. We hope to show that there is in fact a Rhetoric of 'everyday speech' by examining the interactions between parents and children, and between members of peer groups. On the other hand, the business of learning to write in school, and of participating in the institutions of the Christian Church and of the law, can only be illuminated once we expose their various connections with Rhetoric. Both Church and law can be said to possess their own 'sacred texts' which appear on the surface to put both institutions above the pressures of argument, address, and interpretation. Finally, we shall consider briefly the notion of the sacred text in forming the academic 'disciplines' of philosophy and literary criticism.

It should follow from the discussion so far that in our view there is no such thing as 'ordinary' or 'everyday' language that can be used as a benchmark in the analysis of utterances. Ordinary language is often assumed to lack formal patterning, ambiguity, and wordplay, and to be capable of carrying in an unproblematic way the 'message' sent from speaker to hearer, who in turn are assumed to be equals sharing the same cultural norms. Against these idealized projections certain institutions are held to have 'special' languages. An influential doctrine in twentieth-century thought has been that literature, for instance, is marked off from other kinds of utterances by its unique qualities of language. In part this has been motivated by the desire to justify literature as a separate and special category of texts. Religion and law are also held to have special languages. There is of course some truth in this, in that linguistic minorities, or speakers of non-prestigious languages, in many parts of the world often find that court proceedings are conducted in an alien language. Even in England, law was for a long time after the Norman conquest conducted in French, as were parts of the Christian service in Latin; the association of a particular kind of language with religious worship can be so strong that attempts to 'reform' or up-date usage have met with strong resistance (even, as in the case of Greece, riots). We have already noted an example of such 'audience power' in relation to the revised prayer discussed in Chapter 1. Even where vernacular languages have been adapted to legal and religious proceedings, there are often linguistic features that are distinctive. In English perhaps the most obvious examples are archaisms, a retention of usages from the sixteenth and seventeenth centuries when vernacular legal and liturgical utterances were being formulated. Common to both spheres is the doublet, a yoking of synonyms or near-synonyms, such as 'rights and remedies' (law) and 'erred and strayed' (religion). It is important to acknowledge, however, that these forms are restricted to certain *genres* of text only; they cannot be said to be representative of religious or legal utterance in general. The notion of 'special languages' is therefore of limited usefulness, partly because it involves us in thinking of language as a system (rather than a process), partly because there are no clear *linguistic* reasons for distinguishing many so-called legal or religious utterances from other kinds. As we shall see, what counts as a religious or legal (or, for that matter, political) utterance is often something to be contested rather than merely received.

One very interesting and instructive aspect of the argument in favour of special legal or religious languages is its reliance on a kind of analysis that today is most likely to be associated with literary criticism. Patterns of repetition, rhythm, and alliteration have been found, for instance, in legal contracts, while certain recent revisions of Christian texts have been judged as though they were poems: the substitution of 'alien soil' for 'strange land' in the well-known psalm, for example, not only loses the alliteration on /s/ with 'sad song', but conjures up (it is claimed) the wrong connotations in the ear of the listener. Here we see arguments traditionally used to justify a special status for literature (more precisely, poetry, which has often been made to stand for literature in general) being adopted to underpin a similar claim on behalf of other kinds of utterance. The association of this kind of analysis with literature, however, is not essential but historical. Such analysis is actually part of Rhetoric, but a part that over the centuries has become specialized to only certain kinds of texts, those called 'literary'. Part of the purpose of this book is to move back, as it were, to an earlier position which sees Rhetoric as something central to all utterance in general rather than marginal and restricted to only certain specialized kinds.

It might be remembered that one of Cicero's categories was style (*elocutio*). Some of the ancient Rhetoricians were interested in distinguishing levels of style, such as High, Middle, and Low, and relating them to particular kinds of oratory, or stages in a particular oration. One of the more unfortunate consequences of the specialization of Rhetoric noted above has been the tendency to think of 'style' as something 'added on' to ordinary language, which in turn is considered styleless. In our view, style is an aspect of *all* language, an inevitable consequence of seeing any act of utterance as worthy of sustained attention. As we shall see, all utterances, once seen in their contexts of use, are equally complex, subtle, and at times even fraught.

Parents and children

'It is in the nature of language to be overlooked', wrote the linguist Benveniste. While it is a major function of formal education to try to overcome this tendency, there is one area of common experience where language is not likely to be taken entirely for granted. This is child-rearing, at least in the dominant culture of Britain, and especially in relation to the first child, in whom so much is invested: we want it to be 'normal', to function efficiently, even to be like us. And some parents, especially those who were successful at school, also see their offspring as potential schoolchildren, and through their patterns of interaction prepare them, however unconsciously, for the routines of the classroom.

But we must beware of proposing norms. Regional background, social class, gender, and age are all of them sources of variation in child-rearing practices. These also vary, needless to say, across cultures. The principal care-giver, for instance, need not be the mother, but the father or older siblings. In some cultures the child's attempts at speech are either ignored or their existence denied. The line drawn between childhood and adulthood also varies, and we must not forget that most infants throughout the world are likely to grow up in a bilingual community, so that they will be socialized by more than one language. Even in a predominantly monoglot culture, such as England, a child usually experiences more than one linguistic code. Mothers may speak a variety of English different from that of the father, and older siblings may use one that is different again (particularly if they have been brought up in an area new to both parents), and occasionally a child may be brought up by paid helpers (nannies, child-minders, even servants). But some, perhaps most commonly just one, of these care-givers will be more dominant in the socialization of the child, and the more persistant in establishing dialogues with it.

For from the moment of birth the infant is involved in dialogue with others. The earliest exchanges of eye-contact between the baby and the principle care-giver (who in our culture at least is likely to be the mother) provide the unconscious foundation of a major principle of verbal interaction which can be called turn-taking. Feeding time, moreover, tends to be accompanied by extended bouts of eye-contact and smiles, routines which reinforce the turn-taking pattern. Judging by the amount of talk and touch directed at the child, it appears that parents set great store on winning the child's attention and getting it, by one means or another, to respond. Dialogue, then, is there from the start: to quote Bakhtin once again, 'verbal interaction is the ultimate reality in language'.

It is therefore not surprising that parents are keenly interested in whatever emissions – vocal or otherwise – are produced by the infant. The child's behaviour is already being 'coded', in a sense, by its care-givers. Every cry, gurgle, or gesture is *interpreted* by its parents as in some way communicative. It is assumed that the child has something to communicate and that it uses whatever 'raw material' is available as a kind of primitive signalling system. The child's actions reactivate, in a sense, what the care-giver knows about the possibilities afforded by language and gesture – what kinds of meaning may be generated and in what way.

Already, then, the parent seems to be operating with a particular model of social interaction: that the baby, as an individual, has certain feelings, needs, and desires which it wants to communicate to another person. Thus the infant's every emission is treated as though it represented an *intention* to signal something to somebody. Crying, for instance, might mean that the child wants to be fed, or cuddled, or given something to help its digestion, and so on. The important thing is that the child's behaviour is interpreted according to one view of *adult* interaction: that language is a means of enabling speaker A to transmit a message to listener B. What the child so far lacks is the ability to *refer* to whatever it is that it wants. Since it is words, principally, that have this function, the arrival of the first word is awaited with enthusiasm (an impulse reinforced by, perhaps even stemming from, the emphasis placed by school on the word as the minimum unit of language).

From the very first, then, the child is implicated in a framework of communicative behaviour. It has no choice in the matter; its every action is at the mercy of adult inference. The child accordingly learns that certain vocalizations and gestures are interpreted in particular ways, whatever feelings or preferences it may have had. The infant's utter dependency puts it entirely in the power of the adult, whose expectations (that the child will eventually learn language) and desires (that the child will learn language, and that it will respond to and be cheered by her presence) are only strengthened by the sight of the child's vulnerability. But it is because of adult interests and desires that only some emissions receive close attention (or are even noticed). Babbling, as discussed in Chapter 2, is often seen, for instance, as a kind of linguistic practising; because the adult knows what the end-point is likely to be, she or he interprets it as a milestone on the road to language acquisition, and in turn this interpretation draws the child in the same direction. One aspect of babbling, however, is invariably overlooked, partly because it seems to be natural and instinctive rather than learned behaviour. Patterns of intonation, the rise and fall in pitch, are unconsciously picked out by the child from the flow of adult speech and reproduced at an extremely early age. Intonation is particularly important to the realization of speech in English, but such is our 'word-centred' awareness of language that is is perceived as meaningful by both adults and children without either side being entirely conscious of it.

Intonation is vital to the production of dialogue, and, as we have seen in Chapters 1 and 2, one of the most powerful interactional moves is the question; nowhere is this more true than in dialogues between parents and children. Parents ask children questions in order to elicit a response, something that the child feels constrained to provide. The earliest questions are typically **polar** (inviting a simple yes or no in reply) and are uttered (at least by speakers of RP) in a particular type of rising intonation. Part of the child's linguistic development is its ability to recognize that the rising intonation of the parent's question needs to be 'completed' by the falling one of its own response. This means that the questioner can facilitate, if not guarantee, a response of a particular kind by means of his or her intonational contour. This principle, known as **pitch concord**, which operates in many different contexts of spoken interaction, can be seen as a kind of persuasive device by means of which a speaker gains the listener's assent.

The question/response pair is an example of the way in which spoken interaction often has a logic of its own above and beyond the particular interests, desires, and feeling of the actual participants. It has a kind of automatic quality, and has accordingly been classified as an **adjacency pair** (see glossary). Another, even more ritualized example of an adjacency pair is the greeting. The utterance of a greeting requires the addressee to respond instantly with another greeting: failure to do this is likely to be noticed and commented on ('What's wrong with him today?'). It is important to note that greetings themselves are often formulaic in nature: 'How are you?' is not a request for information so much as an invitation to say something like 'Fine' and then respond with something similar. Basic greeting formulas such as 'Hello' and 'Goodbye' are also examples of the few linguistic items that children are especially *taught* by parents. Children from a very early age are continually exhorted to make these utterances in the appropriate situations long before they are able to appreciate their meanings. In being taught them the child is being made aware of the need to *accommodate* others; the use of the right formula at the right time is one way of doing this.

This feature of automaticity, the sense that dialogue has a logic of its own, seems to be internalized and then reproduced by both parents and children in their own distinctive ways. So persistent, for instance, is the parents' questioning (moving from polar to *wh-* questions as the infant gets older) that the child learns to retaliate with its own bombardment of questions, often to the surprise and even bewilderment of the parent. And parents themselves often experience the sensation of being 'overtaken' by a particular kind of utterance when they attempt dialogues with their offspring. One example of this is the adoption of baby talk, in which pitch-height and intonation curves are exaggerated, the phonological structure of words reduced, and special diminutive suffixes and patterns of extra repetition are used. (These features are found in as many as fifteen different languages.) Another example can occur when parents decide that a child's questions are inappropriate, unanswerable, or even tiresome. 'Where are you going?' can accordingly be answered by the formula 'to see a man about a dog'; 'How much did that cost?' by 'Money and fair words'; and 'What's that?' by 'A whim-wham for a water-wheel'. These traditional forms have been described as *put-offs*. Proverbs such as 'Listeners hear no good of themselves' can perform a singular function while at the same time setting the child's behaviour against the social norm (or desideratum) implied by the parents. And matters which are beyond the child's comprehension (and, for that matter, that of the adult) can be deflected by the use of such formulas as 'the clouds are bumping together' (used in response to a child's request for an explanation of thunder).

It would be wrong, however, to see the adult's use of such forms as either merely automatic or as the straightforward exercise of power over an inquisitive child. There may also be an element of 'play' involved; put-offs provide the child with a puzzle to solve, since their force will not be immediately apparent. They may accordingly function as informal tests of the child's wit, as well as displays of that of the adult. Like riddles, they can be highly educative, but their educative value is implicit rather than explicit. Exactly the same could be said of the kinds of childlore discussed in Chapter 2. Automaticity, too, can be a source of play. Comic repartee, as in the plays of Shakespeare and also Pinter, depends in part for its effect on the exposure of this quality in conversational interaction.

The automaticity of much verbal interaction should not of course be exaggerated. Dialogue always presents us with problems: sometimes it's difficult to know how to initiate one, at other times there are problems in drawing them to a close. One problem for the parent is actually securing the attention of a child when initiating a spoken exchange. One way the adult can do this is with an adjacency-pair involving what is called a **pre-sequence**. The parent will tell the child what it doesn't want to hear by such a move as this:

PARENT: Debbie.
DEBBIE: Yes?
PARENT: Time to do your teeth.

In naming the child directly the adult gains her attention, forcing a reply: this constitutes the adjacency-pair, preparing the way for the unpopular request. The problem for children, on the other hand, is that of interpreting the **pragmatic force** of their caregivers' utterances. They are, however, quick to learn the general principle that many adult utterances have a directive force when addressed to a child: the goal of the adult is to get the child to do something. The child's recognition of this goal is apparently so highly developed that it operates on a kind of interactional maxim that states 'find some action mentioned in the adult's speech that can be performed, and do it, to show that you have understood and can take your turn'. Sometimes this maxim is over-applied, so that the polar question 'Can you jump?' is interpreted as a request to perform the actual action rather than a question to be answered with either a yes or no.

But the general lesson the child has learned by about the age of two is that the same goal can be realized by means of more than one linguistic form. A request, for instance, can take the form of a direct imperative 'Give me that', an **interrogative** 'Can I have that?' or a **declarative** 'I want that'. The so-called indirect forms – the declarative and interrogative ones – are understood no less readily than the direct imperative.

What the child has in effect learned is the rudiments of a system of *politeness*. The basic principle of politeness is that linguistic form is varied to suit particular addressees and particular interactional goals. By the age of three, for instance, the bilingual child has learned which language to use with particular addressees, and is also capable of using baby talk to address younger infants. At an even younger age some children are able to vary the form of directives: direct imperatives to peers of the same age, imperatives + 'please' to three-year-olds, interrogatives for four-year-olds, and declaratives and interrogatives for adults. 'Indirectness' here seems closely associated with the power of the addressee, where power is defined by age. Indirect forms may be used by adults to children as a means of 'softening' a directive, but in the final resort, of course, the asymmetries in the interaction will be manifested once the child attempts to challenge the adult's will.

Power, of course, is by no means always wielded in a flat-footed and transparent way. Parents may choose an indirect approach so as to avoid embarrassing the child (or themselves). In subtle games of hinting, for instance, intonation plays a vital part. A mother might genuinely want to know who ate the last biscuit, but is unwilling to confront her child with an accusation in case it wasn't him. So she says, 'Someone's eaten the last biscuit.' The child recognizes the hint, and signals his recognition by replying 'It wasn't me', with a **fall-rise** (see glossary) intonation on 'me'; this indicates that he doesn't want to force his mother into a defensive posture in which she would have to say something like 'I wasn't accusing *you*.' The use of a particular intonation pattern makes the issue at stake seem open and indeterminate, allowing both parties to maintain their self-respect.

Power and politeness

We have already seen the importance of both power and politeness in examining child-parent interaction. Both concepts, however, need further explanation. For although the relationship between parents and children is marked by inequality of power, family relationships are, broadly speaking, relatively close. Power relationships are probably more usually associated with those characterized by greater social *distance* than family ones: pupils and teachers, for instance; or workers and employers; doctors and patients; 'clients' and 'officials' of various kinds. Relationships which are distant, however, are not always power-coded: on a scale of closeness-distance, for example, we can possibly place kin, friends/peers, workmates, neighbours, and, moving beyond one's normal range of contacts, that amorphous category we label 'strangers'. Close relationships likewise often lack a difference of power in this social sense, as in the case of siblings, close friends, and spouses. In sum, we can use this bi-polar grid of unequal/ equal, close/distant as a very crude means of categorizing interactional events.

As children grow into adulthood they must learn to steer a way through these different kinds of interaction. They will accordingly learn, in an unconscious way, that people in positions of authority enjoy certain interactional privileges: introducing topics ('How's the wife, Jones?'), interrupting, initiating a change in the status of the relationship ('Ellen, do call me Joan if you like'), and, in certain contexts like admonishing, demoting, or supervising a subordinate, specifying the pragmatic force of their own utterances and commenting on, defining, and even redefining the force of another's. Thus, a police inspector 'dressing down' a constable might say: 'I'm warning you, Barry, that this is not the way to go on at all' (where he is drawing attention to this utterance's force with the word 'warn') and then go on to ask 'Are you claiming that no one has ever pointed this out to you before?' (where he is trying to define the force of his interlocutor's earlier comments). Ploys like these succeed in dominating the subordinate interactant because they confront him with what he has said, whereas in more equal encounters the force of a turn is more usually left to the interpretation of the listener. And even in power-coded encounters the superior participant will often choose to mask his/or her own position by exploiting the ambiguities available in the language, as in the case of the mother and son previously described. Thus, a research supervisor to a student says: 'I was wondering if you could come over here this evening between five and six, because I'm rather tied up in the early days of next week?'. The student replies: 'I haven't got the car any more.' The supervisor doesn't want to place the student in the invidious position of having to make an outright refusal, and so makes the force of his utterance ambivalent, somewhere between: 'are you able to?' and 'are you willing to?'. The student doesn't want to refuse flatly, and chooses to interpret the supervisor's utterance in the light of the first alternative.

The strategies we have been discussing are those associated with the phenomenon of politeness. Such linguistic routines are possibly universal in all known languages, although they may be realized in different ways. It is not true, however, to say that some languages (and therefore some speakers) are more polite than others, only that *systems* vary across cultures. Politeness, however, means a great deal more than simply remembering to add 'please' and 'thank you' or not pointing at strangers, and avoiding mention of such words as 'death' when expressing condolences. It can also involve third parties as well as one's addressee: I can show disrespect for my addressee's husband as I am talking (politely) to his wife! In order to understand the complexities of polite behaviour it has recently been suggested that people are generally motivated to protect the *face* both of themselves and of others. When addressing another, furthermore, the speaker may choose whether to respect the addressee's personal 'territory' by not imposing on them, or to appeal to their common humanity and similarity of need and interest. The two strategies can be exemplified by the following example.

Borrowing someone else's car, even in the closest and most equal of relationships, is something that is likely to cause all kinds of tension. The aspiring borrower's reluctance to inconvenience the owner, the possible insurance problems, and the owner's reluctance to refuse the request – a position likely to be anticipated by the borrower – all contribute to the problematic nature of the interaction. A borrower may accordingly choose the strategy of negative politeness, characterized by such markers as hesitation, indirectness, and deference, as 'Er, I was wondering whether it might be possible for me to borrow your car for a little bit – if you wouldn't mind?'. Here the onus is placed on the speaker to borrow (rather than on the owner to lend), the use of past tense in 'was wondering' makes it less direct that the present, the use of 'might' and 'if' signal possibilities and conditions that respect the owner's freedom of movement in replying (e.g. you can borrow it *in principle*, but it's got a flat tyre, etc.). It is negative politeness of this kind that most speakers of English tend to think of as constituting politeness in general, and it is this, also, that tends to give many people from other cultures the impression that in certain circumstances the English are excessively polite. What is vital to bear in mind, however, is that this strategy is more common among middle-class speakers of English. For it is quite possible and feasible to adopt a different model when asking to borrow a car. 'Lend us your wagon, will you?' appeals to a sense of solidarity between owner and borrower, with its strategic use of slang vocabulary ('wagon')', informal plural form of the personal pronoun ('us') and **tag question** ('will you?'). The face addressed is that which desires recognition of its friendly, human aspect. Such positive politeness is more common amongst working-class speakers and may be regarded as rude by those who would not adopt this strategy in the same context. A bricklayer at work in a building site who pauses to ask a passing stranger 'Got the time, mate?' may attract this response.

Similar appeals to positive face are made in such contexts as complimenting or thanking someone on their own ground: thus, 'What a *super* garden!'; 'Thank you for that *wonderful* meal.' From a Rhetorical point of view what is interesting here is the use of exaggeratives, or *hyperbole*, in situations where such utterances are entirely predictable. Amongst speakers of English (though not of some other languages) these utterances are likely to be accepted in an accommodating spirit, even though they may be met with a ritual 'Oh, it was nothing' or the like. Similarly acceptable are those instances of **bald imperatives** which accompany equally stereotyped interactions. When the addressee is in some danger, 'Watch out!' can be taken as polite since the needs and interests of the addressee are paramount; likewise invitations such as 'Sit down' and 'Have another sandwich', and well-wishings such as 'Take care'.

The widespread use of polite forms suggests that a high premium is placed on the avoidance of conflict, unpleasantness, offence, and criticism. It is enough that many social encounters proceed in a relatively innocuous and predictable way, where potential disagreements are softened by the use of such formulas as 'Mind you' or 'Well, they do say that . . .'. We often feel the pressure to keep talking simply to maintain contact, even though we are conscious of sounding vacuous, because on such occasions silence would feel awkward and even rude. 'You've had your hair cut', for instance, seems an entirely redundant utterance, telling the addressee something he or she cannot fail to know, yet signalling that the speaker has noticed something about them and therefore offering them the opportunity to confirm it, thereby establishing agreement.

A number of Rhetorical devices are used to signal disagreement, criticism, or disapproval in indirect, and therefore not impolite, ways. A proverb such as 'Listeners hear no good of themselves', for instance, allows the speaker to soften criticism of an inquisitive interlocutor. Metaphors such as 'John's a real fish' (he drinks too much) and understatement, or *litotes*, as in 'I wasn't exactly bowled over by his speech' can be used for similar purposes. Finally, one of the most adaptable figures to be used in these ways is irony. Certain expressions such as 'Well, I like that!' and 'That's *all* I wanted!' when uttered with a predictable 'marked' intonation have acquired the status of formulas, so that the so-called literal meaning of the words (the exact opposite of that intended by the speaker and received by the listener) is virtually lost to sight.

Another use of irony involves uttering a polite formula in an inappropriate context. 'Do help yourself' addressed to someone who is already tucking in to your food without waiting for an invitation to start is a 'polite' way of censuring impolite behaviour. It is a strategy of 'mock politeness'. The opposite of this, mock impoliteness or *banter*, is actually cultivated in relationships which are both close and equal, where it is felt that politeness is neither necessary nor desirable. A weak version of this would be the use of a bald imperative such as 'Put the kettle on', uttered in an appropriately 'friendly' intonation by a woman to her lover. Utterances like 'Shut your face', 'Here comes trouble!' and 'Look what the cat's just brought in!' suggest that a relationship is felt to be durable enough to survive such studied offensiveness. Banter is often an important element in verbal games played in male peer-groups, such as the mock insult sessions of Turkish youths and Black American teenagers. As in childlore, these games serve to distinguish the in-group from the out-group; as usual, however, the 'play' often has a more serious side. Occupational solidarity among such groups as miners, moreover, is a necessity, if only because working conditions are uncomfortable and often dangerous. A kind of banter known as 'piliking' is found amongst miners in Durham and Yorkshire when they are at work in the pit. Its use even extends to contexts where more conventional expressions of sympathy might be expected. A miner whose arm has just been amputated after an accident is carried out of the pit past a workmate who addresses him with: 'Whey ye silly bugger, what's tha dey that for? It'll take six months ti grow anourther one.'

Learning to write in school

Within linguistics there has been a strong tendency to group together many different kinds of spoken interaction – some of them discussed above – under the general category of 'conversation'. Associated with the informal, equal encounters of everyday occurrence the notion of conversation implies a rather open, freewheeling quality in opposition to the constraints of so-called 'institutional discourse', which drastically *restricts* the kinds of interaction possible. Similarly, the emphasis in much child language study until recently has been on the notion of acquisition, a process supposedly inspired by the innate creativity of the child, and characterized by a relatively fixed sequence of grammatical 'stages', as though what the child learned was a linguistic *system* rather than ways of speaking to others. We have tried to suggest, however, that *all* interactions are part of certain institutions, including those of family and peer group, and are therefore fraught with problems of address and interpretation, even though participants may be less conscious of these than they might be in more formal, hierarchical, and professionalized settings.

As already outlined in Chapter 1, the schoolroom is a well-known setting for the restriction of speaking rights and the privileging of certain kinds of utterance. Traditionally, another dimension of language favoured and promoted by schools is the medium of writing. The skills of literacy – reading and writing – have for so long been the staple of formal schooling that during the 1960s educationalists felt it necessary to stress the significance of 'talk' in the child's intellectual development. As might be expected from our discussions of speech and writing earlier in this book, the acquisitional characteristics of each medium tend to be seen in terms of opposition. Speech is learned effortlessly in contexts where its functions seem obvious and where the child is actually unaware of what it is learning, while writing is explicitly *taught*, in controlled conditions, the child's attention being constantly focused on the tasks, since a great many different skills, both physical and mental, have to be learned simultaneously. One result of this is that the act of writing encourages the child to use language as an entity in itself, something to be shaped and manipulated, analysed and reflected on.

While there is much to be gained from this dichotomous approach, we would like to suggest that learning to operate both media is a matter of Rhetoric, and therefore of shared concerns. In fact, it is the business of written composition that gives the term its most common meaning in the USA today. But the Rhetorical foundations of writing tend to get obscured during the early stages of its acquisition, and many schools unfortunately have tended to underplay, ignore, or even repudiate them. When enthusiasm for so-called 'creative writing' was at its height during the 1960s it was usual to ask children simply to 'express themselves' in writing, as though each child had within it some creative urge that needed satisfaction in language. In short, the principle of expressivity, by that time a given in English studies, had found its way into the practices of the schoolroom as well as into the theory of the lecture hall.

It is worth pointing out that the demand for creative writing from schoolchildren is far in excess of demands ordinarily made of adults. This is not to say that educational practice should simply be a carbon-copy of practices in the 'real world'. What matters is that the context of production and reception is usually clear when adults put pen to paper. The *point* of writing a letter, filling in a form, or making a list is self-evident. Even if the actual recipient is unknown, the writer knows what the *role* of the addressee is. One of the problems involved in learning to write is that the child has to be taught the potential functions of writing as well as the mechanics. Its acquisition is therefore very different from that of speech. Since we learn speech as part of interaction with others we unconsciously build up for ourselves a picture of its possible purposes and functions. A major task of the teacher, then, is to try to re-create a sense of *dialogue* between writer and, on the one hand, readers, and on the other the arguments and positions which precede and even give rise to the act of writing in the first place.

One kind of writing that children find little difficulty in doing, however, is telling stories. This is a genre known to them from books – either read aloud to them or read silently *by* them – and from oral performance, as described in Chapter 1. Stories not only have an internal logic, based on the sequencing of events in time, but the role of the audience, or *narratee*, is also known to the child. A teacher who asks a pupil how s/he spent a recent Saturday is playing the same addressee-role as the parents who want to know what their child did at the nursery. In writing a 'reply' to such a question, however, children often produce what have been called 'reports' of events rather than the kinds of narratives favoured by the teacher. In a report events are 'chronicled' rather than shaped to fit a pattern of initial situation + complication + resolution as in the example discussed in Chapter 1. One such report from a primary school child begins:

> Yesterday Pamela came to tea. First we went into the garden and played on the climbing frame but it was cold. So we went in and sat down to watch TV. So I turned it on but there was nothing on. So we went into the front garden to play on the bikes . . .

and carries on in this vein until the end. While the co-ordination with *so* recalls the oral narrative the events in this account do not develop towards any sort of climax. Another example starts similarly by appearing to list a number of activities – peeling vegetables, washing and drying up, cutting the grass – undertaken by the writer and her gran, but then goes on to say that when gran gets the cake out, there is only enough for the two of them and not for the menfolk as well:

> . . . after all we were the ones who did the work. they were watching cricket on television in the front room. we was in the kitchen. so we eat the cake in secret with our cup of tea.

Thus, it is only at the end of the narrative that the jobs are presented as necessary work, something that, unlike sitting around watching television, deserves a reward.

Teachers are likely to respond favourably to the second example because it conforms more to their expectations of a well-formed narrative. In effect, the models of narrative they privilege tend to be literary ones, but the evidence suggests that teachers are often unaware of this. Thus what the teacher prizes in the telling of a story – features which are a matter of genre and technique, however unconsciously applied – is not made explicit to the child. This is one consequence of the emphasis on 'expression', as though this could occur in a social and linguistic vacuum, unfettered by the demands of form and audience. For children's writing, unlike that of adults, is invariably subject to evaluation by teachers. It is crucially important to be clear, therefore, about *how* a piece of work is to be marked. But teachers' norms vary widely. In a now-famous example, a piece of child's writing entitled 'The Balte of Wacster' (The Battle of Worcester) received radically different evaluations by different groups of teachers. Some who appeared to base their judgements on Grammar rather than Rhetoric deplored its 'poverty of language' and 'peculiar spellings'; others praised its sense of rhythm and the 'appropriateness' of its language in reflecting the usage of a common soldier:

> I was on my hase the Balelt begun someone Bule off a dirteygrat gun. my mat was hit on the are and the hed and he fell to the grawnd. and of cuse he was ded anuther was hit and a nuther was Hit.

What is clear is that different teachers interpreted the piece of writing in different ways, as either 'factual' or 'imaginative'. In so doing they were struggling to activate a naturalized yet questionable distinction that conditions the production of writing during a great part of school, particularly at 'O' level.

One area where children will almost certainly need some technical assistance is in the writing of non-narrative texts. They need help in discovering what sorts of things can be said about a given subject, in establishing a relationship between what they are saying and what has been said before, in making assumptions about what the teacher can be expected to know already and have an interest in, in finding – loosely speaking – a 'point' for writing, and in maintaining some kind of linguistic or conceptual relationship between propositions. 'Chapter One: A Collie Dog' from *The Book of Dogs* seems to fall down on many of these points:

> Collie dogs are used on Farms they were used to control sheep. Spaniels are also used on farms. Some collies are kept as
> Pets all sort of dogs are kept as pets. Lassie dogs are also kept on farms.

The writer's interest seems to hover between collie dogs, what kinds of dogs are kept on farms, and what kinds of dogs are kept as pets. One way of concentrating his focus would be to submit his 'chapter' to the scrutiny of his peers – something already practised in many classrooms. Once a 'dialogue' with actual readers is established a writer begins the painful process of learning what can and cannot be taken for granted in the assumptions and interests of an audience. On the way the writer may even learn that you often discover what to say in the course of actually writing. The conventions and restraints of textual organization force you to find connections between ideas and arguments, so that writing of this non-narrative kind usually needs to go through more than one draft, even for the most fluent and experienced writer.

The sacred texts of Christianity

In Chapter 1 we saw something of the range of genres that help constitute the Christian religion. In addition to sermons and prayers there are also hymns, tracts, and commentaries; in addition to different genres there are also many different *attitudes* to language within the institution, such that religious utterances are often open to argument and even conflict. Both these concerns are relevant in considering the cornerstone of Christianity, the Bible. Its alternative designation as Holy Scripture is a reminder that the Bible is written, and is, therefore, something that possesses the aura of fixity and permanence, but is also something that in an age of mass literacy can in principle be read by anyone. As an instrument of religion, however, the Bible needs an institution, the Church, to interpret it in ways that are compatible with the needs and interests of that institution. In interpreting it the leaders of the Church, to whom we can loosely refer as the priesthood, are sometimes brought into conflict with ruling secular elites. In the final analysis, therefore, the public pronouncements of men such as the Bishop of Durham are every bit as political as they are religious, since for many Christians what we might call 'social policy' is as central to their religion as it is – or should be – to governments.

The Bible can therefore never be 'above' the concerns of Rhetoric, and as a first step towards substantiating this argument it is helpful to consider the way that the text itself has come down to us. The Bible can usefully be seen as a compendium of different kinds of utterance: narrative, prophetic, legal. It contains psalms, proverbs, parables, genealogies and histories. In part these distinctions are signalled in the original text by changes in linguistic organization: the Old Testament, for example, is a mixture of verse and prose passages. The seventeenth-century translation into English known as the 'Authorized Version' dispensed with this distinction, however, and rendered the text into a kind of poetic prose, in which considerations of layout were as important as for verse. The Authorized Version was set out in numbered paragraphs that were usually very short (often only a sentence in length) and one effect of this has been that preachers have been able to *abstract* Biblical quotations very easily and readily (as in the example of the sermon analysed in Chapter 1). Perhaps the most obvious impact of the Authorized Version lies in the rhythmical properties of the language itself, which are often claimed to be the source of its great power – qualities which are widely felt to have been erased from modern versions.

This 'compendious' aspect of the Bible might appear to undermine its status as a sacred text in that such texts are ideally *unities*, the product of an overarching and single intelligence or power. It is of course perfectly possible to read and enjoy the Bible as a collection of entertaining stories, mind-provoking aphorisms, and poetic delights: indeed, such 'literary appreciations' are quite common. It is also possible, and not at all uncommon, to seek out inconsistencies and contradictions within the text in the belief that these undermine any credibility it might otherwise possess. The issue of the Bible's unity, however, is no different from the general issue of unity with respect to *any* text: it is not that texts themselves can be unities, but rather it is our decision as readers to read them as such. The ideal of textual unity, which we discussed briefly in relation to literature in Chapter 2, is closely linked to that of value: if we can demonstrate that the individual parts of the text all contribute to the whole, perhaps producing something greater than the sum of its parts, we are also showing that it is a good piece of work. Needless to say, a positive value can also be placed on works which appear to be full of contradictions and frictions.

To read the Bible as a unity, then, is to read it within certain conventions of interpretation: and those conventions arise not from the text itself but from the institutions of the Christian Church that invest it with sacred status. In short, the Bible needs a *priesthood* to control the number of possible readings. The Bible can be unified, for instance, on the grounds that it moves in a dimension of *time* different from that ordinarily experienced: it posits an absolute beginning (creation) and an absolute end (judgement). Another argument concerns the relationship between the Old Testament and the New. Events and roles denoted in the Old predict and bring into being those of the New. And the most fundamental argument of all concerns the authorship of the Bible. Despite the fact that there is no single human author the Bible is still claimed to be a unity because behind all the variety in form and in the circumstances of its writing there remains its sole source, its Author, God Himself.

To argue that the Bible is the word of God does not, however, guarantee that its readers will actually agree on its meaning. A common argument found in literary criticism holds that the meaning of a text is what was intended by the author, but this has never stopped readers from generating new interpretations (if only in the name of the 'author's intention'). If the meaning of the Bible is whatever God intended it to mean, then we can only conclude that this intention is obscure (but no more obscure than those of the all-too-human writers of poems, novels, and plays). As in the case of literary criticism, 'authorial intention' or just 'the author' are used as an argument to justify one particular interpretation rather than another. The history of Biblical interpretation is the history of different readings associated with different priesthoods, each the product of a particular time and place (and therefore politics). At different periods of history, certain parts of the Bible have been interpreted in such a way as to demonstrate the wickedness of certain people (the New Testament was used as evidence against the Jews), or as an injunction to act in certain ways (*Proverbs* was quoted in justification of beating one's children); and where an apparent injunction might prove inconvenient or embarrassing, as in the case of the Old Testament dietary laws, it might usefully be interpreted as allegory. In short, Biblical interpretation faces the same problem that confronts any sacred text: the diversity of human experience in different times and places has to be forced to fit into the categories laid down – the World has to be fitted to the Book.

It follows from what has just been said that all readings of the Bible are historical: there can be no single, authoritative reading that is true for all time. Needless to say, this is not an argument that many Christians have generally found acceptable, although their actual practice over the centuries confirms it. Once again, the issues are similar to those so often raised in literary criticism. People tire of the accretions of commentary, explanation, and exegesis, and demand a return to the text. Listen to what the words actually say, they urge. Such was the Protestant reaction to centuries of Catholic 'dogma', which was supposed to have obscured the text behind a veil of doctrine, drawing on it only for purposes of illustration. In our own time the Fundamentalist emphasis on 'literal interpretation' has also been very strong. But we have already identified some of the problems involved with the argument that the Bible means exactly what it says. One is the sheer diversity of utterance within the Bible, which makes the issue of meaning so thoroughly bound up with that of genre. Another problem concerns the text's Author: God does not write, but speaks, is heard but not seen, and it is claimed that the Bible is a record, in writing, of God's spoken utterance. This is problematic, partly because it places the text's original 'moment' *before* the act of recording was actually undertaken. Also, the fact that it is *written* means that conventions of textual organization needed to be followed, and those conventions link the text willy-nilly to other examples of utterance both written and spoken. Finally, it must also be remembered that in the twentieth century we experience the Bible as the product of a long and complex series of translations. Each translation bears the traces of a particular culture at a particular time – Hebrew, Greek, Latin, and the English of different periods – and it is easy to see how meanings get added or lost in the process. One problem for translators is the fact that the original texts abound in the kinds of Rhetorical devices that today we tend to associate with poetry, such as metaphors and puns. In the Greek of the New Testament, for instance, there is a pun on Peter and *petra* (rock) in 'Thou art Peter, and upon this rock I will build my church', a pun impossible to preserve in English but one which, interestingly enough, is also possible in Aramaic, the language that Jesus spoke (perhaps) when he uttered the words. And we owe the tendency to think of Adam and Eve's forbidden tree as an apple tree to the Latin version's use of *malum* to translate 'the tree of evil' – the word itself is a pun, meaning both 'evil' and 'apple'.

If the 'original texts' are so full of puns and word play it doesn't really help to return to them in the hope that God's 'true meaning' will thus be revealed. Word play reminds us of the slipperiness of language, the fact that irrespective of authorial intention an individual word can preserve ambiguities or acquire them in the context of the other words with which it is linked. But the problem of translation runs deeper still. To a large extent the actual grammar of a particular language will enforce certain choices in presenting information, with the result that we tend to see things in certain ways. The reader may already have noticed that a few paragraphs ago we wrote 'God Himself', testimony to the fact that the English pronoun-system makes it difficult to avoid specifying gender, particularly in usages such as this where a pronoun is placed in final position to provide emphasis.

It follows from all that we have been saying that the Bible, like any text or utterance, cannot simply 'mean what it says', as though meaning were something locked away inside the words themselves. There is anyway a major problem involved with the notion of 'meaning what it says'. By this people usually have in mind what in Chapter 1 we called 'referential' meaning. It was incidentally this layer of meaning that both St Augustine and St Thomas Aquinas wished to promote as the means of controlling interpretations of the Bible. The problem, however, is that we tend to associate referential meaning with particular linguistic forms. To put it crudely, we expect propositions like 'oil floats on water' to be referential because it is precisely structures of this kind that are always cited as examples of such meaning. Similarly, the advertising slogan 'Persil washes whiter' *looks* as though it is making a referential, testable proposition, since it reminds us of the examples we have internalized. The problem is acute when we consider examples from Christian discourse, such as 'God is good'. This seems to invite what we might loosely call a referential interpretation, but when non-Christians question the validity of the proposition (on the grounds, say, that famines and wars are evil but are allowed by God to happen) they are met with the argument that God is beyond human understanding, so that the proposition still holds. The argument often strikes the sceptical as bewildering because it wants to have it both ways: God is both incomprehensible, but at the same time is capable of being talked about in language. This sense of it-is-but-it-isn't is by no means restricted to religious utterance. It is at the basis of metaphor, a Rhetorical figure that has for a very long time been most closely associated with poetry (but which, as we saw earlier, is a characteristic of all utterance). When I. A. Richards argued that poetry communicates in its own, special, non-referential way he used an example of a metaphor – 'My soul is a ship in full sail' - and went on to say that in order to respond to poetry the reader had to ignore the 'literal' meanings of the words, which make the utterance actually nonsensical.

What we can loosely term religious utterances, then, occupy part of the same cultural space as literature: both make use of the idea that things can be known or understood which are beyond the power of language to verbalize in the form of referential propositions. Religion, however, sometimes takes this insight one stage further: as Northrop Frye suggests, 'the agility of language in chasing red herrings has caused some religious traditions to make a cult of the wordless'. Even when they are not silent, many traditions rely on uses of language that cause difficulties for audiences, expressing themselves in paradox or metaphor (which enable audiences to see and feel different things at different times). In short, they see meaning as neither finite nor paraphrasable but as something to be struggled for: like the church service discussed earlier, they promote the idea of *change* in the religious subject. But this Rhetorical stance is limited to neither religious nor literary utterance. Some philosophers, like Socrates and Nietzsche, work with the same principle: in the words of the German thinker Climaticus 'if anyone imagines that he understands it, he can be sure he misunderstands it'.

As we said earlier, however, religious utterances are not uniform but diverse in function. Many have what the ancient Rhetoricians would call and 'epideictic' function, that of praising or celebrating; few make novel assertions of referential value, but serve to *remind* congregations of what they are already supposed to know. Some of them function as declarations, as in 'with this ring I thee wed' where the uttering of the words actually performs the act of marrying. And many can be said to exhort people to do things, often in ways which are a permanent reminder of the gap between ideal and practice: the stern baldness of 'Love thy neighbour as thyself' makes the action sound so straightforward, so easy to accomplish, until we actually try to live it. But the wording needs to be tough, because we can always find all sorts of mitigating excuses and justifications for making an exception.

The law as Rhetoric

Earlier in this chapter we referred to the relationship between religion and state. In some societies, for instance Islamic ones, the relationship is very close, and in practice this means that the law, one of the major concerns of state, has divine sanction. In contemporary British society the law still bears traces of Christian precept, as in the cases of Sunday trading and observance of Christian festivals such as Christmas and Easter, but while non-Christians may know something about church services and ecclesiastical matters – and may even read the Bible for its great cultural interest – they will seldom be *required* to participate in Christian worship. But there is a sense in which we all have to participate in the law. The law is inescapable because we are bound by it: we are likely to encounter its institutions – courts, solicitors' offices, the police force – directly in one form or another in the course of our lives. Although the Christian religion pervades the dominant British culture it can still be marginalized or rejected in a way that the law cannot.

The law, like religion, can also be said to have its sacred texts, although these are unlikely to be read by anybody except its professional practitioners. Throughout much of western Europe outside Britain the corpus of legal texts associated with the sixth-century Roman Emperor Justinian acquired the status of Holy Writ. Discovered by accident during the medieval period this 'vast compilation of foreign legal scripts written in an alien language and directly applicable only to a past culture' became, according to Goodrich, 'the basis of Western legal tradition and method'. These texts were held by an emerging legal priesthood to enshrine the 'spirit' of Law, something which later came to be associated with rationality. In reality this 'spirit' was the imperial *power* of Justinian: the Emperor bore the same relation to the Law as God did to the Bible. We find a similar tradition of commentary and doctrinal dispute as we saw in relation to Christianity: a comparative fondness for quotation and citation, the same struggle to narrow down the meanings of the sacred text to conform to an 'official' interpretation. And as in the case of the doctrinal disputes of the Reformation period, we find the same urgings to return to the 'original text', to find out 'what it really says'.

In asserting law as a 'system' based on reason the legal priesthood is claiming a quality of timelessness that, as we have seen, is also held to be characteristic of Scripture. Even those legal traditions which are not based on Roman Law appear to regard Law itself as a sacred 'text', the voice not of a particular author but of Authority, a concept endowed with a quasi-divine aura. The English tradition puts great emphasis on the notion of reason, and bases its criteria of acceptable conduct and attitudes on the notion of the 'reasonable man'. This notion, however, is far from being timeless: it is the product of a particular time and place (seventeenth-century England) and is highly specific in relation to social class and gender. As we shall see, it is also very instructive to ascertain the identity of the reasonable man in particular instances.

Associated with the emphasis on reason is the growth of so-called 'forensic science', a corpus of techniques and procedures that emulate those of scientific discovery, producing 'evidence' that can 'prove' innocence or culpability. One effect of this development is to convince the lay-person that legal judgements often result from proof rather than probability, and that the ascertaining of proof is a matter best left to the experts. Professionalization has made the law an institution in itself, for itself, and by itself, and nowhere is this more true than in matters of language. The actual forms of utterance, their permitted meanings, and their targeted audiences all appear to have come under the control of the legal priesthood. And not only have lawyers made the rules, they also seem to enjoy the privilege of breaking them as well. Courtroom discourse, for example, places what seems to the lay-person an enormous (and often bewildering) emphasis on form. As in the case of the Church, this is not exclusively a matter of linguistic form: even in the English magistrate's court, where justice is administered not by a professional but by a 'lay' official, there is a precise regulation of space and physical deportment: magistrates are seated above the rest of the court, who must rise not only to speak but also whenever magistrates enter or leave the room (except for the defendant, who must stand throughout the entire proceedings). Dress is also formal: ushers, for instance, are robed. Linguistic formalism goes far deeper, however, than the use of particular verbal rituals such as swearing-in, or formulas such as 'Approach the Bench' and 'How do you plead?' and the fixed phraseology of the death-sentence (now abolished in English law). Turn-taking, for example, is rigidly prescribed: only lawyers have the right to ask questions, and witnesses are not allowed to interrupt. In managing a dispute, however, lawyers often exploit these rules to the advantage of one side or the other. While interrogating a witness a lawyer may pause in mid-question in order to provoke a response from that witness: this can then be made to look like an interruption. But lawyers sometimes go much further than this. In the Israeli rape trial referred to in Chapter 1, the defending counsel uses a number of techniques aimed at provoking the woman into saying things that suggest she is a manipulative schemer rather than the helpless victim of assault. The lawyer uses mock polite forms to her, and at one point deliberately draws attention to the phonetic qualities of two of her words by repeating them in sequence, in an attempt to trivialize her experience.

Like a church service, therefore, the court can draw on all the resources and functions of language in the conduct of a dispute. While at one end of the spectrum a counsel may exploit the ludic possibilities of utterance by playing with the words of a witness, the judge at the other end has, like a priest, the power to issue declarations by pronouncing a sentence. For the lay-person, the effect of courtroom etiquette is to restrict drastically what can actually be said, and one possible consequence of this is the loss of face. The female plaintiff in the Israeli rape trial, for instance, is eventually found to have suffered assault, but she had also had to endure the opposing lawyer's attempt to blacken her character. Rather than being instruments for the establishment of truth, many trials can therefore be seen as ceremonials of degradation. Rape trials can be said to symbolize, reproduce, and reinforce the denigration of women, a process continually enacted at many different levels and places in a great many cultures.

Another aspect of legal power is the privilege of defining the meanings of words, or contesting particular definitions. One example concerns the issue of abortion in the USA. In one trial, an abortionist faced the charge of 'murdering' an 'unborn child'. The prosecuting lawyer consistently avoided the term 'foetus', which lends a dehumanizing and quasi-scientific aura to a highly sensitive and, to many, a highly moral issue. Other terms, however, like 'unborn child' or 'subject', load the dice heavily in the other direction, enabling the lawyer to construct a narrative in which 'murder' becomes an appropriate term. There is no neutral word available, and the legal classification of abortion depends extensively on the actual vocabulary used. The court's function, then, is to fit the world to particular words, a struggle which necessarily makes the legal process part of a much wider social and political one.

A further example, this time from the UK, shows the impossibility of separating the act of semantic definition, as undertaken in the court, from a prevailing social and political ethos. In the early 1980s the Labour-controlled Greater London Council attempted to implement, in line with its published policy, a 25 per cent reduction in public transport fares. The attempt was challenged by the (Conservative) London Borough of Bromley, with a Court of Appeal finally ruling in Bromley's favour. The Appeal Court's judges based their decision in part on their interpretation of the Transport (London) Act of 1969, a text which apparently had all the characteristics of one that was sacred: it was, in their opinion, 'opaque and elliptical', 'lack[ing] clarity', and 'baffling'. Nowhere were these qualities more evident than in those sections dealing with the discretionary powers of the GLC in providing 'integrated, efficient, and economic transport facilities'. The judges chose to concentrate on the word 'economic', which was admitted to have several meanings – even to be 'chameleon-like, taking its colour from its surroundings'; indeed, its meaning was even regarded by one judge as contested, in accordance with the interests of particular parties. In the event the judges ruled that the 'reasonable' interpretation of 'economic' was one that respected the interests of the ratepayers (of Bromley, and, in principle, of all London boroughs) to the exclusion of other groups or interests. In so doing the judges reflected and also reinforced a particular view of social and economic relations that became hegemonic during the early and mid–1980s; the word 'economic' became a key word during the 1984–5 miners' strike over the closure of pits deemed uneconomic according to criteria established by the Conservative government.

The final issue to be dealt with here is that of the audience, in respect of both legal judgements and written legal texts such as contracts. It is instructive to ask who judges are actually addressing when they pass judgement. Clearly judges have to pronounce with an eye on the future, since what they say will in effect constitute the law on a particular issue. Officially, then, judges address the institution of Law itself, and there are supposed to be restrictions on talking to the media, for instance, or writing books for 'the general public'. But judges will know that the media and governments may be very interested in many of their pronouncements since they will often have a clear political and social relevance; they know, in short, that a judgement will be 'overheard' by institutions other than the law, and that politicians and journalists may be saying things that impinge directly on the case at issue. They may therefore be conscious of addressing different audiences simultaneously. In this respect they are placed in a similar position to bishops, whose utterances are supposed (by governments, at any rate) to be directed towards their congregations, and should not therefore be 'political' in content.

A judge's sensitivity to these issues can be demonstrated by a case, again from the UK during the present decade, concerning the use made of government documents by a civil liberties organization during a court hearing. The solicitor acting for the organization was held to be in contempt of court for allowing a journalist to read out in court Home Office documents which had been obtained for the purpose of writing an article critical of government policy. During the 1980s the issue of governmental secrecy (giving rise to calls for more 'open' government) was widely aired; knowing this the judge, Lord Diplock, pronouncing on the case, strives to distance his judgement from this issue. A close analysis of part of his judgement not only shows how his 'discovery' of appropriate arguments is based on this strategy, but also the centrality of traditional Rhetorical techniques in general:

'My Lords, in a case which has attracted a good deal of publicity it may assist in clearing up misconceptions if I start by saying what the case is *not* about. It is *not* about freedom of speech, freedom of the press, openness of justice or documents coming into the 'public domain'; nor, with all respect to those of your lordships who think the contrary, does it in my opinion call for consideration of any of these human rights and fundamental freedoms [contained in] the European Convention on Human Rights . . . What this case *is* about is an aspect of the law of discovery of documents in civil actions in the High Court . . . The case in my view, turns on its own particular facts, which are very special.'	Rectification (*Correctio*) Anticipation (*Prolepsis*) Antithesis (*Contrarium*) Amplification (*Auxesis*) Identification (*Allusio*) Arrangement (*Distributio*)

According to Peter Goodrich, the Rhetoric is used to identify the 'correct' audience for the judgement by asserting (without either argument or explanation) the *autonomy* of legal utterance, method, and more generally, form. *Home Office* vs. *Harman*, in short, is a technical matter best left to the priesthood to resolve.

So far we have limited our attention to the role of law in dealing with disputes. But law also has what is called a 'facilitative' function, involving such practices as the drawing up of wills and contracts. A common objection to the language of such documents is that it is impenetrable to the lay-person. The usual response to this objection is that legal language must be as it is to prevent the unscrupulous from finding ambiguities which they can then exploit. Underlying this notion is the belief that 'ordinary' or 'straightforward' language is slippery and inexact; in order to be clear, legal language has to be so *extraordinary* that it is almost impossible to make it mean anything at all. This paradox is not at all dissimilar from those we have discussed in relation to the utterances of religion.

What follows is taken from a discussion of an American legal contract, a loan form, by Brenda Danet. Its linguistic characteristics will be familiar to anyone who has tried to interpret legal documents:

> In the event of default in the payment of this or any other obligation or the performance or observance of any term of covenant contained herein or in any note or any other contract or agreement evidencing or relating to any obligation or any collateral on the borrower's part to be performed or observed, or the undersigned borrower shall die; or any of the undersigned become insolvent or make assignment for the benefit of creditors; or a petition shall be filed by or against any of the undersigned under any provision of the Bankruptcy Act; or any money, securities or property of the undersigned now or hereafter on deposit with or in the possession or under the control of the Bank shall be attached or become subject to distraint proceedings or any order or process of any court; or the Bank shall deem itself to be insecure, then and in any such event, the Bank shall have a right (at its option), without demand or notice of any kind, to declare all or any part of the obligations to be immediately due and payable, whereupon such obligations shall become and be immediately due and payable, and the Bank shall have the right to exercise all the rights and remedies available to a secured party upon default under the Uniform Commercial Code (the 'Code') in effect in New York at the time and such other rights and remedies as may otherwise be provided by law.

On the fact of it the contract purports to address the lay-person who will be bound by its conditions; the language used, however, ensures that the text will seldom, if ever, be read by anyone except lawyers. Not only are there strange terms (often deriving from French or Latin) such as 'distraint', and unfamiliar meanings of well-known words such as 'assignment' (the transference of a right, interest, or title) but both layout and **cohesive devices** are so distinctive that few of the lay-reader's expectations about textual organization are actually met. There is hardly any variety in punctuation (sentences accordingly are often inordinately long) nor any use of pronouns to refer back to concepts already mentioned (*the Bank*, for instance, is never substituted by *it*). As a general consequence, it is only too easy to get lost in mid-sentence and overwhelmed by the sheer density of unfamiliar items.

But it is also possible to find linguistic characteristics of a different order. Alliteration, together with other patterns of consonant repetition, occurs in 'covenant', 'contained' and 'contract', and there is a regular anapaestic rhythm in 'in the evént of defaúlt in the páyment of thís . . .' (where a stressed syllable is followed by two unstressed ones). It has often been argued that such devices (which are used intuitively rather than consciously) 'thicken' the language of the law, distancing it from the everyday. Like poetry, legal utterances express meanings that are meant to be taken seriously; extra patterning therefore lends them a solemnity (and also perhaps a memorability, so that if necessary they can be repeated in an unchanged form). A fixed, distinctive form brings order to an ever-changing, protean reality.

From here it is only a short step to the argument that legal utterances are much the same as religious ones: as far as the lay-person is concerned, they have to be experienced rather than understood. This view, however, tends to reify the law as a kind of timeless force, in the process endowing its practitioners with the qualities of priests. As in the case of religion, the more the emphasis is put on the qualities of ritual, the easier it becomes to argue that law is so distinctive as to be autonomous, separate from (perhaps even opposed to) the concerns of politics, religion, or anything else. The 'unambiguous' meaning encapsulated within the loan form remains therefore within the sole ambit of the law, and guarantees a perpetual role for the expensively-trained lawyer. But it is only fair to add that to rewrite the loan form in such language as:

I'll be in default
1) if I don't pay an installment on time: or
2) if any other creditor tries by legal process to take any money of mine in your possession

would not only allow the lay-person access to legal affairs, it would also throw an enormous burden of responsibility on to the shoulders of everyone. In effect, it would restore to all of us the ancient association of law with the business of Rhetoric.

Sacred canons, sacred cows?

The sanctification of texts is not a process limited to the institutions we have discussed. Political creeds also have their sacred texts, such as Marx's *Das Kapital*, as do institutions of a different kind, those closely associated with formal education and conventionally known as 'disciplines'. Both philosophy and literary criticism have their 'canons' of indispensable texts, which in a sense help to constitute the very disciplines themselves. Philosophy we shall discuss in greater detail in the next chapter; here we shall briefly trace some aspects of canonization with respect to literary criticism.

Of great significance in the formation of both disciplines, however, were the epic poems of Homer: the *Iliad* and the *Odyssey*. For both Plato and Aristotle, who each wrote about a great deal more than what we would today call philosophy, the epics had already achieved a quasi-sacred status, and were consequently a constant source of reference and quotation. They came to be seen as models of literary form and of 'pre-logical' thought in the disciplines of Rhetoric and, later, Classics, which are the precursors of literary criticism. But like all revered texts, the Homeric epics continually posed problems of interpretation and evaluation, particularly as ideas about what constitutes Great Literature changed. The formulaic language seemed an affront to literary creativity, the apparently inconsistent characterization an embarrassment to the notion of psychological realism. The unity of the texts came to be doubted: was Homer a single author, or merely a handy way of referring to several different ones? The crowing irony was the possibility that the epics were not consciously written by an 'author' at all, but were actually transcriptions of oral performances by a singer.

Literary criticism as a distinct discipline depends on the prior categorization of texts as literature – a development that was not consolidated until the nineteenth century, by which time Rhetoric in most of its traditional senses had been discredited. Literature came to be seen as encapsulating the values once associated with religion, now that scientific enquiry, particularly that of Darwin, had put the precepts of Christianity in doubt. It was literature that increasingly came to be identified as the preserve of the soul or spirit; the poet was now a priest. Literature was 'spilt religion', literature alone could oppose the values of science, only literature could heal the social divisions caused by the Industrial Revolution. It was during the nineteenth century that literature as the object of a distinct discipline, literary criticism, came to be promoted – except that the name given to this innovation in the educational curriculum was 'English'. To study English increasingly came to mean learning to appreciate a 'canon' of texts that were considered to epitomize in some way certain values of timelessness, organic unity, and, somewhat contradictorily, 'Englishness'. During the twentieth century the mantle of 'science' itself was appropriated to the service of literature: the latter could be defined as a particular kind or use of language, the properties of which could be unambiguously and systematically described. And central to the teaching of English was the canon of great texts or, even more elusive, Great Authors, at the apex of which stands Shakespeare – another irony since, like Homer, so little is known about him, yet so much is made of his work that his importance transcends the institution of literary criticism and the teaching of English. Shakespeare's writings have been made to speak for several different political ideologies, not the least of which has sought to make of parts of his plays a kind of constitution for the English 'nation'. Try as they might, the institutions and disciplines of English and literary criticism have been unable to keep Shakespeare away from what is often disparagingly called the public sphere – which is in our view where he belongs.

The sanctification of texts and authors is so often an issue of power and social control, an attempt to fix human affairs and knowledge in a timeless mould. Yet within English Studies the process of canonization has in some quarters been recognized for what it is, and has been actively resisted. One response tends to argue that since no text can have a fixed and inherent value 'literature' is accordingly no different from any other kind of writing (whether history, philosophy, or workshop manuals). We would want to reject this view, while acknowledging that the value of a text can never be above argument. Another response argues that the values involved in the canonization of texts are not timeless and universal after all, but are western, white, middle class and, all too often, male. Indeed, it is feminists – for whom in general terms the sacred text is a patriarchal one – who have been so successful in exposing the hidden aspects of English Studies, a subject so often taught by men to a female student population. It has been impossible to exclude from the canon the writings of women, as our discussion in Chapters 3 and 5 shows; feminist thought, however, inevitably finds itself debating the *value* of those texts in relation to other works in the canon, and this process keeps the *constructedness* of the literary canon in front of our eyes. It is something of a paradox that the Rhetorical tradition, for so much of its history an instrument in the training of males, can be seen as an important counterbalance to the processes of sanctification.

Notes and further reading

An influential source for this chapter was Leech's *Principles of Pragmatics* (1983). Pragmatics, to put it simply, is the branch of linguistics that tries to accommodate within linguistic theory the functional and interactional aspects of language. Leech's book interprets many of the major concepts of pragmatics from the perspective of Rhetoric. Thomas (1985) was an invaluable source of examples and analysis.

The view of child language acquisition propounded here has to a large extent been influenced by Vygotsky (1962). See Coulthard (1985, Chapter 8) and Saville-Troike (1982, Chapter 6); both books have extensive bibliographies. Stubbs (1983, Chapter 3) and Romaine (1984) have useful material. For linguistic accounts of children learning to write see Kress (1982) and Harris and Wilkinson (1986); there is an interdisciplinary – and especially stimulating – account by Carolyn Steedman (1982), for whose own examples of children's writing we are most grateful. For an account of 'piliking' among miners see Douglass (1973).

On Christian discourse see Donovan (1974), Doody (1980); see also Frye (1982)), on whom much of the discussion of the Bible is based (although we disagree with many of his arguments). See also notes to Chapter 1.

The section on legal discourse is heavily indebted to the Rhetorical approach of Goodrich, whose *Reading the Law* (1986) and *Legal Discourse* (1987) are indispensable. Other studies include those of Harris (1984a, 1984b), Atkinson and Drew (1979), Bennett and Feldman (1981) and O'Barr (1982). See also Danet (1980) and notes to Chapter 1. An entire issue of the journal *Text* is devoted to legal discourse, and contains the piece by Liebes-Plesner, together with other useful articles (vol. 4, 1/3, 1984).

The notion of English as a discipline of thought is addressed by Leavis (1976). On the canon in English studies see Williams (1982) and Baldick (1983). Eagleton (1983) covers much of the same ground and is one book among many that calls for a return to Rhetoric: our chapter is in part a response to his (entertaining) polemic.

Chapter five

Interpreting stories

In this chapter, we move to a problem of a different kind; the interpretation of stories. Two fairly extensive claims might be made by this transition. One claim would be for a Grand Theory which connects all the subjects. Another would be for an extreme virtuosity which can disregard the boundaries of study. Grand Theory and great virtuosity are legitimate claims, but the present argument relies upon neither. Instead what we offer are 'linked practices'. We wish to suggest ways of interpreting stories which are linked to ways of analysing language-in-society, linked by a style of thinking.

Certain reference points are important for our argument at this point of transition. First, there is classical Rhetoric. Here what matters is how some classical Rhetoricians made claims that are relatively modest for their discipline. Aristotle's *Rhetoric* offers no final rules, no answers that are inevitable for all contexts. Plato criticizes Rhetoric when it forgets about its limits, and claims to become a Grand Theory. Only philosophy can do that: but even philosophy needs Rhetoric on the way. Rhetoric properly resists the obligation to propound a Grand Theory of its own before discussing problems across a range of contexts. A second reference point, then, is Grand Theory itself, in its modern forms. One thing that distinguishes such theory is the master concept, the idea which applies universally. We are certainly influenced by several concepts of that kind. One that has been discussed is Bakhtin's notion of 'dialogism'. What makes 'dialogism' a master concept is how Bakhtin uses the idea to formulate *laws* of genre, including laws of historical development. He prescribes how novels differ from other narratives, for instance; he also divides all discourse into 'dialogical' and 'monological'. He emphasizes the relations between voices, and to that extent his work is part of the approach which we are presenting, but Bakhtin makes the idea of 'dialogism' do things which are far beyond the scope of an approach that is Rhetorical in our sense.

In so far as our concern is with asking questions rather than stating laws, there is a third point of reference: the work of the German thinker Hans-Georg Gadamer. Gadamer is consciously concerned with classical Rhetoric, though he has many other interests. Here what matters is his emphasis upon 'the priority of the Question'. In our Chapter 3, Gadamer represented one approach to argument and society. He insists that questions are what matter; the 'dominant opinion' threatens questions. Here we want to draw upon the principle of questioning:

> Only a person who has questions can have knowledge . . .

Questions permit us to know things, but questions must always have answers that differ:

> Only a person who has questions can have knowledge, but questions include the antitheses of yes and no, of being like this and being like that . . .

In the moment of seeking to know, we must recognize that other answers are possible. Gadamer's principle of questioning is radical: knowing is fundamentally inseparable from being uncertain. This view of knowledge is profoundly Rhetorical: knowing belongs within an arena where different voices speak, where conflicting views are possible.

In particular, Gadamer is concerned with knowing what texts mean, with interpretation. He insists that we interpret texts by asking questions; and then he insists that questions have answers that vary. Consequently, he asserts,

> It is part of the historical finiteness of our being that we are aware that after us others will understand in a different way.

Gadamer's ideas are central for our approach to interpretation. Rhetoric can suggest questions, and questions can enrich interpretation. But this questioning is not a temporary phase. The questions never vanish; although answers do occur, other questions could still arise. This is an idea of questioning that is very different from the scientific model, where questions do become answers, definite answers. The question, for us, is far larger than any answers – no answer exhausts the question. Therefore we are not proposing a system which ties up interpretation. On the contrary: there are always other answers, and indeed other questions.

Rhetorical questioning

'What does this mean?': that might be the basic question for interpreters to ask. But interpretation is an art because there is no way of asking that question bluntly and directly. The challenge is to find other questions which will take the place of the great problem, of 'What is the meaning?', other questions which will lead towards meaning without being so blankly coercive. We are going to suggest two questions, or ways of questioning. These are two of many possibilities which Rhetoric provides, for Rhetoric can be seen as a heritage of questions.

First, there is the question 'Whose words are these?' How should we identify the voices by which we are being addressed? Identifying voices is always tricky, and stories make the problem especially difficult, and rich. Our aim is to explore how meanings become possible, not to produce categories of voice. Rhetoric can be associated with lists of devices, including complex categories of voices. To analyse a story Rhetorically would then be to abstract these devices from the flow of the storytelling. Gerard Genette (in the essay 'Frontiers of narrative' and in *Narrative Discourse*) has found a way of reconciling that kind of Rhetoric with a sense of the process of telling. Our approach is different, and simpler: we would not claim to challenge or revise Genette's achievement. The purpose here is to find the simplest way of adopting an approach that is both Rhetorical and interpretive. The approach can then be connected with other practices, such as the preceding analyses of language in society, and it can also be assimilated more fluently by a wider range of readers.

'Whose words are these?'. A great deal can be done with a question that is derived quite simply from reading. Of course many things will be beyond the reach of such a question – but it can become complex enough to be genuinely interpretive. Questions also overlap: identifying voices links with other problems.

One question that is related is: 'To what is this voice replying, to what are these words replying?'. What matters is not keeping the questions distinct, but understanding the whole way of interpreting, of interpreting by asking questions and by using the idea of address to focus the questioning contructively.

Neither of the questions is hard to conceive: each derives from the experience of reading, derives quite directly from that experience. This is an Aristotelian way of proceeding:

> Rhetoric is, in a manner, within the cognizance of all men . . .

Other Rhetorics can be more complex than ours, but if they are something is lost, something which has been essential at times. Rhetoric has relished staying close to the familiar, deriving its ideas and questions from the verge of the usual, the ordinary.

The questions we are focusing on are basic, yet they also have the sanction of Rhetoric's traditions. Asking the question, 'Whose words are these?' Rhetorically is an ancient practice. In Aristotle's *Poetics* the enquiry is into whether a story's wording belongs to a central narrative, or to both a narrative and characters, or whether there is no external narrative but only voices from within the story. In that way Aristotle distinguishes drama (no external narrative) from epic (mixed narration). 'Whose words are these?' is therefore, for Aristotle, the central question about stories. Such a question can be very powerful when asked Rhetorically, that is, with a sense of address. The question was also asked with vigour in the Middle Ages. The thirteenth-century Franciscan friar, St Bonaventure, when starting a commentary on another theologian, has to decide the precise status of his subject. That decision is taken by thinking about 'Whose words are these?':

> There are four ways of making a book. Sometimes a man writes others' words, adding nothing and changing nothing; and he is simply called a scribe (*scriptor*). Sometimes a man writes others' words, putting together passages which are not his own; and he is called a compiler (*compilator*).

St Bonaventure grasps profoundly the force of the question 'Whose words are these?' and renders it practicably askable by talking about the voices and how they address us:

> Sometimes a man writes both others' words and his own, but

with others' words in prime place and his own added only for purposes of clarification; and he is called not an author but a commentator (*commentator*). Sometimes a man writes both his own words and others', but with his own in prime place and others added only for purposes of confirmation; and he should be called an author (*auctor*).

Burrow, introducing this fine passage, comments that there is no one who writes purely his own words. Everyone writes with *other* voices. It is true that while Aristotle, here, is dealing with stories, St Bonaventure is not. But both accounts show *how* the question 'Whose words are these?' becomes askable, and therefore each contributes to the present practical enquiry.

Modern thinkers have also considered identifying voices to be a problem that is tricky and important. Both Bakhtin and Genette re-ask 'Whose words are these?' in new ways. The moderns have emphasized what Bonaventure notes: there are no simple answers – voices overlap and the same words will, generally, have several 'owners'. Bakhtin and Genette elaborate their ideas in ways which overlay the link with earlier Rhetoric. These elaborations lead away from the concerns that are essential here. Bakhtin poses problems of genre: what makes the novel distinctive, formally and historically? Genette offers a system of voices, a system that is general though illustrated specifically. These are higher level projects, in terms of the hierarchy of theory.

Here we are concerned to see how much can be done by keeping the questions basic, and so retaining something of the spirit of earlier Rhetorics. Still, it is important that even advanced writers should have reworked the basic question rather than leaving it behind altogether. Indeed, some theorists have generalized the question 'Whose words are these?', extending the problem further. Jacques Derrida argues for a recognition of the already used and in that sense 'quoted' quality of all utterance and all writing. If you ask 'Whose words . . . ?', you will always find that the answer is complex. Voices always quote each other, and words belong to more than one voice at a time. One can still feel how this idea connects with St Bonaventure: no one writes (or speaks) in simply his own words. The question is also asked more sociologically – here is Bourdieu, as cited by John Thompson:

> To speak is to appropriate one or another of the expressive
> styles already constituted in and by usage . . .

Words belong to 'expressive styles' as well as to a particular
speaker or author or passage. The question becomes richer and
richer. Barthes elaborates more psychologically:

> I read the text: . . . This 'I' which approaches the text is
> already a plurality of other texts . . .

'Whose words . . .' can be asked of the reader's mind as well as
of the text. Yet even here one can feel the link with ideas such
as Bonaventure's: no one thinks just their own words. . . . The
question has become more and more complicated, until it is not
easy to recognize that there is a question there at all. Answers
begin to shut out the questions from which they spring. Of course
these answers are vital, but keeping hold of the question is important too.

Questions do not come singly. In the readings which follow,
'Whose words are these?' overlaps repeatedly with another set of
questions. This set focuses on the problem of replying. As we saw
in earlier chapters, speech and writing almost always involve some
elements of responding to other views. Even the lecturer delivering what seems a monologue will be replying, implicitly and
explicitly, to all kinds of possible voices which might be associated
with the matter at hand. The whole of argument is an extension of
the basic phenomenon of voices replying to each other: Aristotle,
Plato, and many later thinkers were considered in that context.
Types of reply can also be related to power and status in society
– indeed the previous chapter uses reply as a central concept in
social analysis. Now 'To what is this a reply?' becomes a question
that is central for the Rhetorical reading of stories. There is no
need to match particular examples from stories with philosophical
concepts of reply, or with sociological ideas. What matters is that
the question of reply is as complex and essential in interpreting
stories as in other spheres of Rhetoric.

Now we come to some readings. First there is a reading of
Mary Shelley's *Frankenstein*, a reading which also considers some
aspects of the history of science. 'Whose words are these?' is the
main question asked in this reading. 'To what is this voice replying?' comes in as well, but the novel is richly responsive to the first

question. Then there is a reading of Dickens's *Martin Chuzzlewit*, where questions of reply become more central. There is an important point here about questioning and reading. Questions must not be imposed mechanically; yet readers necessarily decide in advance what questions to ask. Rhetoric merely formalizes that choice, making it more explicit. The art of reading is to adjust questions, to decide when and where to pose them and when to try a line that is different.

Here the questions are the most basic possible: yet they can still be refined in a reading. *Meaning* is the goal – that is the important point. Such questions only become mechanical when meaning is ignored. That does happen in many attempts to define methods of interpreting – especially methods which are 'scientific', some of which are noted at the end of the chapter.

Reading *Frankenstein*, reading science: 'Whose words are these?'

He then told me that he would commence his narrative the
next day when I should be at leisure . . . I will at least make
notes. This manuscript will doubtless afford you the greatest
pleasure; but to me, who know him and who hear it from
his own lips – with what interest and sympathy shall I read it
in some future day! Even now, as I commence my task, his
full-toned voice swells in my ears . . .

A story is about to begin – 'he would commence his narrative the next day . . .'. Someone is going to speak a tale, which a writer will then transcribe:

I will at least make notes.

But consider that 'at least': how accurate will the transcript be? Are we going to read 'his narrative', or will that be rewritten first? Then, even if the manuscript is faithful to 'his narrative', what about 'his . . . voice'?

This manuscript will doubtless afford you the greatest
pleasure; but to me . . . who hear it from his own lips . . .

No reader will hear the voice properly, 'his full-toned voice'. So, 'Whose words are these?' will be a question, necessarily. Victor Frankenstein is the man who 'told me that he would commence his narrative'; the transcriber is one Captain Walton, who has rescued Frankenstein from the Arctic wastes. Mary Shelley's *Frankenstein* is about to start the great story. So far there have been 'letters' which Captain Walton has sent to his sister, letters describing a journey to the pole and a meeting with the lone stranger who now takes up the story. These letters are Walton's words, one might feel, whatever complications follow with 'his narrative'. Yet the letters contain many more voices than that suggests; the novel even teases us about the plurality of voices in these passages:

> I have read with ardour the accounts of the various voyages . . . These visions faded when I perused, for the first time, those poets . . .

Walton is an avid and suggestible reader: he has read explorers' journals and he has read poetry. Naturally, given the novel's linguistic wit, he writes of the Arctic in words which sound partly like 'accounts of . . . voyages' and partly like 'poets':

> . . . it ever presents itself to my imagination as the region of beauty and delight . . . you cannot contest the inestimable benefit which I shall confer upon mankind to the last generation, by discovering a passage near the pole to those countries . . .

Some words suggest poets' voices ('My imagination . . . region of beauty and delight'); others sound more like explorers' ('a passage near the pole'). In between, voices overlap: 'the inestimable benefit' may sound like voyagers' voices, but 'to the last generation' feels more as if it came from poets' voices.

Walton's 'voice' is not one voice but many voices: poets' and explorers' explicitly.

What happens when Walton proceeds to 'take notes' of the 'narrative' – Frankenstein's tale? The story is familiar to everyone – at least in outline – and includes episodes as famous as any in storytelling. Frankenstein recalls discovering how to bestow life on dead tissue:

> I was surprised that among so many men of genius who had directed their enquiries towards the same science, that I alone should be reserved to discover so astonishing a secret . . . I

became myself capable of bestowing animation on lifeless
matter . . .

Is there not a reminiscent ring to the words which follow?

The astonishment which I had at first experienced on this
discovery soon gave place to delight and rapture . . . What
had been the study and desire of the wisest men since the
creation of the world was now within my grasp . . . my
imagination was too much exalted . . . A new species would
bless me as its creator and source . . .

Do we not also hear certain echoes in the account of his hopes
just before?

. . . more, far more, will I achieve treading in the steps,
already marked, I will pioneer a new way, explore unknown
powers . . .

Whose words are these? The 'narrative' is 'his', Frankenstein's;
but Walton has 'at least' been making 'notes', and transcribing
the tale. There is a teasing doubleness to the narrative because
Walton has described his own voyage to a region which 'ever
presents itself to my *imagination* as the region of . . . *delight*';
he has hoped for 'the inestimable benefit I shall confer upon
mankind . . .'; he has even declared

I shall satiate my ardent curiosity with the sight of a part of
the world never before visited, and *may tread a land never
before imprinted by the foot of man.*

There is more than common ground here: 'imagination', 'delight', new regions, benefits for whole races, the image of
treading. . . . Walton has felt how Frankenstein's great voice
'swells in my ears'; now Walton's voice rings insistently in the
reader's ears, as we try to hear the words of Frankenstein – and,
elusively yet memorably, Walton's voice then resounds with the
voices of others, of poets and explorers. So the voices of 'Walton'
will not withdraw from the text and let it be purely the words of
Frankenstein.

The puzzle is richer still, because Frankenstein is also speaking
to Walton, warning him:

> Learn from me, if not by my precepts, at least by my example,
> how dangerous is the acquirement of knowledge . . .

Frankenstein directs these words at Walton, and Walton sends
the message on to us. Clearly, Frankenstein is doing the telling;
but Walton as transcriber has one claim on the words, and Walton
as interlocutor has another claim, having specifically provoked the
warning by being so aspiring himself. Then consider the moral
itself: 'how dangerous is the acquirement of knowledge'. No message could be more proverbial: this truth is familiar, which is part
of why it is so strong. Novelty is derided in practice, as well as
rejected in principle:

> Learn . . . how dangerous is the acquirement of
> knowledge . . .

Learn *that*, the old truth, rather than pursuing anything new.
Voices overlap, voices that are individual and also voices that are
cultural – and this overlapping enters into the meaning of the
story.

'Whose words are these?': this becomes a problem that is
explicit as well as implicit. Frankenstein grandly recognizes that
his voice is not the best agent for his idea: 'if not by my
precepts . . .', he concedes, except that the 'concession' is so
forceful. Coming from him, these traditional words may seem
strange: so he urges Walton not to dwell on how these can be
Victor Frankenstein's words – to dwell instead on their ancient
truth and on an example beyond anyone's words. As Frankenstein's words, these ideas may seem peculiar; as a proverbial
saying, they will apply forcefully to the story. *The authority of ideas
can depend on how we decide to identify a voice*: these choices
matter, that is part of what reading such a novel reveals to us.

The problems are radical: even time can be problematic when
we try to identify the voice. 'Time' sounds like an abstract question
– but it becomes palpable as Frankenstein recalls what he used to
think:

> A new species would bless me as its creator and source: many
> happy and excellent natures would owe their being to me.

Now, that seems ridiculous – and worse: 'would bless me . . .
would owe . . .' makes it clear that the hope is past (not 'will . . .

will . . .'). Yet some phrases resonate still: 'new species . . . bless . . . creator and source . . . happy and excellent . . .'. The hope is over, but the hopeful voice is audible still, especially in patterns which remain alive ('creator and source . . . happy and excellent'). Frankenstein is trying to be ironic at the expense of hopes that are lost: 'happy and excellent . . .', yes, but just remember what happened. . . . Yet the hope rivals the irony: the ideal can still speak, the other view is still there. So these words belong to a tale in the present, and that tale is caustically rejecting the ideal; but certain phrases and patterns are still loyal to that ideal, and so bring the dead past back to life. There is a dialogue, a strange interplay of present and past, of disillusioned wisdom and energetic idealism. As well as identifying voices, then, we are also tracing a process of replying: the experience of reading is so rich that it needs to be thought through in terms of many questions together.

Yet the trickiest problems of defining voices are maybe still to come in the novel. Frankenstein recalls making the monster, deserting him, and being pursued by his own creature. The monster learns to speak: he addresses speeches to the scientist, who reports the words. Then the monster is given a narrative that is extended, describing his life to Frankenstein, who conveys the episode to Walton. . . . Once the monster has a voice, Franken- stein's own voice has to be identified as 'not the monster's words', as well as being 'not Walton'; and it is no easier to separate Frankenstein's voice from the monster's than from Walton's. Con- sider, briefly, some examples where the need to tell the tale fully forces the inventor to let his enemy find words. For instance, the monster has a long account of his formative experience, told to a past Victor and 'now' retold to Walton and by Walton to his sister and to us. The monster is reported to have addressed Frank- enstein, speaking as, 'thy creature', and lamenting its unique misery as 'a blot', then a whole new series of lines are drawn and un-drawn between voices. For a start, the monster's 'thy creature' is evidently not in Frankenstein's words but still is being reported by Victor. More suggestively, there are many echoes and overlaps linking this voice with what that 'hero' himself says. Victor as the present teller wails 'no creature had ever been so miserable' and he is referring to himself. But 'whose voice' is that? There is no way of separating present narration from past outburst, ('no creature *has* . . .') since either could claim 'creature' and 'miserable'. But then again, would those words be possible without the monster's voice, which has brought the word 'creature' into play?

Frankenstein has previously identified himself with the word 'creator', but he becomes a 'creature' – he, now the most 'miserable' of creatures, who had hoped 'many happy . . . natures would owe their being' to him. The monster has caused the change, and not just at the level of events. There is a 'monster-ring' about the telling voice, with 'creature', 'miserable', and the idea of being uniquely wretched. The words read as if they were being taken over by that 'otherest' of all other voices. Certainly, not to hear the monstrous tones is to register only part of the answer to 'Whose words are these?'. That question has, therefore, proved more and more relevant. Now what can be *done* with all those tempting patterns?

Often the novel does not address the story to the world in the words of one 'owner'. Still more importantly, sometimes there is not even a definite hierarchy of 'owners'. 'Whose words are these?' therefore does not reveal a static system of tellers and speakers. On the contrary, the question becomes a way of exploring a *process*. What does that sense of process indicate about the power of address itself? That the whole enterprise can work, must work, *without* a simple answer to a basic question 'Whose words are these?'. In fact, as far as the current example goes, there seems to be an actual gain, rather than a loss, of focus. What we are considering here is not, then, any particular interpretation so much as the grounds of all interpreting.

The story becomes strangely objective in such telling. No viewpoint is uncoloured by subjectivity, often a named subjectivity such as 'Walton', 'Frankenstein', 'monster'. But no single voice representing an individual point of view can take over the tale. The narration is always contested. Such effects are not particular to *Frankenstein*, though the impact is distinctive here: one potent element of storytelling is its capacity to conjure a feeling that certain events are, or were, objectively real. That can, paradoxically, be done very effectively by addressing tales without fixing their narrative source. In *Frankenstein*, for instance, the play between the present Victor and the past idealist, between creator and creature, between the insider and Walton the outsider, is such that nobody gets to stamp a definitive view on events. Therefore, what 'happens' seems to exist independently of the competing voices.

This is magic: a spell is cast and it makes an objective world out of overlapping subjective positions. As such it is one variety of what the Greek sophist Gorgias considered the sorcery of words (in his case speech, but we are extending his meaning):

> The force of the charm [of speech] meets the conviction of the mind and bewitches, persuades, and changes it by sorcery . . .

Persuading has a magical quality: that is a vital point. Rhetoric, and indeed analysis more generally, is often thought to strip away 'charm'. But here, asking 'Whose words are these?' about *Frankenstein*, dispels nothing. Being precise does not mean explaining away the experience which readers have when 'the force of the charm', in this case the play of voices in the telling of a fantastic story, 'meets the conviction . . . and bewitches, persuades, and changes . . .'. What would have seemed ludicrous becomes temporarily real. In recognizing that strange 'other' reality, we gain space to make interpretations of a different world. Meanings can play back over familiar worlds, the usually real, the historically real. The persuasion arises in and from play, and then yields scope for more play, play of interpretation.

Many, though not all, of the examples from the novel can now be drawn into the net of *quotation*. Walton quotes Frankenstein, Frankenstein quotes the monster. That applies both to snippets of 'speech' and to longer narrations. These are *explicit* quotations, vouched for by the book's structure, including chapter divisions. But then the inventor's earlier voice turns up inside his later (present) account; and monster-resonances get into what 'should' be Victor's narration. These might be called implicit quotations, with the monster-in-Frankenstein being the most deeply buried. These are 'quotations' in the sense that one voice presents or contains another. As ever, the quoting and the quoted identify themselves as *not* the other, and yet overlap (even more so than in, say, the sermon). Asking 'Whose words are these?' consistently defines a part of the experience of the novel's address. The term 'quotation' may serve for a large part of that rendering, and so it seems reasonable here to talk of Quotation-Reading. This kind of terminology is helpful if not used over-zealously. Such an idea of a 'reading' is an outline, a 'model', not a formula or a prescription. It is a reminder of *some* important elements in reading. So far, Quotation-Reading has indicated one magical power of address.

This process of reading is flooded with meanings; suggestion saturates every move. Frankenstein wants to be an originator, making a fresh start on a 'new species'. Yet these desires are recalled in an endlessly receding pattern of voice-in-voice. Where is the 'source' of the telling? That source is Victor himself, but also the earlier scientist, and Walton, and the monster. At a different level, the novel's subtitle is *The Modern Prometheus*: the whole work is referred back to the Greek myth about the stealing of fire (enlightenment). So all the named quoters are living and telling inside a quotation from another culture. But echoes of the Christian fall are everywhere, too – Biblical and Miltonic. Therefore, the Greek myth isn't *the* 'source', only *a* source. Accordingly, even 'Mary Shelley' is not *the* source, since so many other possible answers are in play, such as 'Greece', 'the Bible', as well as the characters. Nothing originates the story itself, in the important sense of there being a single 'source'. No one can truly originate utterance: there are always borrowings. Therefore, in a way, language is Frankenstein's great adversary. Language forbids pure origination. The novel can therefore deploy the texture and idea of quotation against the idealist's desire to be a fresh source, a pure originator. The whole process of address-as-quotation *answers* the voice of the idealistic inventor who longs to be the true 'source'. Quotation-Reading cannot be separated from this other emphasis, which (for symmetry's sake) could be called 'Reply-Reading'.

Scientific voices and the meaning of *Frankenstein*

Meaning is what matters: asking questions is a way of *interpreting* stories. The questions here are 'Whose words are these?' and 'To what is this a reply?': but the answers are meanings, not categories of voice. Another problem arises here. If meaning is the aim, then when should the reading stop? An account which classifies voices ends when all the voices have been classified, when the grid is in place. But where does meaning end? Consider Frankenstein's discovery further:

I saw how the fine form of man was degraded and wasted: I beheld the corruption of death succeed to the blooming cheek of life; I saw how the worm inherited the wonders of the eye and the brain. I paused, examining and analysing all the minutiae of causation, as exemplified in the change from life to death and death to life . . .

These words belong to several voices in the novel: the speaker now, the protagonist then, the transcriber. . . . But we can also hear other voices, voices of a different kind: 'examining and analysing . . . the minutiae of causation . . . exemplified . . .'. *Science* speaks in the words, a discourse that is empirical ('examining') and rational ('analysing'), meticulous ('minutiae') and explanatory ('of causation'), objective and technical. There are, of course, other discourses too: 'the worm inherited' has the sound of preaching, 'the eye and the brain' hovers tensely between preaching and science.

Now here is a scientist, the great Robert Hooke, using a voice that is analogous in certain ways to *Frankenstein's* scientific tones:

I could perceive, through the transparent shell, while the animal surviv'd, several motions in the head, thorax, and belly, very distinctly, of differing kinds which I may, perhaps, elsewhere endeavour more accurately to examine . . .

Hooke is writing in the late seventeenth century – and his work is not a source for the novel. But the novel has reproduced the manner in general: '. . . more accurately to examine' corresponds to the fiction's 'examining . . . all the minutiae'. The passages resemble each other because they share a vocabulary; but this is a vocabulary that is more than just words, it is a way of thinking as well.

Hooke also raises an issue about science that is central in the novel: 'while the animal surviv'd'. He is only observing a water insect but he is still conscious of how science needs to find a way of including death in its discourse, since the observer may often kill the observed as he examines it. Hooke recommends caution: indeed he warns that the discourse of objectivity may betray itself by being falsely objective about death:

when we endeavour to pry into her [Nature's] secrets by breaking open the doors upon her, and dissecting and mangling creatures whil'st there is yet life within them, we find her indeed at work, but put into such a disorder by the violence offer'd, as it may easily be imagin'd, how differing a thing we should find, if we could quietly peep . . .

Death *distorts* Nature: therefore science must not be indifferent to the death of its subjects, for in dying they become misleading. And Hooke's words apply even to insects . . . !

So Hooke is aware that what, from one point of view, is examining, may be, from another point of view, endeavouring to pry. Being objective is necessary, but there must be limits or science will become self-destructive. Hooke insists that the word 'life' must retain an ethical value as well as being a central term in biology: 'dissecting and mangling creatures whil'st there is yet life within them'. He is conscious of how easily the word 'life' could slip, becoming merely a technical term. Ironically, at that point science would begin to mislead itself. Here the comparison with the novel is pertinent. Frankenstein has had a language which made 'life' into merely one more term, a term for naming part of the observed process:

. . . as exemplified in the change from life to death . . .

'Exemplified': as if *that* could be just one example!

To repeat: the novel is not quoting Hooke. But both Hooke and the novel are quoting science – the 'objective', the analytic discourse. And both *Frankenstein* and Hooke are concerned with the limits of that discourse, with its relation to the rest of language and so to the rest of experience. Hooke replies to others who dissect and mangle happily, who are misled by the idiom of being analytic until they have lost sight of what is being analysed. Eventually, analysis destroys its subject: the analysed becomes something else, something that is merely parts, bits, fragments. The novel is exploring similar dangers: 'examining and analysing all the minutiae'. Science needs to talk about parts, and therefore to talk as if breaking things down is the way to understand them. Yet there are limits: if things break down too far, they are changed into something else. Science must keep a sense of *wholes*, even while examining parts. Scientific language can make wholes difficult to remember: 'minutiae', 'analysing'. . . . 'Life' is a quality of wholes: thus warns Hooke, and that is precisely what the earlier

Frankenstein forgets, letting the word 'life' become just one term in a process. The religious voice in the novel hints at that error – 'the worm inherited' – but we can still hear the appeal of the scientific voice when it was pure. (And, of course, the novel lets Frankenstein succeed, up to a point . . .)

We can recognize the discourse of science, and what we recognize is not just the words, at least in the superficial sense of that phrase. The novel can quote a central idea as well as a central vocabulary: *the analytic vein*. Other examples abound in science: for instance, Humphrey Davy refers to uncovering 'minute properties' (Davy being a famous discoverer and inventor of the late eighteenth and early nineteenth century). Frankenstein's 'minutiae' belongs in the same repertoire as these 'minute properties'. The link is the idea that breaking things down is the way of revealing their nature. *Frankenstein* allows us to hear the voice of analysis, to hear how it is exciting, and also to sense that it could be dangerous and limiting. In a way, therefore, the novel replies to that voice, as well as quoting it. Other scientists have themselves made replies that are similar: to criticize science may be to play a part in the process rather than merely to be one of the enemy.

But science is more than just the analytic vein. Does *Frankenstein* reproduce any more voices which are scientific? Here are Victor Frankenstein's first feelings about what he has achieved (or his memories of those feelings):

> The astonishment which I had at first experienced on this discovery soon gave place to delight and rapture . . . But this discovery was so great and overwhelming that all the steps by which I had been progressively led to it were obliterated . . . What had been the study and desire of the wisest men since the creation of the world was now within my grasp. Not that, like a magic scene, it all opened up to me at once . . .

He has found 'the cause of generation and life'; he feels 'delight and rapture'; the 'discovery' is 'great and overwhelming'. The discoverer stands out from all other men: so here is the scientist as hero, experiencing feelings more intense than those of ordinary mortals, feelings which accompany a great moment of insight. The 'cause' is never clear: it is a way of 'bestowing animation . . .'. In fact, scientists *had* discovered a force analogous to this 'animation'; here is an account of such a discoverer at his moment of insight:

> October 1806
>
> . . . The extreme delight which he felt, when he first saw the metallic basis of potash, can only be conceived by those who are familiar with the operations of the laboratory, and the exciting nature of original research; who can enter into his previous views, and the analogies by which he was guided, and can comprehend the vast importance of the discovery, in its various relations to chemical doctrine; and, perhaps, not least, who can appreciate the workings of a young mind with an avidity for knowledge and glory commensurate . . . when he saw the minute globules of potassium burst through the crust of potash, and take fire as they entered the atmosphere, he could not contain his joy - he actually bounded about the room in extatic delight; and that some little time was required for him to compose himself sufficiently to continue the experiment.
>
> (From *Memoirs of the Life of Sir Humphry Davy* by John Davy, 1839)

Humphry Davy has discovered electricity and he feels 'extreme delight' beyond the ken of ordinary people ('can only be conceived by those who are familiar . . .'). His 'discovery' is of 'vast importance'; the breakthrough testifies to 'a young mind with an avidity for knowledge and the glory commensurate'. These words are no source for *Frankenstein*: the *Memoirs of the Life of Davy* only appeared in 1839, twenty years after the novel. Why, then, does the memoir overlap so closely with the novel? Again, *Frankenstein's* 'narrative' has quoted something which is central to the idea of science in general: in achieving a leap forwards of 'vast importance', the scientist becomes a hero. This is the idea of scientific genius, the genius of the break-through.

'Genius' is still only one idea of the scientist, or one way of talking about what the scientist can achieve. The scientist can also be presented as a *producer*, a maker of things. The novel certainly includes this way of defining what the scientist does:

> Although I possessed the capacity of bestowing animation, yet to prepare a frame for the reception of it, with all its

intricacies of fibres, muscles, and veins, still remained a work of inconceivable difficulty and labour.

So the scientist discovers – but he also produces; he is an explorer, but an explorer who brings back tangible riches from his travels. The scientist is objective and experimental, he is inspired, but he is also a practical maker of new things:

> Mr. Hooke produced a contrivance to try, whether a mechanical muscle could be made by art . . .
> (Royal Society Minutes)

These new things are likely to be anomalous, by natural standards. Science will invent products which are artificial, yet these products will *perform* like natural organisms. There will be 'a mechanical muscle' (Hooke); there will be 'the creation of a human being' (Frankenstein). The scientist will re-produce the world; like the artist, he will make a copy of nature, but the scientist's copy will act upon nature in new ways. The novel is quoting another idea of the scientist, the idea of the scientist as (re)producer of nature, as reinventor of the world. Science observes and experiments, but science ultimately aims to re-produce the world.

Here, then, are three ideas: analysis, genius, re-production of nature. These ideas are also *voices*: they are ways of talking, not just notions in the abstract. Without these ways of talking, there can be nothing which would sound recognizably like scientific discourse. In this context, scientific discourse includes both what scientists say and what is said about science. Of course, that discourse has results that are real: knowledge emerges, and knowledge has consequences. But science is more than just knowledge, science is an *idea*, a way of using language, a way of thinking about the world. Therefore, if we ask 'Whose words are these?' of *Frankenstein*, then the answer will sometimes be: these are the words of science (as well as those of certain characters). The novel *quotes* science, and in doing so, the fiction is revealing something important, which is precisely that science *can* be quoted, because it includes voices as well as knowledge, images as well as experiments.

There are other ideas and voices which are necessary for science, although they are more general, perhaps. We can hear one such voice when Frankenstein recalls being the idealist who would explore unknown powers and unfold to the world the deepest mysteries.

There are any number of analogues. One cited (by Vassbinder) is the Elizabethan philosopher Francis Bacon. Equally, we could choose passages from the Renaissance alchemical sage Paracelsus, who is in fact a hero of the earlier Frankenstein:

the legitamit [sic] Interpreter of Nature, who alone searcheth out its oeconomy, and the universal latitude thereof, prying into all things . . .

It is a property of truth to increase, when properly pursued: that is the idea, the way of speaking and thinking which *Frankenstein* has reproduced. One might call this idea a principle, the principle of 'expandable knowledge'. That principle has its voices and its images – especially voices which talk of 'explore' and 'unknown', or of 'searcheth out' and of 'prying into all'. 'Expandable knowledge' is an idea that is larger than science, and that idea needs voices that are larger than scientific discourse. What are we hearing, then, in *Frankenstein* or in Paracelsus? Perhaps the best term would be 'enlightenment', a whole ideal of progress through knowledge.

That ideal has always had its critics. Paracelsus may be eager, but nearby, other voices are more sceptical:

for the true felicitie consisteth not in understanding, but in lyving with understanding: for not the good understanding, but the good wyll, toyneth men unto good . . .

That is Cornelius Agrippa, another Renaissance sage. Interestingly, the novel mentions both Paracelsus and Agrippa. The student Frankenstein has his heroes, and these include both Paracelsus and Agrippa, who pursued alchemical research as well as writing *Of the Vanitie of Artes and Sciences* from which the extract above comes. Here Victor has been speaking with a professor:

He heard with attention the little narration concerning my studies and smiled at the name of Cornelius Agrippa and Paracelsus, but without the contempt that M. Krempe had exhibited. He said that 'these were men to whose indefatigable zeal modern philosophers were indebted for most of the foundations . . .'

There is no need to think of Paracelsus and Agrippa as specific sources for the novel. But *Frankenstein* is quoting a whole debate, between the ideal of enlightenment and the counter-voice of warning and of tradition:

> Learn from me . . . how dangerous is the acquirement of knowledge . . .

Paracelsus and Agrippa are forerunners of this debate, and their presence in the text can symbolize for us the novel's power of quoting from western culture. Ultimately, in *Frankenstein*, relations of conflict and reply are part of the fabric of quotation.

Science of course is not static. But these general *ideas* of science and of enlightenment are still recognizable, still influential culturally. Reading the story of *Frankenstein* becomes a way of exploring ideas of science, both historically and pertinently. Rhetoric does not create the novel's engagements with science-as-quotation – but thinking Rhetorically is one way of being responsive to those potentialities for meaning. Ultimately, the story fosters two kinds of response to science. One is a *critique* of scientific discourse, of its dangers and limitations. But there is also room for simple excitement, as we sense the persuasive power of the voices of science. Perhaps power is the crux: Frankenstein himself says

> When I found so astonishing a power placed within my hands, I hesitated a long time . . .

That 'power' is real: though the events are fantastic, the voices are representative. In the end, perhaps, the meaning of the story *is* the process of listening to these voices and ideas – listening to them in a context set apart from the familiar world. How, then, does all that meaning relate to the layering of the narration as a whole? That layering of voices is precisely what encourages the reader to listen intently: and what we hear is partly Victor and Walton, Victor and the creature, and partly the discourse of science and enlightenment, and of their critics. To read this story is to *hear* a culture – and Rhetoric both enters into such a reading and benefits from it.

Narrative and the dynamics of reply: *Martin Chuzzlewit*

'Whose words are these?' is one question; Quotation-Reading is one part of the reading process. Other questions must be asked in the course of interpretation, such as 'To what are these words replying?' (or to what is this story replying?). Such questions arose in reading *Frankenstein* and are now central. As with the question 'Whose words are these?', the general heading should not be treated as a fixed form, but only as a helpful indicator of possibilities. One kind of reading could concentrate upon finding opposing positions, without much (or even any) concern as to whether any of those positions directs attention towards its opponent/opposed view. Then 'reply' would have a single sense of 'reacting against', rather than any double sense of being both 'against' and 'towards'. Another version of 'To what is this replying?' would be useful in exploring how far a story formulates reactions against views prevalent in the wider culture. On the other hand, there can be a kind of 'Reply-Reading' which is very strict about the double sense of 'reply against/towards'. The major literary example is M. M. Bakhtin's work on Dostoevsky.

The idea of reply in the present chapter lies between the simpler notion of 'reacting against' and the strict double sense of Bakhtin's concept. The basis for our idea of replying in narrative derives from our treatment of argument.

To argue against a position always induces *some* feeling of address towards another who holds the opposing view. The feeling may amount to no more than that: an imaginative impulse towards an absent or abstract opponent. Or the opposing view may be located in someone arguing from within an audience that is actually addressed. Words are hurled towards/against opposing positions in different ways and these ways may be infinitely complex and elusive, as part of many different kinds of address. Consider this extract from *Martin Chuzzlewit*:

> nobody ever dreamed such soup . . . or such fish; or such side
> dishes . . . or in short anything approaching the reality of
> that entertainment at ten-and-sixpence a head . . .

Three people are here found enjoying a meal – the humble Tom Pinch, dashing young Martin Chuzzlewit, and someone who has donated the feast. In what sense can this description of a meal be interpreted as a reply? To what does it reply? As with all interpretation, it is essential to consider the whole context. All three have been passing through the hands of scheming Pecksniff, who was enjoying another meal some chapters earlier. At that meal, Pecksniff memorably disguised his gusto for food as ethics . . .

'. . . the worldly goods of which we have just disposed . . . even cream, sugar, tea, toast, ham . . . have their moral.'

These two meals obviously contrast. Critical interpretations often settle for patterns of contrast, but such patterns are static and inaudible. They do no justice to the experience of address. The young men's meal can be interpreted as replying to Pecksniff's sly relish. The hypocrite half dismisses the word 'worldly' and then wraps his tongue lovingly round the words 'cream, sugar'. He then slides onto the higher ground of 'their moral'. Mr Pecksniff's great allure is in the way he delights fiercely in 'worldly goods' and at the same time energetically uses 'worldly goods' as other-worldly arguments. The humbler feast replies to that attitude, an attitude which gains credit by transcending the worldly. At the same time, Pecksniff is getting his hands on bigger and bigger slices of the world. The entertainment at ten-and-six replies to Pecksniff's greed, and the emphasis on 'reality' replies to Pecksniff's moral pretensions. No, food *is* first an entertainment, not a 'moral' issue (so is fiction), and credit should not be looked for in transcending reality. Those who claim to be above 'worldly goods' are the ones who consume them most extravagantly. Those who enjoy their meal at 'ten-and-sixpence' are truly generous spirits. The real moral is *lived*, not pronounced, lived in giving and taking generously, in the entertaining and the being entertained.

'Reply' here can be understood in two senses. First, the truly moral entertainment *counters* the inflated idea that 'goods . . . have their moral'. It is not 'goods' which have morals but people and deeds. Second, 'reply' can suggest actually speaking *to*, a response *back*. Pecksniff's presence is so persistent that many passages and episodes easily come off the page as if hurled back *at* him, at the eloquent villain. The novel explicitly suggests that replies are being made to Pecksniff:

. . . one would not have been disposed (unless Mr Pecksniff said so) to consider him [Tom Pinch] a bad fellow . . .

And on another occasion Pecksniff says:

'You will excuse Thomas Pinch's want of polish, Martin . . .'
'He is a very good fellow, sir.'

Both of these passages concern Pinch, who is mild and good, and in each case the novel is replying to Pecksniff's calculated snootiness. In the first example, the words 'one would not' draw the reader into play and pit us against the parenthesized Pecksniff. (He of course soon breaks out and bounces back.) In the second example, young Martin delivers a rebuff on our behalf. The feeling of replying against and towards Pecksniff *diffuses* through the story.

Asking the questions 'Whose words are these?' and 'To what is this a reply?' does *not* produce a final interpretation. What results is a reading, or a map of possible readings. No reading is final because different questions are always available. Some questions, about whose words these are, are already implied. One might ask of the passage 'such fish . . . such soup' whether the enthusiasm for these things was being shown by a narrative voice or by the intruding voices of the characters. Such questions could also be extended: Reply-Reading and Quotation-Reading go together.

As *Martin Chuzzlewit* goes on, the oily moralist claims more power over others *and* in the text:

. . . assuming the position of the Chorus in a Greek Tragedy, [he] delivered his opinion as a commentary on the proceedings.

And Pecksniff says to the elder Chuzzlewit:

'Shall I give expression to your thoughts, my friend?'

Consequently he becomes a still more obvious target *for* replies. In the end, events, final events, make several such responses: they show Pecksniff that his calculating method does not work. The world is not, as he implies, infinitely open to deception and calculation. Another kind of reply to Pecksniff's views occurs when some of the characters *do* behave honestly and selflessly. The effect, then, is of the whole story answering Pecksniff's sneering proposition:

'Oh! let us not be for ever calculating, devising and
plotting . . .'

In that remark he meant just the reverse of what he appeared to
be saying. The moral is reclaimed from his words by the actions
of good servants such as Pinch. Reading their virtue means 'experiencing a reply to Pecksniff', and that feeling prevents the good
and evil from becoming static. In an active interplay, the story
makes virtue a *reply* to hypocrisy, not merely a contrast. The
treacherous voice finally comes unstuck. The elder Mr Chuzzlewit
is talking to Pecksniff.

'Hear me, rascal!'

And the old man then goes on to retell the events, defeating
Pecksniff's 'commentary', and substituting for the thoughts which
Pecksniff has attributed to him very different thoughts.

Thus a long story can address itself by replying against and
towards a strong character. That possibility was glimpsed in the
reading of *Frankenstein*, and is often worth examining. Several
characters can share the position of being replied to, in which the
character is both privileged and exposed. The reader experiences
such characters as inherently 'replyable to'. It is not automatically
clear where the process of replying to Pecksniff stops in the novel.
When young Martin Chuzzlewit goes to America, he hears many
voices which sound just like Pecksniff's:

'You air now, sir, a denizen of the most powerful and highly
civilised do-minion . . .'

In a way, these voices *side with* Pecksniff. Such speakers confirm
the oily orator's view of the world . . . fine goods are all. So
long as you talk about virtue, anything goes. When the narrative
denounces 'America', and characters flee that country, the story
replies to American speakers who have proclaimed the virtue of
America and their own share in it. The question arises: is the
world a place where morality is only verbal? 'America' and
Pecksniff say 'yes', other voices (and deeds) respond with many
'noes'. All those 'noes' are hurled back at the magnificent villain
directly in moments such as those in which old Mr Chuzzlewit
speaks: 'Hear me, rascal!'. Such a reading is *contestable*: many
others would be possible. Rhetoric is not an escape from making

judgements about interpretation, but is a way of defining what is to be judged in the reading.

When 'replying' is the issue under consideration, *Martin Chuzzlewit* explores a major problem, that of subjectivity. Mr Pecksniff, talking to someone who has done a wicked deed, excuses it as 'natural':

> Touching which remark, let it be written down to their confusion that the enemies of this worthy man unblushingly maintained that he always said of what was very bad, that it was very natural; and that he unconsciously betrayed his own nature in doing so.

The novel is launching another counter-move to Pecksniff. The words 'unconsciously betrayed his own nature . . .' are rich in possibilities for interpretation. One possibility is that Pecksniff lets down ('betrays') human nature and all human nature is basically good. Another, more central idea is that the hypocrite *reveals* ('betrays' in that sense) his own *bad* nature. The tell-tale sign of a bad nature is a low estimate of what is 'natural'. By contrast and in reply, Pinch elsewhere uses the words 'quite natural' when talking of good things. But is each view just revealing the speaker's own nature, good as well as bad? Do both express subjective origins? Does this mean there is no objective truth? Is there only Pinch's nature against Pecksniff's? The opposing views of what is natural are not equal; but are we always to be left making moral comparisons between speakers rather than finding out the truth about the issue they are considering, for example, what is natural?

Here Dickens' novel raises the most central problem for any reply model, whether in story-reading, or philosophical debate, or in, say, legal dispute. It looks as though the choices they offer always lie between the 'natures' of the disputants as revealed in their views. That makes all judgements between 'sides' ethical: which is the better, or the healthier, or the more noble, or the more beneficial . . . ? Or can an answer be found to the issue under consideration itself? Do we want to know which is the true view? Does the truth always coincide with the better nature? How much attention should we pay in a dispute to the natures of the parties concerned and how much to seeking the truth about the issue in other ways (scanning the rest of the story, for instance)?

A reading of *Martin Chuzzlewit* here confronts a major problem in the history and philosophy of dispute. When it comes to the problem of evaluating replies, Plato's Socrates gives relevant advice:

> Those who attend to discussions of this sort ought to listen to both speakers impartially but not equally . . .

On this principle it is possible to avoid premature verdicts on the one side and, on the other, empty open-mindedness. A reading of *Martin Chuzzlewit* can explore the same territory. We do not need to treat Pecksniff and opposing tendencies equally in order to experience the story in terms of replies. At times it is assumed that it is necessary to suspend judgement in order to appreciate dialogues, and some assume that this state of suspension is preferable to the process of judging. That emphasis on suspension of judgement encourages the pursuit of 'polyphonic' novels. In our view, however, novels are as polyphonic as the reader makes them. Polyphony is in the ear of the reader. The collision between a 'Pecksniff world' and opposed world views *encourages* judgement. But the whole process of replying must be gone through in order to discover the judgement's meaning.

Reading *Martin Chuzzlewit* Rhetorically defines an experience of persuasive address, but to experience *Martin Chuzzlewit*'s responses to Pecksniff is also to be thoroughly at play. The 'Pecksniff world' is playfully elaborated partly by what he says and does, by his claims on the text itself, and partly by a widening network of affinities. Counter-moves can be experienced all over the story, as narrated reactions, as characters' answers, as opposed behaviour, as the reclaiming of words, and the retelling of events. What makes the process playful as well as persuasive is the diversity of the conflict. That diversity enhances persuasion while threatening to freewheel: 'Pecksniff' becomes a glorious show, as well as the object of determined opposition.

Rhetoric and reading stories

The question 'To what is *this* replying?' may be asked of a passage or a whole story. 'Replying' may take the form of a fully addressed reaction to something previous, or may be a simple negation of something previous without directly addressing what has been negated. The readings move between these different definitions of a reply. The 'reply' might be more or less strongly opposed to what is previous, more or less hostile. Within the reading of Dickens the degree of conflict suggested in the 'reply' varies from statements of a downright negative kind to an emotional tension raised between different attitudes. The question, asked Rhetorically, is interpretive; the answers are interpretations, not categories that apply to the novel. The aim is to explore how meanings become possible as a story's address is experienced. The result of asking the question repeatedly is a kind of map of readings and meanings, not a system of categorized devices. Interpretation remains contestable, cannot repeat itself again in an identical form, or find sanction from 'linguistic devices'. Repeatable patterns do not emerge from the present use of Rhetoric; no such patterns here try to make interpretation less subjective or less contestable. Rhetoric *explores* the subjective process of interpreting; it organizes but does not automate. Therefore with each reading the precise form of the interpretive question must be allowed to vary.

Reading is a process. Questions must enter into that process if questioning is to lead towards meaning in a helpful way. Any approach or theory which stops the process is bound to hamper interpreters, rather than help them. Rhetoric's questions may seem simple, in our version, but the advantage is that such questions do not distort or overburden the processes of reading. Furthermore, 'Whose words are these?' and 'To what is this reply?' turn out to be richer in practice than in the abstract. Above all, reading can re-create these questions; each story can reshape the approach rather than the other way around.

The notion of 'method' is often dangerous when it comes to interpretation. A method that is consistent is liable to keep discovering the same meanings: method finds the same truth everywhere, a truth which is contained within itself. Up to a point, that circle is inevitable. But the art is to try and keep the circle from closing too neatly, too tightly. These questions can impose themselves lightly on the text; the circle forms, but not mechanically. 'Whose words' alters as the story dictates; 'reply' can mean many different things in differing contexts. Consequently, the approach can be recognizable, and yet read *Frankenstein* and *Martin Chuzzlewit* differently.

Therefore such a Rhetoric can learn from each reading, instead of applying itself to 'cases'. Interpreting becomes reciprocal, as it should be: the approach and the text both contribute actively. Reading stories, then, expands Rhetoric's own horizons. To interpret *Frankenstein* can be to explore science itself, as well as to understand more about quotation as a process. At the same time, the interpreter is also at play. Many Rhetorics have acknowledged play (see Chapter 3) – and without pleasure, excess, freewheeling possibilities, there is no understanding of language at all, let alone of stories. To understand quotation in *Frankenstein* is to enter into the excess, the freedom of language. To interpret *Martin Chuzzlewit* is to explore the ways in which voices oppose each other; but one can only do that exploring by recognizing play, that is, by being open to language's pleasures, and to the freewheeling lightness of words as they dance across a story, from voice to voice. So Rhetoric can let reading remain a process, a process which is different for each story.

Questioning history: ideas of history

The purpose of Rhetoric, ultimately, is to encourage thinking, thinking about language in the world. Genette stresses the way Rhetoric and thinking share the same beginnings, start in the same space:

> The Rhetorical fact begins when I am able to compare the forms of this word or this sentence to that of another word or sentence that might have been used in their place . . .

Or as Genette puts the idea even more forcefully, discussing the ideas of Fontanier:

> . . . there must be at least two terms to compare . . . a space in which thought can operate . . .

Rhetoric is a way of discovering spaces 'in which thought can operate'; our questions show how stories are 'a space in which thought can operate', pre-eminently. Reading stories, then, is a way of thinking – and Rhetoric must seek to enrich and encourage such thinking, while being enriched by it.

We want now to explore how reading stories can be a way of thinking about problems, specifically here the problems of history.

What is history? That is one of the most ancient problems, and one of the most important. Some problems are for solving, but 'What is history?' is a problem to explore, not one to solve. In ancient thinking, history is often thought of as essentially a kind of storytelling. That idea is present centrally in Aristotle, and recent work by Kennedy, Eden, and others has re-explored that thinking. Another classical writer who conceived of 'What is history?' as basically a question about stories was Lucian in his *How to Write History*, which Russell and Winterbottom have translated and reproduced in full. The problem keeps returning, and has passed down to the moderns.

E. H. Carr's book, actually called *What is History?*, finds itself reconnecting history and storytelling. For Carr, to tell a story is to select, and the question then becomes: how do histories select from the range of material, which is potentially limitless? What kinds of stories do historians find themselves telling? Kenneth Burke has addressed these same questions in a way that is even more explicitly Rhetorical. In his *Attitudes toward History*, Burke thinks of histories as stories told to enable people to 'accept' the world. Some ways of 'accepting' may be better than others, of course – closer to realities which are important, liberating more choices. . . . This line of thinking has been extended by Hayden White, who argues that histories are stories for making the world cohere. Like Burke, Hayden White suggests that these stories can be seen Rhetorically: as arguments, as forms of address.

Isn't it dangerous to see histories as argumentative stories rather than simply as facts? Hayden White is aware of the danger, and he insists that to call history Rhetorical does not mean endorsing 'the assimilation of history to propaganda'. To consider history Rhetorical does not involve talking about it as 'propaganda', unless Rhetoric is taken to mean merely manipulative trickery. White wants to emphasize Burke's idea of history being Rhetorical in a sense that is constructive. Histories vary; the stories differ. But these stories are not all of equal value; we can still make judgements:

> . . . it is not a matter of choosing between objectivity and distortion, but rather between strategies for constituting 'reality' in thought so as to deal with it in different ways, each of which has its own ethical implications.

Histories make worlds, and not all worlds are equally valuable. White urges historians to think ethically: a far cry from reducing history to propaganda.

Hayden White also emphasizes another side of Rhetoric: the theory of figures of speech. He seeks to define and list basic figures, figures from which all discourse and all thinking arise. He wants to suggest that figures, especially metaphor, hold history's stories together – figures rather than logical reasons, even in the case of an extract from Ranke, famous for being meticulous and objective:

> Now, it might seem that what I have done here is to engage in an unmasking . . . But . . . my point is that, although the passage lacks any kind of logical rigour, it possesses perfect figurative coherency.

We are not pursuing Rhetoric in that way, perfectly legitimate though it is. Instead of figures, we are offering questions. But we do share Burke's and White's idea that to see the problem of history Rhetorically is not 'to engage in an unmasking'. History is not exposed as or by Rhetoric, but rather explored Rhetorically.

Ideas of history differ: Carr is discussing history very differently from, say, Hayden White. Carr would not accept the idea of history lacking 'logical rigour', and being saved by 'figurative coherency'. Carr also wants to salvage an ideal of facts as the criterion – facts that are constituted by the storytelling as *historical* facts. He might well feel that White's call to examine 'ethical implications' was still too close to 'the assimilation of history to propaganda'. White might respond that Carr's selected facts are still too close to an idea of history being scientific, an idea that misses the human dimension. What matters here is that each thinker recognizes that an idea of history is necessary, and each links that idea to storytelling.

Particular histories are only conceivable if there is an idea of history in general. Further, these thinkers consider that the idea of history is an idea of a story, essentially, though each has a different view of stories. Carr's stories are far more indebted to logical reasoning. He is close to the Aristotelian tradition in this respect: stories are essentially ways of giving reasons for things which happen. White, on the other hand, is far less Aristotelian about stories: his stories are essentially figures. We are not going to try and decide between these rival views. Instead we are going to explore the idea of history by reading stories Rhetorically. But how is it possible to explore an idea by reading stories, let alone an idea as complex as 'history'?

Between the Acts: history, gender, childhood

Characters in a novel are gathering to watch a play, or a pageant, about the history of England. The performance will be outdoors, and the scene is being set:

> The ground sloped up, so that to quote Figgis's Guide Book (1833), 'it commanded a fine view over the surrounding country . . . The spire of Bolney Minster . . .'
> The Guide Book still told the truth. 1833 was true in 1939.

Narrative quotes words that have become history, and confirms that this history is still 'true'. But what status does 'true' have?

> If Figgis were here now, Figgis would have said the same. So they always said when in summer they sat there to drink coffee . . .

Truth becomes opinion, doubly: first, this truth is what 'Figgis would have said', and then *that* is 'what they always said'. So, the characters 'always said' that 'Figgis would have said' the same now as he said then, in 1833. 'Whose words are these?' is a question we must ask about

> . . . it commanded a fine view . . .

These are the words of Figgis (1833), the likely words of Figgis (1939 and after), and the words which the characters quote and reattribute to both of these Figgises, actual and hypothetical.
'True' becomes a problem: whose words, whose truth? It is a great problem:

> 1833 was true in 1939.

What force does this idea have? Later, a character in the novel writes and presents a play which suggests a very different view. The world of 1833 is still 'true', if it is, because

> No houses had been built

to alter 'the view'. But Miss La Trobe's play will suggest that these things are changing: other words will skim through the minds of the audience when they see and hear her scene presenting the aftermath of the Great War:

Suddenly the tune stopped. The tune changed. A waltz was it? . . . The swallows danced it . . . The swallows – or martins were they? – the temple-haunting martins who come, have always come . . . Yes, perched on the wall, they seemed to foretell what after all the *Times* was saying yesterday. Homes will be built. Each flat with its refrigerator, in the crannied wall . . . So abrupt. And corrupt.

The world does alter: things will be different, and 'homes will be built', to quote what 'the *Times* was saying yesterday'. True, the plays of Shakespeare are still half-alive ('temple-haunting martins' for 'temple-haunting martlet'), but other voices are springing up, and old symbols will take on new meanings. These martins will represent the future, a world where every 'flat' has 'its refrigerator'. The audience, maybe, replies

So abrupt. And corrupt.

But these words still belong to the future, acting out the change by their rhythm, even while rejecting it with their sense.
Consider the sentence:

Homes will be built.

Whose words are these? They are linked to

what after all the *Times* was saying yesterday.

They are also, perhaps, from the pageant, its scene after the Great War when England promised 'Homes Fit for Heroes'. Then the words enter the text by entering the audience's minds. Furthermore, the statement replies to the earlier idea of a world that is unchanged because

No houses had been built . . .

The play replies to the characters (and to Figgis, their authority); the characters as audience reply to their ordinary selves; the future replies to the past; the novel replies to itself. So, returning to the view that

1833 was true in 1939

we must now ask whether that statement itself is 'true' later in the novel. For whom is this idea true, and for how long?

Virginia Woolf's *Between the Acts* is a strange novel. The pageant actually fills much of the narrative. We are shown the play's author, Miss La Trobe, pacing irritably behind trees and bushes while the performers spoil her effects and the audience misses her meanings:

'Curse! Blast! Damn 'em!' Miss La Trobe in her rage stubbed her toe against a root.

Yet hers is the text, in many passages – indeed she holds the text before we see it.

Miss La Trobe was pacing to and fro between the leaning birch trees. One hand was stuck deep in her jacket pocket; the other held a foolscap sheet. She was reading what was written there.

She gives the novel many of its words; but the novel finds her ridiculous: 'pacing to and fro' and 'in her rage'. This author is absurd: yet she still provides much of our text.

So the novel writes itself by quoting Miss La Trobe, the ridiculous author. Here is a scene, from earlier than the post-war episode described above:

From behind the bushes issued Queen Elizabeth – Eliza Clark, licensed to sell tobacco . . .

The Queen of this great land . . .

– those were the first words that could be heard above the roar of laughter and applause.

Mistress of ships and bearded men
(she bawled)
Hawkins, Frobisher, Drake,
Tumbling their oranges, ingots of silver . . .

The narrative mocks its text, quoting from the script ('issued Queen Elizabeth') and then from the shopfront of the performer who is reciting that script ('licensed to sell tobacco'). The narrative interrupts the speech, mimicking the way 'laughter and applause' blot out passages. Parentheses bring everything down to earth: '(she bawled)'. Yet the script *is* quoted, still: and whose words *are* 'Mistress of ships and bearded men . . .'? They are Miss La Trobe's words, Eliza Clark's words, the words that are heard by the audience, the narrative's words.

But history too has claims:

Hawkins, Frobisher, Drake,

Is Miss La Trobe mocking the solemn lists of the histories? Or is she unable to control her own text? These men are 'bearded', but they are also like children:

Tumbling their oranges . . .

The novel quotes Miss La Trobe; her play quotes 'history'. Maybe the play uses history's words as mockingly as the novel re-uses Miss La Trobe's script. Those names are solemn and romantic, the names of great men. Yet the speech turns the heroes into children, still trying to impress mother, even though they are now 'bearded men'. So the speech *replies* mockingly to the history which is being quoted, just as the novel replies mockingly to the play. But mockery does not extinguish the mocked originals. The play still resonates, and those old history-names are still magical.

For we, the audience, are children too: history is what we learn about 'the past' as children. Those images persist, even though we later mock them and try to outgrow them. The colours are still bright for us:

Tumbling their oranges, ingots of silver . . .

We know that the performer has 'bawled', that the author 'cursed', that there is a 'roar of laughter'; we know that these 'bearded men' are absurd, 'tumbling' their plunder before their mistress. Yet the images themselves reply to all mockery: look, the colours are still bright, whatever you know as grown-ups. There is no escape from the voices which impressed history on our childhood: that is a blessing and a curse.

Woolf's novel is full of histories: the play is only one of many such stories. At the start, we meet elderly Mrs Swithin, reading 'her favourite reading – an Outline of History'. She

. . . had spent the hours between three and five thinking of

rhododendron forests in Piccadilly; when the entire
continent, not then, she understood, divided by a channel,
was all one; populated, she understood, by elephant-bodied,
seal-neck'd, heaving, surging, slowly writhing and, she
supposed, barking monsters; the iguanadon, the mammoth
and the mastodon . . .

Histories have lists of special names: 'the iguanadon, the mammoth, and the mastodon' are like 'Hawkins, Frobisher, Drake'. To think about history is to quote these special names. This passage explores the way we quote history's magic words – explores this mockingly *and* romantically. Many of these words clearly belong to the Outline of History: 'not then . . . divided by a channel'. Other phrases put Mrs Swithin between the history and the novel's reader: 'not then, she understood, divided'. The insert 'she understood' divides a phrase about not being divided. More generally, what is the effect of 'she understood . . . she understood'? 'Understood' seems to reinforce the notion of history: Mrs Swithin accepts and learns and is impressed. But isn't a history thus interrupted also a history mocked?

Do history's images survive? Should they survive? Can the reader avoid quoting the same kind of 'Outline'? The novel challenges us: can we distance ourselves from these images, are we really able to avoid treating them as history? Don't all our minds contain an 'Outline', full of these

. . . elephant-bodied, seal-necked, heaving, surging, slowly
writhing, and she supposed, barking monsters . . .

How far does fantasy have to go before we can really say, *this* is no longer part of history? The novel challenges us to resist these images, to reject them as history. The more fantastic the images become, the less easily we can disown them. Here Barthes has a version of 'Whose words are these?' that is pertinent:

I read the text . . . This 'I' which approaches the text is already a plurality of other texts . . .

The 'I' who reads is already possessed by these histories, by

Hawkins, Frobisher, Drake

and by

the iguanadon, the mammoth and the mastodon . . .

'*I read the text*': but here the 'I' that reads is there in 'the text' that is being read. These names are there in our minds long before we read them again in *Between the Acts*; equally, Miss La Trobe has her 'foolscap sheet' on which she reads these passages before the narrative re-presents their words. We all have much of this text in our heads before we read this novel. The novel quotes histories: these same histories help to compose the 'I' which reads, if that 'I' has ever had a childhood contact with English histories.

History makes us children again: that is old Mrs Swithin's experience, and that is the reader's experience. Yet history is serious:

Had he not read, in the morning paper, in the train, that
sixteen men had been shot, others prisoned, just over
there . . .

So one character thinks, as he watches the others at lunch before the play. Surely *that* is serious? Yet the process of quotation is present here too: 'in the morning paper, in the train'. Those two 'in's' are disturbing. It is as if the man takes refuge 'in the paper-
. . . in the train': he seems to be looking outwards to the Continent, but actually he is retreating into a cosy womb, the womb of masculine dignity. This seems a grown-up history – contemporary history, but actually it is just as suspect as the play, if not more so. Miss La Trobe and Mrs Swithin recognize their histories as fantasies, in part; Giles, the serious and stockbroking husband, takes his history solemnly, wraps himself in it.

The novel also sets up replies to Giles's history, his serious history. The word 'prisoned' deserts Giles in the novel's text, deserts him and goes over to his wife, Isabella:

Giles glared . . . Isabella felt prisoned.

Neither character actually speaks or 'hears' the other in the story world. The word 'prisoned' stands out in each instance, being claimed first on behalf of Giles and then on behalf of his wife, Isabella. Her 'prisoned' counters his, and throws itself back towards the male use of the word. Voice answers voice, across paragraphs rather than across rooms. To decide whether Isabella's 'prisoned' outmatches Giles's 'prisoned' means making all kinds of judgements about public history and private experience. That takes the reader back to the central passages of the novel, those which present the village pageant. How far should we accept standards of 'seriousness' that are part of 'masculine' identity? One older man objects to Miss La Trobe's story:

'Why leave out the British army? What's history without the Army, eh?'

History addresses us as children, partly; but isn't history also the voice of serious men, men speaking of great deeds, glorious or terrible? The audience replies thus to the playwright, Miss La Trobe, and between them they contest the subject of history. This is a conflict of voices which generalizes, but there is a link back to Giles, Isabella, and the word 'prisoned'. *Is* the man's use of 'prisoned' more serious than the woman's? Or is his use of the word part of what imprisons her, part of the weight of masculine dignities? Perhaps, then, history should be freed from the serious voices of men; perhaps insisting on facts and deeds is part of what causes sixteen men to be shot? Perhaps we need to recover the more playful histories of childhood? Or maybe those old stories are just another limiting account, and an account still dominated by great men and their doings ('Hawkins, Frobisher, Drake')?

So what do we learn about history by reading this fiction? History is a story, or a collection of stories: we can feel the magic of these stories even when Miss La Trobe is cursing behind her tree, even when the audience is muttering or deaf or distracted. History is also composed of quotations: these stories are stitched together from phrases that are familiar, from images that are traditional. Above all, though, what we learn is to ask certain questions. When did these phrases first become familiar, where did we first meet these images? If we met history first as children, then how far do histories continue to address us as children? The moment we hear history's old voices, we feel our childhood revive inside us: is that why history is so powerful, and also why it can be so ridiculous? We cannot choose these stories freely as adults – by then, the choice has been made for us. As adults should we, then, resist the old associations? Can we do so? Should we submit to the old magic? Have we any choice about accepting history as we have been given it? We can see Miss La Trobe behind her tree, but that does not seem to dispel the magic. Yet history is also contested in other ways. These stories divide us from each other as profoundly as they compel us all back towards childhood's national consciousness. Perhaps history for men is one thing, while for women it may be another?

We have not been 'applying' Rhetoric to fiction; instead, the idea is to think Rhetorically about the experience of reading a novel. Therefore what results is not Rhetoric's idea of history, but ideas of history that derive from thinking about Woolf's *Between the Acts*. These ideas are responses, ways in which the novel has reacted to Rhetoric's questions. Gadamer proposes an ideal of interpretation which is pertinent here: the interpreter must engage the text in conversation. Questions must be asked in ways which are appropriate to the context: it is no good just flinging the same questions mechanically at all texts. The problem of 'What is history?' becomes a context for engaging *Between the Acts* in conversation; 'Whose words are these?' and 'To what is this replying?' become cues which may draw the text into play.

Ngugi's *The River Between*: objectivity, myth, motive

Rhetoric can be a way of allowing ourselves to think about problems, to think by *reading*. Clearly there are many other aspects to the problem of history, there is much more thinking to be done. For instance, if history is a story, can stories be *objective*? Here we are asking about narration in general, and about how narration limits or shapes what history can be. Again, the best way of exploring the issue is to read a story; thinking Rhetorically can then help to focus the meaning of that experience.

Narration is recognizable, most often by its verbs. Most stories will depend upon certain ways of recounting events, and history is not exempt from this. The standard narration is 'she went . . .', not 'she goes'; not 'The trees are lovely' but 'The trees were lovely'. Narration in the present tense feels different: the reader feels the need to explain the occurrence of the present tense in a story. For instance, the basis for an 'explanation' may often be that there is a narrator or witness taking part in events as they happen. However, even the simple past tense is not, Rhetorically, as simple as might be thought. Ngugi's *The River Between* begins in the simple past tense:

> The two ridges lay side by side. One was Kameno, the other was Makuyu.

Describing landscapes and giving names are standard things to do in that past tense. No one would take such sentences to indicate that the ridges are no longer there or that the names have changed. As the novel continues, these ridges remain in focus:

> They were like many sleeping lions . . . They just slept.

A shudder occurs: 'were like many sleeping' jars against 'they just slept'. Here are two different kinds of past tense, an effect enhanced because 'sleeping' is a temporary state. Does 'they slept' mean they are no longer asleep? Describing and naming continue:

> The river was called Honia, which meant cure, or bring-back-to-life.

By now one wonders whether the river is still called Honia and whether the name still means 'cure'. This is a problem of address to which questions such as 'Whose words are these?' and 'To what is this a reply?' readily apply:

> People saw this and were happy . . .

One voice simply describes these people in the appropriate story manner. Another voice is talking more forcefully about something past – they *used* to see this, and so they *used* to be happy. The voices answer each other: the narration is contested, profoundly contested.

So apparently 'simple' narration provides a rich field for Rhetoric's questions:

> When you stood in the valley, the two ridges ceased to be sleeping lions . . . became antagonists . . . It began long ago. A man rose in Makuyu . . . claimed . . .

There are two reasons why 'slept' may refer to something that is no longer the case rather than simply being the narrative way of describing things in a story's world. One reason is that the observer's position may move. The other is that certain things may have happened to wake the ridges. People enter the landscape:

> Mugo wa Kibiro, that great Gikuyu seer of old, had been born there . . . he vanished . . . Or there was that great witch, Kamiri, whose witchery bewildered even the white men . . . before he was overcome by the white men . . . Another was

Wachiori, a great warrior, who had led the whole tribe . . .
he died, at the hands of a straying white man . . .

The passage is beginning to be more about loss, lost people. In
that context, the voice for which 'ridges slept' and 'people were
happy' were statements about the dead past becomes stronger,
and so does the voice for which the words 'was called' and 'meant'
referred to lost meanings of a lost language.

How does this reading help us to think about history? The
problem is language and time – more specifically, two ideas of
language and time. One idea is that of time as a *continuum*, the
other idea is that of the *break* in time: there is a 'continuous'
world, and there is a 'no longer' world. Writing can describe a
story's setting so as to imply that the same condition continues
still: as we read 'The river was *called* Honia', that is its name in
the story and for the reader. But writing can also describe a setting
so as to suggest that the condition no longer continues – a break
has occurred, and we are now on the other side of time from the
story: 'The river *was* called Honia', but not any more. The first
idea entails particular stories unfolding within a world that stays
constant, a world which has constant settings and names. The
second idea entails a world which changes with each story, radically, so that the reader is on the other bank of the river from
the events. This second idea, which is 'the break', could be considered the more purely historical sense of narrative time: there
is a past in which the story occurs, and a present in which the tale
is told. But what happens to history if continuum and break
overlap? What happens if we cannot distinguish the language of
the 'continuous' world from the language of the 'no longer' world?

And what about objectivity? One might assume that

The river was called Honia . . .

is a statement that is really objective: no choices are being imposed
on the reader, there are just the facts. But there *are* choices: is
this a 'continuous' world or a 'no longer' world? All narration will
involve the reader in that problem, just by the nature of the
narrative mode. Consider next

The ridges were isolated.

These words can belong to a description of the story's world, the continuum which contains story and reader. But, in context, another voice wants to make a statement about something being no longer true. For that voice, 'the straying white man' of the earlier passage marks the end of the time when the ridges were isolated. Polemical and elegiac tones also become audible, despite what seems to be the grammar of statement:

The people there led a life of their own . . .

These words may be neutral, but they may also belong to an angry and sad political orator who is surveying a lost scene. That orator may then be thought of as *replying* to different views of 'the people'. Since the language is English, which means that 'Honia' needs explaining, the orator's voice is emotionally talking towards as well as against the dismissive views of those people who are English. Such views are indeed going to be articulated by characters in the novel.

This storytelling address has both playful and persuasive potential:

Their people rejoiced together . . .

The words are alive with possible address. 'Their' might be the beginning of a loaded contrast against 'other' people – 'their people' were united, elsewhere people lived differently, or even elsewhere enemies were waiting. Accents vary. There is a statement which is simple, as if the passage were mythological instead of historical: people were happy, originally, before all the troubles and the stories began. But there are also statements about a history, about the time before the Europeans arrived to disrupt Africa's world. These historical statements are themselves elusive; they may be sad or angry or factual.

The novel also introduces another idea about histories and stories. Kameno and Makuyu each possess a story which establishes that it is superior to the other:

Kameno had a good record, to bear out this story.

These stories conflict and compete:

So the story ran in Kameno. Spiritual superiority and leadership had been left there.

'Kameno had a good record': these stories have the status of histories in their own culture, and they perform the function of histories. Kameno has its 'good record' to make sure of its right to 'superiority and leadership'. Histories, therefore, are loaded with practical motives: they legitimize claims to power. But listen to the words: 'spiritual superiority and leadership'. These are familiar terms, but not from Kameno's story: 'superiority' and 'leadership' belong to a British voice, a voice which has been telling Britain's story to justify Britain's power. So the idea generalizes: all histories are loaded, because each serves to justify its own culture.

Can history be objective, then? Reading Ngugi, and thinking Rhetorically, it seems that history cannot really be objective. There are several reasons. First, there are problems about narration itself: different versions of time compete within the language of narration, and choices will always be necessary between the 'continuous' world and the 'break' or the 'no longer' world. Then again, historical narrative overlaps with mythological narrative: to assert history is to reject myth, which means making judgements. Next, some sentences may seem very detached from feeling, but few are likely to avoid all hints of attitude and emotion. Finally, stories become histories for a reason: because they serve the interests of a culture, because they preserve the self-image of a nation. Reading Ngugi's magnificent chapter is an important way of thinking around the idea of history and objectivity, thinking more densely than would otherwise be possible. And all the time, to think like this is to be at play among words, to follow voices which dance.

History is our main concern here rather than narration in general. However, reading Ngugi does raise questions about storytelling as a whole, and we should recognize these questions. Some thinkers have argued that it is possible to have 'pure narration' or 'non-narration'. Genette defines 'pure narration' as

the complete absence . . . not only of the narrator, but also of the narration itself.

Or as Benveniste puts it, in pure narration

No one speaks here; the events seem to narrate themselves.

These theorists are proposing laws; Ngugi's writing does not operate at that level. Yet to read Ngugi Rhetorically (asking Rhetoric's questions) is to have doubts about whether pure narration *is* conceivable. If somewhere in language 'events seem to narrate themselves', then somewhere there could be a history that might be absolutely objective. But choices seem hard to escape, attitudes seem difficult to avoid: and there are always contexts which are far from neutral. So how useful is the ideal of pure narration, even as an ideal? To read Ngugi responsively is to think about questions which are central and difficult.

Reading *Science and Civilisation*: from Western Enlightenment to the idea of universal history

Reading fiction is one way of exploring ideas of history; of course, another way is by reading history itself. Usually, we read history mainly to 'find out' about particular subjects. But ideas of history in general are essential before any histories can be written and read. History writing can explore ideas of history as part of telling the particular tale, presenting the specific case – indeed the best history writing will necessarily revise whole ideas of what history is, while engaging with a study that is particular. Hayden White considers histories to be 'strategies for constituting reality'; the great histories force us to revise our whole way of 'constituting reality'. One does not have to dismiss Carr's idea of history selecting facts, either: history may select facts while being a whole strategy for constructing a world. Indeed, the work we are about to discuss could be a paradigm here.

History is a story of progress, and progress has happened in the West: that *idea* has been generally influential. Why has the West advanced? Because Western civilization discovered the sciences and invented technology. That answer defines an idea of history as a whole: many histories that are smaller then follow. Not everyone has accepted that idea of history, though, and some have searched for other ideas, ideas that are less narrow: a major example is Joseph Needham's *Science and Civilisation in China*. Needham has been working for over forty years on this study of Chinese history, working with collaborators both Chinese and English. E. H. Carr has praised Needham's project as the major history being written in Britain since the war; others have concurred with the high valuation in different contexts (for example, Feyerabend in the context of the history and philosophy of science). *Science and Civilisation* is massive, but Colin Ronan has abridged the many volumes, and this abridged version addresses itself to the culture of the West generally, and to our ideas of history as a whole.

Of course, the two volume *Science and Civilisation* is still essentially informative. We read particular stories here, stories which present the thinkers and schools of Ancient China: but as we read these stories, we can re-explore the whole concept of history.

By thinking Rhetorically, we may focus on precisely how *Science and Civilisation* enables the reader to conceive a history different from 'the progress of the West'. Sometimes Needham (for he is essentially the producer of the work) engages directly with concepts of history in general while telling particular stories. For instance, he discusses Chinese technology, and at the same time engages with ideas about the west and progress:

> . . . a belief that much characteristic development of Chinese thought and practice derived from the West still lingers on; among other things early Chinese astronomy, the evaluation of pi (π), or hydraulic machinery, have all been said to owe their origin to the West. This we now know to be untrue.

People assume that China fits in with the idea of history where the West creates progress. Needham presents the assumption, then elaborates it; only then does he deny the idea, subsequently affirming an alternative view:

> Moreover, Chinese inventions and discoveries passed in a continuous flood from East to West for twenty centuries before the scientific revolution . . .

Asking 'To what is this a reply?' is one way of focusing clearly on this text: Needham's words act on us by replying to other voices, voices that are familiar. Then look back at the examples he chooses: astronomy, the evaluation of pi (π) and inventing machinery. These are not just any examples: they are counter-instances to the idea of history as progress, and of progress as Western. The theory of the physical universe, mathematics, machinery: these represent the jewels of (supposedly) Western enlightenment. Replying can be a matter of saying directly: they/you assume this, and they/you are wrong. But replying also governs the examples, implicitly. These examples are emblematic: they challenge central symbols of enlightenment as a Western monopoly.

Needham accepts that pure science does develop in the West after the Renaissance. He is not crudely inverting the old idea of history, substituting China for the West. The idea of history which he is proposing is much subtler: yes, knowledge has progressed, but many cultures have contributed to that advance. He takes the idea of history as progress, and makes that progress into a *universal* story instead of a provincial one. Needham is trying to *defend* the view that history is the story of enlightenment. One way in which that story has become discredited is by its being limited to a single civilization. Needham wants to have history that is human instead of merely Western. So the West has contributed certain key sciences, but China, for instance, has produced other kinds of knowledge that are essentially scientific:

> Technical inventions . . . show a slow but massive infiltration from East to West for the first fourteen centuries of the Christian era, and include such epoch-making innovations as paper, printing, gunpowder and the magnetic compass, to mention only the classical discoveries noted by Francis Bacon in the seventeenth century.

Thinking about this story, we explore what would be meant by a universal history. A whole system of associations begins to shift: 'from East to West' – and so we must shake off our automatic association of the West with 'inventions'. 'The Christian era' is a fine irony here: time itself is Westernized by that phrase. But together with that 'era' there are also 'epoch-making' forces from the East. Time is Western *and* Eastern: it depends on what you use to divide up the years.

The question of 'Whose words are these?' is also coming into play here. The text is quoting when it says 'the first fourteen centuries of the Christian era', quoting from a stock that is shared through the West. Then the text quotes Bacon, the great exemplar of Western enlightenment. At the same time, the East is being recognized for 'paper, printing, gunpowder and the magnetic compass'. The effect is *inclusive*: this history will include Bacon, even while acknowledging the East's claims. The aim is not to be pro-Eastern, and anti-Western, but to be *genuinely* universal. So we must alter our associations, we must listen again to the old voices, to the old phrases about 'West' and 'invention', about 'the Christian era' and 'Francis Bacon'. We do not need to reject these voices, proud and lavish voices, but we must cease to hear *only* these voices, for they have presented as universal a history that was merely provincial.

Needham must produce his idea of history through specific stories - the two levels are inseparable: general and specific. The work is aiming to change assumptions that are popular, influential, and deep-rooted. The reader must therefore be compelled, enticed, and liberated if the new history is to become conceivable. Consider now the way in which Needham presents two great schools of ancient thought in China: Taoism and Confucianism. Surely these are obscure philosophies, esoteric and remote? How can these be part of a history that will *include* (and surpass) our familiar story of enlightenment and the West? Needham is firm:

> The Taoist system was a unique mixture of philosophy and religion that also incorporated magic and a primitive proto-science; it was the only system of mysticism the world has ever seen that was not profoundly anti-scientific.

The story of Western enlightenment runs thus: other cultures stayed trapped in magic and superstition, only 'we' escaped. Needham replies: no, there was (in China) 'a unique mixture . . . mysticism that was not profoundly anti-scientific'. He then glosses 'Tao':

> Its name, Taoism, was not derived after some founding father, as Confucianism was, but from the aim of its followers, to seek a Tao or Way . . .

To seek a 'way': does that sound mystical? Needham is quoting again, quoting generally from voices that are familiar. 'Followers', 'seek': this is the idiom associated with faith. But the text wants us to alter our associations; or, one could say, the text replies that these associations are too narrow, too parochial:

> 'Way' is but a shadow of its full meaning. One could call it the 'Order of Nature', or the immanent power within and behind the universe.

'Immanent power' still sounds religious: but 'Order of Nature' sounds more like science. We are starting to hear things differently: to hear voices of science *together with* voices of religion:

The Tao was the way; not the way of life within human society, but the way the universe worked. It was the Order of Nature. This is shown clearly in the Tao Tê Ching (Canon of the Virtue (Power) of the Tao), written some time around 300 BC, and perhaps the most profound and beautiful work in the Chinese language.

We hear voices that belong to both science and religion: 'the way of the universe' is beautifully poised between these associations. We begin to comprehend how there could have been 'a mysticism . . . that was not profoundly anti-scientific'.

And we begin to conceive of a history that is universal – a history of human advance far greater than that of Western culture, a history in which all cultures will be recognized, and in which science may grow with religion as much as growing out of religion. This is an idea of history as truly inclusive. So we begin to grasp just how narrow our great history has been, how few were its patterns and its possibilities. Thinking Rhetorically can be a way of exploring precisely how the reading of stories may create such ideas of history. Rhetoric's questions may seem simple – questions about quotation or attribution, and about replying and motivation. But these questions can be powerful because they allow reading to unfold, enabling us to be exploratory without inhibiting or distorting the process being explored. Rhetorical thinking becomes part of the thought which the story has released, rather than replacing or repressing that essential *experience* of 'story-thought'. So Rhetoric begins to explore how stories enable their readers or audiences to think – to think about history if they wish. This is what Rhetoric can offer in the 'field' of interpretation – not a new formula, nor even a technique, but clearer access to our own experience. In the end a tradition may live by giving such access – and die by occluding our experience in the name of a system or method that remains external.

To read Needham closely is to follow a thinking process *and* a story. It is worth dwelling a little further on *Science and Civilisation* because it is a story that richly repays the interpreter's attentions. Needham focuses on Taoism more closely, citing the Tao Tê Ching in detail:

Only the *chun-tzu* (gentleman) holding on to the idea of the
One can bring about changes in things and affairs. If this holding
on is not lost, he will be able to reign over the ten thousand
things . . . The *chun-tzu* commands things and is not
commanded by things, for he has gained the principle of the
One.

In this passage, voices overlap as richly as they do in *Frankenstein*.
Here are words which are 'not-the-English-history', yet which
have become part of Needham's historical text. Whose voice then?
The voice is Tao's, also the history's; the sentences are the trans-
lator's and, just briefly, the Chinese writer's 'sound' is audible.
The word '*chun-tzu*', meaning gentleman, is explained – and then
recurs, preventing the text slipping away from Chinese and unde-
tectably becoming English. That hint of an alien voice helps to
suggest that the whole passage has voices which are 'not-English',
'not-Needham', despite the strong claims of the surrounding text.
The extract is *kept* multi-voiced as effectively as if there were
overlapping narrators and characters.

The commentary then responds:

. . . in spite of the mysticism, it is clear . . . that this is an
affirmation of the unity of Nature, a unity (one-ness) that
now, in the twentieth century, lies . . . at the very foundation
of post-Newtonian natural science. (Our parenthesis)

Here is a voice which is 'not-Tao', 'not-Chinese-philosophy', but
which continues to include a Taoist presence. The words 'unity
of nature' clearly replay 'the principle of the One': the 'unity of
nature' phrase, therefore, does partly belong to Taoism, at least
in terms of general ideas. Yet 'unity of nature' is also a general
quotation from a Western scientific discourse, in the same way as
Frankenstein's 'minutiae of causation' was a quotation from the
same source. Needham's writing acknowledges that the phrase is
such a quotation, referring us to 'post-Newtonian natural science'
for the source. The effect is that 'unity of Nature' echoes back to
the Chinese principle while being attributed later in the text to
Western scientific discourse. The voices overlap. The possibilities
of meaning are dazzling. The 'principle of the One' belongs (with
'*chun-tzu*') to voices from ancient Chinese culture, but the same
'principle' also belongs to modern scientific voices. In between

are the many voices of the history, translating and narrating, criticizing and characterizing *both* the Chinese and the post-Newtonian.

Experiencing the history's manifold address we encounter 'unity of Nature' in the new way. The phrase (or figure) does belong explicitly to science, but now Tao has a claim to speak with some of the same discursive figures as 'post-Newtonian natural science'. Consequently, when we consider the 'unity of Nature' and ask 'Whose words are these?' (or 'whose figures?') the answer is actually different after being addressed by Needham's history. Tao now also claims words and figures which would have belonged simply to 'Western' scientific discourse. *Science and Civilisation*, therefore, quotes scientific figures and, without denying Western claims on them, brings into play in these figures the voices of ancient China.

Needham asserts that he wants us to

. . . look at the world through the eyes of the Taoists.

But he does not 'paint' a picture of that world; instead, he works by helping us to *hear* a way of talking. Here is another example, for the process is cumulative:

In his study of Nature, the Taoist became aware, of course, of change, of action and reaction . . . Thus in the Chuang Tzu:

The Yin and the Yang reflected on each other, conceived each other and reacted with each other. The four seasons gave place to one another . . . slow processes and quick jostled each other, and the motions of collection (or condensation) and dispersion (or rarefaction; scattering) were established.

First, there is commentary, offering a discourse which is scientific ('action and reaction'), and including 'the Taoist' inside that discourse. So we listen to the explicit quotation in that context: how far does 'the Taoist' have a voice which corresponds to anything scientific? Clearly some phrases are more mystical in their English terms: 'The Yin and Yang reflected on each other . . .'. Other phrases are half-literary and half-naturalistic: 'The four seasons gave place . . .'. But a scientific voice is audible as well: 'processes', 'motions of collection'. Of course this is a translation, so what we are listening to are echoes. But still the whole text makes us attend closely to those echoes, and we ask ourselves how far 'the Taoist' does belong with the idea of 'action and reaction', or with that kind of voice. It seems there may be a link between the echoes of the Taoist and other echoes of Western science: at least, the reader is invited to consider new possibilities.

Questions of reply become palpably pertinent here in *Science and Civilisation*. Needham next comments that this extract on Yin and Yang

> . . . shows the Chinese were aware of the physical processes
> of condensation . . . Certainly the Greeks knew about
> this . . . but transmission of such ideas was very
> unlikely . . .

Needham's commentary replies to the view that everything scientific originates with the Greeks, the West. As often with the novels, it seems worth giving 'reply' a double sense, since the traditional view is actually being addressed, in the minds of readers, as well as countered. The construction 'certainly . . . but' makes the whole sentence acknowledge the reader's assumptions and then actively correct them.

Replying can be a process which is extremely complex in *Science and Civilisation*. We have seen some local replies, but there are larger structures. For instance, the Taoism chapter follows one on Confucianism, a very different philosophy. There, too, are voices which form their own coherent view of life and knowledge. That Confucian view is allowed to address itself forwards as a reply to the Taoist approach. The Confucian view is identified with a thinker called Hsun Tzu:

> The detailed pedestrian process of scientific logic was not for
> him. That the Taoists might favour, but Hsun Tzu replied:
>
>> 'You vainly seek the causes of things;
>> Why not appropriate and enjoy what they produce?'

First, the commentary replies locally to Hsun, with a corrective intention belonging to debate rather than to chronicle:

> . . . he struck a blow at science by emphasising its social
> context too much and too soon.

Then replying to Hsun will be taken over by the Taoist passage about the *'chun-tzu'* (gentleman) holding on to the idea of the 'One'. For the Tao, only *that* gentleman 'can bring about changes in things and affairs . . .'. The Hsun Tzu Confucian view is that no one should 'delay practical activity for general theorizing and experiment'; the Tao implicitly replies that without 'the principle of the One', no practical activity is possible. Tao and Confucianism debate with and against each other in the history's address. Meanwhile corresponding emphases in modern science on 'unity of nature' (Tao) and on 'social context' (Confucian) contest the same issues. Voices from the two debates overlap in individual phrases and whole arguments. The modern West is not simply being projected backwards. On the contrary, we begin to feel a sense of a very different Chinese context, an autonomous Chinese enlightenment. Ancient China has some claims to historical ownership of scientific discourse, and indeed to some influence on modern debates in science.

Finally, then, reading *Science and Civilisation*, we sense an idea of history even while we absorb particular histories. That idea is present in the process of the writing rather than being an abstract shadow. To follow the story is to begin conceiving of how history *might* become universal, of how the story of Western enlightenment might be retold as stories of human enlightenment. We test this idea by reading the story, especially by listening to the voices, following the echoes and the replies.

Rhetoric, history, and ideology

Each of these works we have examined (*Between the Acts, The River Between*, and *Science and Civilisation in China*) explores what history means, explores that problem so radically that common assumptions come under pressure. Ideas about history, then, are not separable from other ways of perceiving the world, including notions about gender and about 'race' or culture. Questioning history, we must also question other categories: all of that is inherently part of reading the stories, as Rhetoric attempts to demonstrate. For instance, history has often been thought of as the solemn story of great men's deeds. *Between the Acts* can challenge that idea – challenge it exploratively, not polemically or dogmatically. Another powerful assumption has been that history is objective, and further that it tells objectively of progress led by Europe and the Europeans. Ngugi's writing can question those assumptions in many ways, and with an energy at once visionary and experimental. Then there is the assumption of science being modern and Western – the idea that the history of science is included by, and distinguishes, the history of the West. Few assumptions about history can have been more influential, yet Needham's writing challenges the whole idea – challenges it in the turns of phrases and in the play of voices as well as in the mounting of evidence.

Each of these texts could be called 'dissenting', or 'hetorodox' rather than 'orthodox'. Each locates itself in relation to assumptions which are common, and then challenges those assumptions, creating new ideas in the process. Behind such works there is perhaps the dissident's ambivalent hope: now, at least and at last, the major tradition will have to start speaking back, engaging in a debate. Pierre Bourdieu crystallizes that hope as a law of dissent, summarized by John Thompson:

> heterodoxy impels the dominant agents or groups to step out
> of their silence and to produce a defensive discourse . . .

'Impels' seems too mechanical. Maybe the main ideas of history will have to respond and so risk being altered – that is the hope which forms the horizon of these stories. So histories enter into the field of dispute, enter diversely and as diverse *stories*, compellingly and compulsively.

Notes and further reading

Mary Shelley, *Frankenstein*, is referred to in the Penguin edition (1985). The main references are to the following passages: letters on p. 75 and pp. 59–60, discovery on pp. 96ff, ambition on p. 92, the monster's reproach on p. 141, and p. 162 and Victor's misery on p. 237. Jennings (1985) is a key collection of writings on science, and includes the passages on and from Hooke and Davy. Paracelsus and Agrippa are quoted from early translations of 1657 and 1575 respectively.

Charles Dickens, *Martin Chuzzlewit*, is also referred to in the Penguin edition. The meals quoted are from Chapters 12 and 2; Pecksniff is then followed in Chapter 2, where there is the question of Pinch as not 'a bad fellow' and the exhortation not to be 'calculating'; in Chapter 5, where he refers to Pinch's lack of 'polish'; Chapter 43, where he

becomes a 'Chorus' who claims the thoughts of others; and Chapter
51, the scene of his exposure. America features from Chapter 21.

Virginia Woolf, *Between the Acts*, is referred to in the
Granada/Panther edition: Figgis is on p. 42; from the play, there is
Eliza on p. 65 and the British Army on p. 115, with homes on p. 132;
Miss La Trobe and the script appear on p. 45 and her toe meets the
root on p. 72; Miss Swithin and history comes early on, on p. 10, Giles
grumbles on p. 38 and Isabella feels 'prisoned' on p. 52.

Ngugi Wa Thiong'o, *The River Between*, is referred to in the
Heinemann edition (African Writers Series), the references being to
the first chapter.

Colin Ronan's abridgement of Joseph Needham's great work, *The
Shorter Science and Civilization in China, Vol. I* is referred to in the
Cambridge paperback edition: see Chapter 6, 'The travelling of science',
on assumptions and counter-assertions about Chinese science; Chapter 8
on Taoism; and Chapter 7 on Confucianism.

Two sources for histories of the Rhetorical ideas in this chapter are
Burrow (1982), especially pp. 29–30 for St Bonaventure; and Kerferd
(1981), especially p. 70 for Plato's *Protagoras* on listening. John
Thompson (1984), Chapter 2 on 'Symbolic violence', is important on
'whose words', especially for Bourdieu's ideas on expressive styles and
heterodoxy. Barthes, in *S/Z* (1975 translation), considers 'I' and the
text in Section V, 'Reading, forgetting'. Genette (1982 translation) is
essential on the conditions of Rhetoric, particularly the essays entitled
'Figures' for 'rhetorical fact' and 'Frontiers of narrative' for 'pure
narration'. Bakhtin (1984 translation) gives one view of replying and
fiction, an important view articulated particularly in Chapter 2 on 'The
Hero'. On history, Hayden White is influential, and we have quoted
a strong passage from 'History and rhetoric' in White and Manuel (1978)
(p. 22). Kenneth Burke (1961) is inspiring on history and values,
particularly Part I on 'Acceptance and Rejection'. E. H. Carr (1964)
gives a fundamental account of history and narrative.

For our approach to interpreting stories, we have also found the
following helpful in diverse ways: Benjamin (1970 translation) includes
a major essay, 'The Storyteller'; Booth (1983) is a systematic Rhetoric
of fiction; Eden (1986) is a major rethinking of the question of Aristotle
and narrative; Kristeva, in Moi (ed.) *The Kristeva Reader*, has an
illuminating essay, 'Word, dialogue and novel'. On science and
narrative, Beer (1983) is essential. For classical approaches to history,
Russell and Winterbottom (1972) is a rich source, including especially
Tacitus's *Dialogue on Orators* and Lucian's *How to Write History*. The
collection also provides Gorgias on persuasive magic. Lentricchia (1983)
has a stimulating response to Burke's thinking on history and
language.

Newman (1986) gives a different approach to narrative in
Frankenstein; Harari (1984) is illuminating on scientific genius in
French fiction of the nineteenth century; Hillis Miller (1982) includes a
complex response to the narratives of *Between the Acts*. Griffiths (1973)

is helpful on approaches to history; Vattimo (1988) is challenging on history and argument, putting the issues into the context of contemporary thinking.

Chapter six

Reviving Rhetoric

What is the best kind of 'revival'? That question is important for anyone thinking about Rhetoric. Rhetoric is an ancient name, and not a name only, but as Kennedy says:

> a continuous, evolving tradition. Constantly revised and made more detailed . . .

That 'tradition' is no longer 'continuous': gaps separate us from Aristotle's *Rhetoric*, Gorgias' *A Defence of Helen*, and Plato's *Phaedrus*; from Cicero's *De Inventione* and *Topica*. . . . Nevertheless, we have tried to show what ideas these works could contribute now, particularly to the understanding of language. This chapter considers more fully the problems of 'revival'. To consider a problem which is general does not mean merely generalizing: the emphasis is still practical.

Revival has been a problem for many thinkers. Antonio Gramsci for example, a theorist of politics, economics, and culture, reflected deeply about what revival means. How should we best subject ourselves to the influences of ideas from the past?

'Does it mean "to return" mechanically to those concepts?' asks Gramsci. He answers with another question:

> . . . or does it mean to assume an attitude towards art and life similar to the one assumed by De Sanctis in his day?

Gramsci is discussing ideas about culture, specifically the ideas of De Sanctis, an earlier theorist. However, what Gramsci suggests applies to our argument about Rhetoric. No one should try to return, mechanically, to Rhetoric: the tradition cannot be continuous any longer. Instead we can try to 'assume an attitude towards art and life', an attitude 'similar to the one assumed' by Rhetoricians who did belong to the tradition.

No phrases can summarize the Rhetorical attitude, no terms can guarantee it. The essential point is to understand how voices exist in relation to other voices, how there are no voices at all *without* such relations. Therefore 'address' is integral to speaking and writing – not merely formally integral but creatively so. Words point towards the other, who may be silent but who is always a possible interlocutor, even when the 'other' is a crowd. This is the 'attitude' which Rhetoric encourages us to 'assume': to revive that attitude is to practise a new Rhetoric, not return to the 'old concepts'. 'Play' and 'persuasion', and all our other terms, are ways of trying to reassume this attitude now.

What about ideas that are modern? How do they fit into a project of 'revival'? Gramsci is helpful again: he urges that we look at older thinking and ask:

What current moral and intellectual interests correspond . . . ?

Revivals are complex. Gramsci urges that we define the 'exemplariness' of the original, what distinguishes it. Then one must connect that 'exemplariness', linking it to 'current . . . interests'. Different people will answer these questions differently, whether about Rhetoric or any other tradition. There is no one idea of Rhetoric's 'exemplariness', and no one way of defining the 'current . . . interests' that might be relevant. We have given our versions: others are possible, of course. Some, for instance, have seen Rhetoric as a great theory of 'figures of speech', a theory which connects with modern equivalents. Key terms are then 'metaphor' and 'metonymy', 'irony' and 'substitution'. Both Gerard Genette and Hayden White offer such revivals of Rhetoric. Indeed that is the kind of revival which has been most influential. Ours is an alternative: another way, not *the* way.

What are the 'current . . . interests' to which we are connecting Rhetoric? Partly, they are classical interests, newer histories which redefine the 'tradition' so as to make 'figures of speech' less central (witness the work of Kennedy, Russell and Winterbottom, Gadamer, Eden, Kerferd . . .). Trends in linguistics have seemed to share the spirit of this redefined Rhetoric. These are trends which explore closely how people's words interact with the acts of others, including the possible words of others. In connecting this linguistics with Rhetoric we have drawn upon the principles, rather than upon the terminology or the higher theory. We are not rejecting such terms or theory, but here 'attitude' and 'interest' are most important. The links we are making are at a level which is basic, basic in both senses of 'fundamental' and 'introductory'.

Then there have been interests from literary criticism and literary theory. These interests include particular ideas from Bakhtin and from Genette. But more generally, we have tried to draw upon an attitude in some English criticism, an attitude exemplified by the work of William Empson. This criticism has pursued the play of words closely, in ways which are necessary for any revival of the Rhetoric we have presented. Clearly there is no synthesis of all these interests. Bakhtin remains different from Empson; Aristotle remains different from current ethnolinguistics. What we offer is far more limited than synthesis. We are pursuing a certain 'exemplariness', pursuing it in places that are very different in other ways. The connections are real, but they are made, and made in the context of one project.

Two analyses follow, of a television news broadcast and of a philosophical dialogue. The purpose of these analyses is to explore more fully the problems of revival, of reviving Rhetoric. How should classical ideas come into play? This has been one question all through; now it is the main question. Here modern thinking is relevant only as an element in asking that question, in reviving ideas that are classical. Both the news and the dialogue tell stories, and so both examples follow from the preceding chapters. News and philosophy, then, tell stories which claim to reveal truths, though truths of different kinds. The truth of news is particular, that of philosophy is general. The previous discussion ends with history and fiction, so these other forms of truth-telling are necessary as a sequel. How does Rhetoric analyse the discourse of truth – that is itself a classical problem:

> For, in fact, the true and that which resembles it come under the purview of the same faculty . . .
>
> (Aristotle, *Rhetoric*)

So revival begins with problems.

Watching the news, thinking Rhetorically: questions of revival and experience

Television news is analysed by several disciplines already. How does the news work as television? How does the medium shape the message? Media studies ask those questions expertly. The broadcast in question is about a hijacking; media analysts have explored how television as a medium handles terror. Indeed there are analyses which differ. In Davis and Walton (eds), *Language, Image, Media*, several authors discuss how political judgements may be present within what seem to be 'formal' decisions about editing and interviewing. Schlesinger, Elliott, and Murdock's *Televising Terrorism* presents views which are politically subtle on how politics enters directly into the 'technique' of television. Television news can also be analysed sociologically. Who is watching, how are they influenced? Examples of this approach are present in Stuart Hall *et al.*, *Culture, Language, Media*. Or there are more content-centred analyses: how is 'news' defined, and what is left out? The Glasgow Media Group (*Bad News*) has an extremely polemical account of news items about trade unions.

Then there are studies of how the news media cover particular issues. The hijacking occurs in 'the middle east'. There is a passionate analysis by Edward Said in 'Islam and news' (*Covering Islam*), an analysis which could be extended to our example. Or there could be analysis of television news in relation to the institutions of modern Britain: how do the institutions of broadcasting relate to political institutions, and to other forms of communication? Raymond Williams has emphasized these questions for instance, in *Communications* and *Culture*. Or one could try to define 'the language' of television news, the visual and verbal language. Rhetoric may be another approach, one among many. We are exploring how some ideas from classical sources may be revived; we are not claiming to replace or to contest other approaches. Our analysis is relatively playful, even; the finale should be exploratory and not conclusive.

First the news broadcast is considered in relation to oratory as conceived in classical Rhetoric. Then the same broadcast is compared to classical ideas about narration, and particularly to ideas about epic. After that, history is the point of reference, and finally we consider the news and some ideas about argument and the probable. The interpretations vary; they are played off against each other; there could be any number of further angles. That is the idea: to revive Rhetoric can be to multiply possibilities, playfully and teasingly – Rhetoric need not come down to categories that are rigid, interpretations that are frigid.

The ideas of legal oratory which we use have one main source: a handbook called the *Rhetorica ad Herennium*, or 'To Herennius'. This work used to be attributed to Cicero, but is now left unattributed. The *Ad Herennium* looks forbidding – it is full of details about how to make a speech. Yet the work can be suggestive and alive when read in the context of an approach to Rhetoric such as that offered here. *Ad Herennium* advises legal and other speakers on how to arrange their material; that advice compares significantly to the way the news is arranged.

Then for narration and epic, we turn back to Aristotle's *Poetics*, looking for questions that are more specifically classical than those asked in Chapter 5. We want to suggest how Aristotle's own approach can apply to the news in some detail. For history, we turn to Lucian, a theorist from the later classical period. Russell and Winterbottom present the ideas he expounded in *How to Write History*. Here we are concerned with his principle that for the 'potential historian' there is a

single criterion . . . one exact standard, [which] is to bear in mind not his present hearers, but his future readers.

We are interested in the distinction between 'future' and 'present', rather than that between 'hearers' and 'readers'. But how does this idea apply to the news? That will be the question in the third section. Finally, there is argument, for Rhetoric always comes back to arguing. Of course argument is relevant to the account of legal oratory or history; but there are more general points to make about the broadcast as argument. *Ad Herennium* is again a basic source; Eden's work on argument in *Poetic and Legal Fiction* is also central.

All the time the point is to explore how a Rhetoric can multiply interpretations, and create openings for thought. To consider news Rhetorically need not mean asking bluntly, whose side is the news on? Or crudely trying to isolate figures of speech from the flow of the broadcast as a whole. To consider news Rhetorically may be a way of appreciating how rich an ordinary experience can be when inspected closely.

The hostage crisis: a historic broadcast

The broadcast under considerations was an 'extended' one, announcing on a Sunday evening the release of American hostages who had been taken from a TWA flight and held prisoner for nearly three weeks in Beirut. The story of these hostages has become the news equivalent of a folk-memory. The BBC broadcast is part of the process by which these real and moving events have become something to which other stories can be readily referred, an ambiguous symbol both of danger and of escape.

The essence of news stories, as of ballads, is that they are told in many different forms on different occasions. Even within this one news broadcast the story of the TWA hostages' release was told four times in four different ways. Other news items are very briefly inserted between the first and second of these accounts, without noticeably affecting the connections between them. There is a slightly longer insertion of other news stories between the third and fourth renderings. No material from other stories separates the two major versions, the second and third versions; however, formal distinctions between the ways in which the stories are told distinguish the two as narratives of different kinds. To differentiate between these two versions is already to make an interpretation.

Legal oratory and news

To start with, the way the news service presents its story may be compared with a classical theory of legal oration. The news of the release of the American hostages, in its first version, begins:

All the American hostages are safe tonight in Damascus . . .

These words function to 'hook' an audience, to engage their attention and emotions. That is, indeed, the function of an opening according to the classical idea of a legal speech. An example of those ideas can be found in *Ad Herennium*, which states that the purpose of an introduction is:

. . . to enable us to have hearers who are attentive, receptive and well-disposed . . .

The same authority recommends that where introductions are concerned:

We can have receptive hearers if we briefly summarize . . .

Such a summary should indicate the story at issue. The news broadcast, in its first part, does this admirably. Because the news broadcast regularly works in this form, the proceeding is taken for granted. But as the comparison with classical Rhetoric suggests, this familiar convention may testify to the application of a profound rule as regards address. From the opening there emerges the main event and some of the issues for interpreting it as well. So the term 'hostages' (as opposed, say, to 'prisoners') anticipates the moral categories which follow. Taking hostages is a particular crime. (Prisoners could be taken by enemies in war, but hostages are taken by criminals, or by enemies who do not recognize reasonable rule.) This emphasis resembles that of 'a speech for the prosecution'.

A further pointer for introductions arises from the same classical source:

We shall have attentive hearers by *promising* to discuss important, new and unusual matters, or such as appertain to the commonwealth, or to the hearers themselves . . . by bidding them listen attentively, and by enumerating the points we are going to discuss. (Our italics)

Here are criteria ringingly met by the opening summary. In the statement 'all the American hostages are safe' the words 'all' and 'safe' *promise* matters new, unusual and important. The rest of the summary enumerates the points we are going to discuss:

They left Beirut in an armed convoy . . . The missing four hostages speak out about their treatment . . . The Americans insist there was no deal . . . And at home it looks as if the IRA bomb threat to holiday resorts is over.

In this list, the words 'no deal' meet the classical criterion of 'appertaining to the commonwealth', i.e. having political significance. Finally, 'at home' does indeed 'appertain . . . to the hearers themselves'. The story is made significant and urgent, large and directly compelling.

According to classical theory there are two ways in which a full narration of events may be given: in the sequence in which they occurred, known in classical theory as 'the natural order'; or the events may be presented in a different sequence from that in which they occurred, the so-called 'artificial order'. In the second version of the news, which lasts twelve minutes, the events are told out of sequence, not in the order in which they occurred. The news reader begins by telling us about what has happened 'in the past hour'. Using film from several sources the report moves back across the day, dropping in on 'twenty past ten this morning', returning to 'this afternoon', interviewing the hostages after their release, and going back to pictures of them gathering just before leaving Beirut. 'I think we are ready to go', says the hostages' leader. From there we move to a press conference in the present and ahead, anticipating arrival in Frankfurt. However, there are further interviews, this time including one with the then American vice-president, George Bush, when the questions range back again over the whole story.

In the third account, which follows directly after the second, there is a strict and explicit chronological sequence. ('Day one . . . Two days later . . .'). As noted above, classical Rhetoric termed this kind of sequence 'natural order' and the classical notion about such passages is further stated here in *Ad Herennium:*

> Our Statement of Facts will be clear if we set forth the facts in the precise order in which they occurred, observing their actual or probable sequence . . .

What distinguishes the third version of the news is precisely what then seems like a return to the natural order, as a result of which *the story does seem to become clearer.* In terms of interpretation, part of the meaning of the transmission, deriving from this effect of gathering order, is that *things can be clarified.* Stories can be told even under the impact of an unpredictable world. To say this is by no means to denigrate television news. This feeling that the world can be organized into stories is one by which whole societies must live.

The fourth version, or epilogue, occurs after a brief break in which other news items appear, and this version concentrates on one hostage who has already been referred to several times as the group's leader:

He was on just another business trip. Then his plane was hijacked.

Which says, in effect, 'you know this could happen to you'. A lighter note of this sort is another convention of the presentation of news in general, although usually its subject is different from that of the main story. That small emotive irony corresponds to the idea of an appropriate *conclusion* in the classical concept of judicial oratory. Classical theory recommends that a stirring touch should be conspicuous at the end. The name given to that effect was *Amplificatio*, or amplification:

. . . the principle of using Commonplaces to stir the hearers.

Indeed the whole process of reporting the story has emotional resonances, which is also in line with the classical view, which would never consider it useful to pile dry fact on dry fact. For Rhetoric, the human world cannot be truthfully discussed in such a drily factual way. So far as television reporting is concerned, it is sometimes assumed that traces of feeling are a weakness, but it is hard to see what kind of human story could be conveyed without traces of feeling. Nevertheless, in the context of the particular news being dealt with, the feelings involved are powerful ones and their consequences pervasive: for instance, another kind of commonplace may stir the hearers of the following extract from the second account:

The original hijackers . . . gave a chilling warning that for them their holy war is not yet over.

The words 'a chilling warning' direct us towards a fearful reaction (as against, say, considering that the warnings were boastful or arrogant, which indicate a less intense commonplace). The comparison with judicial or legal oration points especially towards the prosecution for crime. The word 'chilling' has associations with 'chilling crime'. According to the classical theory of prosecution, much should be made of the disadvantages which would ensue from being indifferent to the crime. It should be pointed out that if this criminal goes free, others will do similar things. According to *Ad Herennium*, there should be an emphasis that what has happened is:

. . . a foul crime, cruel, sacrilegious, and tyrannical; such a crime as the outraging of women, or one of these crimes that incite wars and life-and-death struggles with enemies of the state.

In the second account we hear that 'President Reagan called them animals' and we also hear that they may be pursuing a 'holy war'. *Ad Herennium* goes on to advise that in establishing 'a foul crime'

. . . we shall examine sharply, incriminatingly, and precisely, everything that took place in the actual execution . . .

The meticulous detail, especially when repeated, is only partly required by objectivity; it also underlines the enormity of the crime.

In our interpretation of television news so far, comparisons have been made with the requirements of classical oratory, and specifically with the classical theory which concerns functions of parts and is known as 'arrangement'. Sometimes there are criticisms of news on the grounds of its organization and composition, which are such as to include emotional impact, and thus might be negatively thought of as manipulative. Such criticisms seem to assume that the news could and should be transparent, literally a 'window on the world'. However, in a Rhetorical view, there is no way of standing outside the constraints and compulsions of address. There is no such thing as an unarranged address. The alternative to precise and explicit arrangement is a more confused version, which might have all sorts of unpredictable effects. It also needs to be said that arrangement is here being considered from the point of view of the audience, whereas *Ad Herennium*, like most classical Rhetoric, is concerned with the point of view of the speaker in relation to the audience. For the present approach, arrangement is in the eye of the beholder. Therefore what is being considered is the way the news broadcast is centrally interpretable in terms of arrangement. There may well be a gap separating these possible interpretations from what seem to the broadcasters to be their intentions. The classical Rhetoric which has been cited concerns how to succeed when you intend to make, say, a prosecuting speech. The same principles are here being applied to the comparative interpretation of a discourse which may well have no such intention. The purpose, as in the readings of novels, is to explore how meanings arise from address, not to attribute intentions to their authors.

Aristotle, Epic, and television news

Rhetorical comparison arises from the story's magnitude as well as from consideration of the voices used in the telling. This comparison is with Epic, again as conceived by Rhetorical theory. Epic is essentially a term for the great story in a culture. For the Greeks that means primarily Homer. In modern times there is no such clear reference point, but news has a claim to produce a continuous sequence of temporary epics week by week. The culture seems to form and re-form itself around these stories. The result is that if one is immersed in that culture one finds it hard to believe that these stories will pass and yet they do, continuously, although this story of hostages has been more resistant to the passage of time so far. Aristotle has a theory about how the great story has been told in Greek culture. He distinguishes (as mentioned briefly in the previous chapter under the heading 'Whose words are these?') three ways of presenting stories. At one extreme there is a single telling voice all the way through. At the other extreme, different voices speak from within the events without any central narrative (Drama). In between, there is a mixed mode in which central narration alternates with voices from within the story. The great story, or Epic, belongs to the mixed mode, as indeed, in our time, do novels usually. It is perhaps less obvious that television news also belongs to this mode, partly because it does so in a very complicated way, owing to the presence of pictures as well as words.

The second telling is a mixed mode in which (just thinking about words) what may be narrative voices alternate with participants' voices, but there is no clear distinction, since various reporters on the spot seem to belong to both categories at once. Where on such a spectrum does one place the reporter's voice which talks of 'a chilling warning' from within Beirut? Is he a narrator speaking from outside the story or is he experiencing the story from within? The ambiguity becomes profound when pictures show a reporter being harassed by people who may have held the hostages. In this second account, all the potential narrators, including the newsreaders in the studio, seem to be trying to slip back and become characters in the story ('in the past hour . . . now . . . first indication'). Within the shifting pattern of narrators, the hostages are presented debating their experiences, very much in the style of formal controversy favoured by classical epic ('revenge . . . will not give comfort' as against 'I would dearly love to get my hands on' the kidnappers). At this point in the news broadcast no outside voice is in a position to resolve that controversy, although the voice which conceives of a 'chilling warning' seems to intervene in favour of action. One advantage for the reporter in being a participant rather than a pure narrator is that the reporter can then express feelings more directly.

The role of central narration varies at other points in the news broadcast. The opening summary does in a sense have a central narration, although it is very brief. The third version renews that central narration, locating it in the studio, from where the script organizes the sequences of the story. The shift between the second and third version has been commented on from the point of view of natural order. What matters here is the reassertion of a central narration. That narration still contains snatches of other voices but has authority over them. The most striking example of such authority comes when President Reagan has been heard to say, from within the story: 'We will not cave in.' The narration replies categorically that the President's 'show of strength' turned out to be 'impotent'. The effect of the renewed narration is that the previous version veers towards the dramatic and the third account towards recitation, the telling of the tale by a single voice. The fourth instalment, or epilogue, is still strongly narrated.

All four tellings have remained in the mixed mode, since voices from within the story interact with the voice of a narrator outside of it. Sometimes the presentation veers towards one extreme within the mode, so that the presence of the narrator is more prominent; at other times dramatic potentialities in the news become more obvious. This mixed mode, as noted previously, is that adopted by Epic. The arrangement of the voices can contribute to the audience's sense of the status of the story. The complex requirements of the great story include the requirements of the great story for excitement: this is the effect produced when the mixed mode veers towards the dramatic. On the other hand, the

great story, in addition to being exciting, is also unusually expansive. A complicated chain of events stretches over large spaces of
time and place. The authority that is required to present them in
their entirety, comprehensively, to an audience derives from the
narration and the narrator. In the *Iliad* itself there is such a
modulation between the dramatic and the more authoritatively
narrated sections. Clearly such a formal pattern cannot be separated from the content (and Aristotle, who was dealing partly with
the *Iliad*, would never have tried to do so). No composition of
voices will turn *any* event into an Epic, but it is an important part
of the effect of a great story.

The epilogue, or fourth instalment, of the news, though it *is*
still strongly narrated, moves back towards a point of view closer
to the story:

> Tonight they have been praising the calm authority with which
> he led them through the ordeal.

Both opening summary and closing epilogue have a strong narrative voice; however, the urgent and comprehensive announcement
of the opening has become a touching and almost intimate gesture
of farewell, another effect of Epic, and one found in a great epic
much closer to our own times.

To readers of epic poetry, the sequence of voices, and their
shifts through the mixed mode, may sound oddly familiar. Milton's
Paradise Lost begins with the most urgent and comprehensive
viewpoint:

> Of Man's first disobedience, and the fruit
> Of that forbidden tree . . .

The aesthetic value of these words may not compare with that of
the news broadcast. But the issue in this interpretation of the
television news broadcast is simply the relevance of epic patterns
to understanding the process in which news tells stories. In that
respect the comparison with Milton may be stretched further.
Paradise Lost does produce an effect (among many others more
important) of shifting from categorical opening summary to a
narration which seems intensely involved within the story and
where participants' voices (though what participants!) threaten to
take over the whole account. In Books I and II of the poem, there
is a less clear line between external narration and participating

emotion. The rest of the poem uses a wide variety of devices to reassert a clear sequence of events and meanings within which that opening makes a different kind of sense.

One of those devices is an extended chronological narration (but what chronology!) by the angel Raphael which re-establishes a definite succession of events:

> Evening and morn solemnised the fifth day,
> The sixth, and of creation last arose . . .

This angelic narrative does become a kind of stabilizing voice for the whole poem, whereas the initial books seem to contain destabilizing and ambiguous voices. The earlier books also contain heated debates. The comparison afforded with the news broadcast is not one of text with text, but shows a link in two different directions back to an epic theory of telling the great story. Among the meanings which become possible for an interpreter of the news's address is precisely the idea of a great story.

Rhetoric, history, and news

The news story has a prosecutory ring, and an epic resonance. Other echoes also inhabit this garden. From within the news broadcast come claims for the historical status of these events, and these claims are all the more striking when made by a reporter on the spot:

> The lessons of this affair will be studied for a long time to come, the reverberations felt.

There are two sides to this claim to historical relevance: first, 'this affair will continue to be studied for a long time to come'; and second, 'the reverberations will be felt in other events to come'. By now the reporter seems to have been proved right. There is a complicated relation between the force evident in his speaking this judgement from the spot and the fact that it seems to be accepted as history. Obviously, many other reporters and commentators reinforced the feeling that history was being made, and that was possible only in the light of what was already accepted as history. Not everything which happens becomes history, and not everything which happens becomes news, but it is now very difficult for anything to become history without first becoming news. (An American television news service had an advertising slogan which claimed that they brought the news 'before it becomes history'.) History always has to be proposed, and by making the proposal the news service is performing a creative function. A problem would arise if the news service were to have a monopoly of that function. In particular there would be a problem if the news were to determine not only *what* becomes history but *how* it became history.

There is insistent pressure towards historical status. Here is part of the central narration, in the third and chronological account, which is distanced from the events and strongly centred in the telling of a single narrator, the newscaster:

> President Reagan insisted he would not negotiate . . . 'We will not cave in' (Applause) . . . But the show of strength by part of its Sixth Fleet off the Lebanese coast served to underline how impotent the superpower was in the face of this fanatical terrorism.

The statement has great authority; partly because the distance from the events seems enormous (it is a few days) and in that gap history has become possible, and partly from the effect of the strong central narration. Consider the words: 'to underline how impotent the superpower was . . .'. They do not just state what happened but make claims to the status of *historical pronouncement*. Evidently a story which means that America is 'impotent' is likely to demand attention in the future as well as in the present. The newsworthy has become the historic, in Lucian's Rhetorical sense of being addressed to the future.

Story, argument, and news

But there is yet another kind of meaning which Rhetoric generally would expect to find when interpreting a story, whether in the form of oration, or Epic, or history:

> We shall develop an argument as follows: we shall show that Ulysses had a *motive* for killing Ajax . . . (Our italics)

This extract from *Ad Herennium* is about a general relation between all kinds of stories and argument. *Motive* is a link between story and argument. If a story is told in such a way that motives become plausible for the actions, then for Rhetorical theory the story will acquire probability. If the news story does not include motive among its meanings, then, Rhetorically, the news broadcast would not even enter the area of probability. It might be thought that technology would render this ancient criterion irrelevant, because the pictures on the film would make the criterion irrelevant, because the pictures on the film would make the story convincing whether or not motives were raised. The film does show *something* has happened, but it is necessary for the broadcast *to give an account of what happened* which makes sense, and that account will need to be convincing. For the story to be plausible, motives are necessary.

In the case of the TWA story, there are three areas where an interpretation in terms of motives is possible. The first area concerns the release of the hostages: what was the hijackers' motive for releasing them? That is the main issue in this particular broadcast, and possible motives are clearly accessible in the broadcast. After the opening summary has said what happened, it adds: 'The Americans insist there was no deal . . .'. In the second telling, Vice-President Bush is shown in an interview taken from American news, and he is asked by an American interviewer: 'No deals were made? . . . No deals?'. And he replies to this pressing enquiry, which has been repeated, with repeated denials. But this does not put an end to the question. At the end of the second telling, the studio newsreader announces:

> The Israeli cabinet today put off a decision on whether to release the 735 Shi'ites they are holding. The defence minister, Yitzchak Rabin, said they would look at the situation once the American hostages had arrived safely in Europe.

From these three sources a clear motive for the kidnappers to release the hostages becomes available: a deal, a deal in which the Israeli government might release 735 Shi'ites if the kidnappers release their hostages. What keeps this idea alive is the way it keeps coming up to be denied again. There are no positive statements about motive. But the deal becomes a possible motive, partly because it is repeatedly raised and denied, and partly because we all share Rhetoric's view that no story is plausible without a motive: we are tempted to acquire a motive in this way, unless we are to regard the release as improbable or inexplicable.

The second area for interpretation in terms of motives concerns the reason why the hostages were taken in the first place. What motive was there for taking them? This motive is only part of the background to the present events, which concern the release of the hostages, and is therefore less essential. But an interpretation of motives for taking the hostages does arise in the course of the programme, though it is only accessible by a circular process of reasoning. When the reporter describes the vehicles containing the hostages leaving Beirut, he suggests that those responsible for the hijacking 'can claim that their hijacking humbled America', from which it may appear that the motive for the act was to humble America. They 'humbled America': therefore their motive was to humble America. *Ad Herennium* identifies this kind of argument as 'tricky', saying that:

> A reason is weak when it appears to be presented as the
> Reason, but says precisely the same as was said in the
> Proposition . . .

Here the proposition would be that they 'humbled America'; and the reason would be that they did it to humble America. Clearly this interpretation is an analysis of what *may* happen when the programme is watched, and is not necessarily a criticism of the report, since the programme has to make explanations available for the background of the story.

The third area where an interpretation may be made in terms of motives that apply to what was done is still more difficult to deal with. This interpretation involves ideas of the global situation. The problem is to decide at the most general level what may be motivating groups in the middle east. That problem is further complicated by the difficulty of identifying the groups involved. The way in which this news broadcast tries to identify the groups involved in the hijacking indicates a general feeling that there are large motives with a religious background. The opening summary refers to 'Shi'ite gunmen' and to 'Muslim extremists', and then the bulletin refers to the 'Amal militia', and also to 'the radical Hesbollah Shi'ite group'. The terms themselves suggest a wide field of reference in which certain events in the middle east have a religious context. It is not clear what the connection between the groups themselves is, or between all of them and the whole tradition of Islam as manifested in the middle east and the rest of the world. It is not clear to what extent religious affiliations supplied motives, but the question is raised by the repetition of the religious categories. This news report is not responsible for *creating* these uncertainties, but they arise in the process of address as it reaches out towards the audience.

What, then, about truth? To analyse the news Rhetorically is not to deny that information is conveyed and received. But truth is never distinct from the text which conveys it, and that text has its own life in our receiving minds, a life full of persuasive impulses and playful invitations. Therefore, truth remains as ideal; no message will convey just the truth, the truth alone and in isolation. As the news audience, we learn that something *has* happened; we know, indeed, that some people are dead and others safe. But that truth never walks naked into the world: the truth-telling powers of news cannot be separated from the rest of the text; the truth-receiving powers of the audience cannot be separated from other responses. The story involves truth-telling, but the news cannot simply tell the truth; saying what happened is only an ideal.

Rhetoric seeks to explore the whole experience of the news, without trying to distil a factual essence from the text, or to distinguish 'being informed' from 'the rest of' watching television. It is only habit which makes us overlook how dense the experience is, how flooded with possible meanings. True, the TWA episode is exceptional, explicitly; but the exception only serves to reveal the potential of the news in general. We follow the story instantly – yet the interpreting can be limitless. The classical *attitude* is valuable because it encourages us to explore the depths without obscuring the surface. The revival is precisely about that attitude: the concern with the whole experience of attending to the story, being informed and being entranced, understanding instantly and reflecting endlessly. Above all, the Rhetorical attitude keeps the whole experience in view by refusing to reduce news to simply persuasion or to ignore the persuasive force. Here classical concepts have been deployed directly: the arrangement of legal oration, the modes of Epic, the address of history, the elements of argument and narrative. But those concepts always were a means to an end, when used properly; the end is the attitude, the critical sense of the process of address and understanding.

Revival: Rhetoric and modernity

Classical Rhetoric can be revived liberatingly, so that meanings multiply, and the sense of experience expands. Under the sign of Rhetoric, analysis may diversify – and, as the news analysis attempts to suggest, to revive this tradition does not mean ignoring the present. There is always the question of how Rhetoric corresponds to current 'moral and intellectual interests', as Gramsci puts it.

Some modern reference points that are more theoretical are pertinent after discussing news. First, there is Kenneth Burke again. He proposes an 'interest' that is constant for any would-be revivers of Rhetoric. Every society must produce a 'code of names', according to Burke, 'names' which 'suggest how you shall be for or against'. We all live within these codes:

> Call a man a villain, and you have the choice of either attacking or cringing. Call him mistaken, and you invite yourself to attempt setting him right.

One notes some terms which are important in the broadcast: 'chilling', 'called them animals', 'fanatical terrorism'. The vocabulary is rich, but it is also powerful, and Burke's ideas remind us not to treat too lightly the prosecutory logic. Burke also reminds us (like the best Rhetoric) that choices exist, choices are made: 'Call a man a villain . . . Call him mistaken . . .'.

Burke's thinking is also beautiful; singly, he generates a vision as subtle as a whole tradition, a tradition of Rhetoric. So 'codes' involve choices (politics), but they also serve functions that are universal or existential. Here is Burke on Epic, one kind of 'code of names':

> The epic is designed, then, under primitive conditions, to make men 'at home in' those conditions.

We need these stories, and such stories need codes: nothing is possible at all outside the codes, and the codes require stories. Any given code may be limiting, or worse; but codes are necessary in general. Burke is offering a view that is Rhetorical; he is also giving a theory of culture. Cultural theory is a reference point more generally, and here the work of Raymond Williams is a 'current interest' that is most relevant. Williams suggests that we may see

culture as the signifying system through which necessarily (though among other means) a social order is communicated, reproduced, experienced and explored.

We would not want to assimilate 'signifying system': our account operates at a level that is far less expansive. But there is an idea of meaning being created, collectively and continuously – an idea with which our analysis might connect. Williams is also generous in a way we would like to assimilate and recommend. An 'order' is 'communicated' and 'reproduced', but it is also 'experienced' and 'explored'. In Williams's terms, our worlds are complex: the texture of experience is dense. Culture may communicate to us; but we have an experience that is active as well. An 'order' may reproduce itself, but people also explore the world in ways which have value.

Why not let the theories conclude for us? Theory is a tempting way to conclude: vistas expand, and yet patterns can burgeon. But to end theoretically would be to misrepresent the project. To let theory alone finish would imply that practice was a means to which theory is the end. But the essence of our approach is that theory cannot be separated from practice, any more than practice can proceed without considering theory. There are general concepts, principles, and questions which together do comprise a consistent attitude. Yet every example also alters the approach, actively; each analysis re-creates Rhetoric differently. Revival is therefore a problem which will always become practical, which can be defined but not solved at a level that is general. To revive classical ideas must be to *use* them – and in using, to change them. Other theories provide essential points of reference, but without examples there is nothing to connect.

One must try 'to assume an attitude towards art and life similar to the one assumed . . .' by the tradition, as Gramsci suggests about revival generally. To define what that attitude might be now, one needs a sense of the classical models, an idea of modern thinking in related areas, and also, above all, one needs the process of analysis. The practice of analysis is still the only way of testing the revival, of making the connections count.

Berkeley's philosophical dialogue: Rhetoric, truth-telling, and enlightenment

The final example is designed to review the connections, to re-explore the possibilities. The subject is a dialogue, a philosophical dialogue entitled *Alciphron*, after one of the protagonists. The author is Bishop Berkeley, a philosopher from the early eighteenth century. Why choose this case for an ending? First, we are still pursuing the problem of stories, and here is another kind of story. The *Alciphron* dialogue is a type of story which claims to be underwritten by truth. The news underwrites itself by claiming truths which are particular; a philosophical dialogue lays claim to truths that are general. So we are still revolving the question of stories and truths first raised by juxtaposing fiction with history.

There are other reasons why Berkeley's dialogue is a fitting end. Berkeley is often associated with an idea of a historical period called 'the Enlightenment'. History always proves 'periods' false: the exceptions endlessly overtake the rule. But still, behind the cliche of 'the Enlightenment' there is an important idea: the idea of a time when reason became authoritative for many people and when science seemed likely to resolve many disputes and problems. In the Enlightenment view, knowledge advances, and people may trust that the advance will continue and accelerate. Some may then resist the march of knowledge, of course, but they will be *resisting* – that is what the ideal concept of 'the Enlightenment' represents. We have touched in places on the problems of enlightenment – as in Needham's account of civilization. The concept can be useful, at least negatively. In recent times, there has been in many disciplines some feeling of ceasing to inhabit 'the Enlightenment' – at least, many thinkers have explored such a feeling. Interestingly, some of the writers who feel themselves to be 'post-Enlightenment' have turned towards Rhetoric, or towards ideas that are Rhetorical in origin. Feyerabend is one example, and Gadamer another, much more conservatively-minded. Why does Rhetoric appeal to those who feel that an enlightenment age is passing? Perhaps because Rhetoric considers the world to be inevitably full of disputes which no knowledge can settle. Returning to Berkeley, we can reconsider the relations of Rhetoric to enlightenment, putting the whole project into some degree of historical perspective.

Berkeley rejected 'all controversies purely verbal' – as such he can be seen as an enlightenment spirit, for whom many of the old disputes will be settled or shaken off. A world free of verbal disputes would be an un-Rhetorical world. But the poet and critic Geoffrey Hill remarks acutely that

Berkeley's eschewing of 'all controversies purely verbal' is . . . in part, a verbal gambit, a bid to score in a controversy.

Berkeley is himself, in this view, a great Rhetorician, even as he claims to be above 'controversies purely verbal'. If an enlightenment is ending, or at least changing, that might be one reason why 'current interests' contribute so freely to a revival of Rhetoric. In that case, it seems only fair to let the enlightenment provide the last example, giving the approach a final twist. At least, the fancy is appealing, and suggestive – provided one recognizes that talk of enlightenment and post-enlightenment is a speculative way of placing oneself and not a way of pinning down history. In any case, Berkeley turns out to be a great reflector on address . . .

Berkeley's Alciphron *(Fourth Dialogue): a story of address*

So the account of Rhetoric turns towards enlightenment, finding there, we will suggest, not a simple opposite but many of its own concepts and concerns. Berkeley's Dialogue is a fine site for re-exploring story and argument, so fine that it is worth bringing into play another of the ancient ideas. According to Aristotle, a story must be a 'whole' and

By 'whole' I mean 'with a beginning, a middle and an end'.

The idea of 'beginning . . . middle and . . . end' occurs in the *Poetics*. But this view also connects closely with the *Rhetoric* – as Kathy Eden has shown. Stories need this form in order to address themselves most convincingly to an audience. Aristotle understands 'convincing' in a sense that is very wide, a sense in which persuading cannot be separated from playing, logic cannot be separated from vividness. It turns out that Berkeley enables us to draw creatively upon Aristotle's idea - and also to turn again to Rhetoric's questions about 'Whose words are these?' and 'To what is this replying?'. Berkeley lets us re-explore the revivability of Rhetoric, reaching back across our project as a whole.

225

> Early the next morning, as I looked out of my window, I saw
> Alciphron walking in the garden with all the signs of a man
> in deep thought. Upon which I went down to him.

A story begins – or a new episode opens. The passage is telling
us the time in a way which implies that there is 'a past' ('the
next morning'). The tempo seems to be rising (*'Early* the next
morning'); things are *about* to happen. The place must be known
already: 'in the garden' is familiar. There are characters, who *act*;
what we are told suggests that we have met them previously. The
narrative moves to 'I went down' without explaining who this
Alciphron is, or who the 'I' is, or what they are doing here. The
writing is presenting a 'next' event; the story is continuing, in a
new chapter (Fourth Dialogue), which is about to offer a new
episode.

Narratives need to keep restarting; they often have to start
again. They must assume that we know some things already, that
we have 'followed the story' so far. The passage addresses a reader
who has followed, a reader who is waiting for what comes 'next'.
By what are we being addressed? One answer would be: a voice
which is telling a story, a storytelling voice. Storytelling voices
convey action, although there are many kinds of action. The 'I'
looks out and sees 'Alciphron' walking: that is action. Other things
make the voice sound like storytelling: 'with all the signs of a man
in deep thought'. These characters have inner lives, which we
need to know about in order to understand what they are doing;
Alciphron does not just walk, he shows 'signs' as well. Why 'with
all the signs . . .'? Why not just say 'Alciphron was walking and
thinking'? 'Signs' are part of storytelling: all narratives tell us
about signs as well as about actions. Ancient theorists pointed out
that signs are necessary for narratives, in poetry, and also in law
and in political oratory. Aristotle explored how storytellers need
signs; his idea passed into medieval theories and is important to
the work of modern critics such as Erich Auerbach and Wayne
Booth. Stories can show people doing many things, 'walking', for
instance. But other activities must be *deduced*: there is evidence
to suggest that Alciphron is thinking, where 'I' can see him walking. The storyteller must present actions, but he can also read
signs, or report reading signs: that is true of literary stories, and
also of legal narratives, or of histories. Some things need inferring

from evidence: feelings and thoughts must be inferred, unless the story claims special powers to 'see inside' other people. Likewise, the past often needs deducing.

What are these 'signs' which imply that Alciphron has been 'deep in thought'? There is hardly any need to specify: furrowed brow, remote gaze . . . we share an idea of 'all the signs of man in deep thought'. 'Signs' are public. So a voice which says 'all the signs . . .' is addressing a reader who shares in a pool of meanings, a reader who can (re)visualize the evidence from which 'deep thought' is deduced.

A storytelling voice is addressing readers who have followed the story and who share the culture. The voice is one kind of storytelling voice: there is an 'I' in the narrative, an 'I' who is down there reading the inner lives of others from the 'signs'. It may be more important to recognize that here is one kind of narrating voice than to know anything else. But that is not the only way of identifying the voice. The passage could come from a novel, except for the name, perhaps (Alciphron?). In fact, the passage comes from a work of 'Philosophy', rather than 'Fiction', as usually defined. These words begin the 'Fourth Dialogue' of a book called *Alciphron*, by Bishop Berkeley, the eighteenth-century philosopher. That makes an important point: story-telling happens in many kinds of speech and writing. It is best to think of a process which can be part of many other processes. A voice is addressing us in one storytelling way: it is also part of a work of philosophy.

Those 'signs' are important to Berkeley's philosophical case, as well as to the feeling of narrative. There is going to be an argument involving 'signs' in general. That argument will be part of a dispute about God, but the theory of 'signs' will be central in itself. The point will be that language consists of signs which are 'arbitrary'; language signifies and yet there is no natural link between the signs and what they signify. A word conveys an idea: 'garden', say. But it is purely arbitrary that this word conveys that idea. The same is true of the way we see the world – that is going to be the argument. We see signs, and interpret them to discover the world. We see signs that we can interpret as a hill, or a tree, or a person. But we have to learn the trick of interpreting these signs as tree, those as hill. . . . The argument will be that we see signs, not objects; but signs are language. Whose is the language

that we see? Language must be used by a speaker. If we are
seeing signs, then someone must be uttering them, intelligibly:
God. The argument is tricky, and we will return to it. Here the
important point is that 'signs' belong to the voice of storytelling;
but they are also part of the philosophical argument. Even the
detail is as relevant to the philosophy as it is to the story. The
reader can move backwards from 'all the signs of a man in deep
thought' and 'see' an image of a person. The path leads back from
the idea, the 'deep thought', to the signs which reveal it, visibly.
But everyone has to *learn* what these signs are: there is no inevitable link between furrowed brow and 'deep thought'. The reader
experiences the fact that some signs *are* arbitrary, at least: people
do in some ways deduce the world rather than see it directly. So
the detail is prepared for the general theory that signs are arbitrary, and that this applies to what we see as well as to what we
say. The reader is being addressed by a philosophical case as well
as by a story, yet the two cannot be separated.

The episode continues, and this 'I' talks about his feelings:

> Alciphron, said I, this early and profound meditation puts me
> in no small fright. How so? Because I should be sorry to be
> convinced there was no God.

Alciphron argues against God: he claims to disprove the diety. 'I'
believes in God, evidently, hence the 'fright' at seeing the atheist
in 'early and profound meditation'. So then 'I went down to him',
because of being afraid? What seemed to record a neutral action,
going down, now presents the results, or signs, of having felt
afraid. The swiftness might suggest fear: no sooner did I see
Alciphron, than I rushed down, hastily ('Upon which I went down
to him'). The words begin to sound anxious, as they record 'my'
anxiety. So the voice might be nervous; the syntax might reflect
that hasty feeling, the nerves themselves. By what were we being
addressed, then, when we were told about 'I' seeing the other
person? There has been an impersonal voice recounting events;
there has been a philosophical case, which needs the idea of
arbitrary 'signs'; and now there may be a voice of personal
memory, even feeling.

But is the speaker really 'in no small fright'? Isn't there something unconvincing about his words: 'I should be sorry to be
convinced there was no God.' 'Sorry' seems too weak: is that the

voice of someone anxious? Perhaps the atheist Alciphron is being teased: then what about the 'deep thought'? 'Deep' might even be mocking – the atheist is thinking deeply, but to what effect? How ridiculous – no wonder he is out early! All the details could fit: Alciphron is up because *he* is worried, he is losing an argument about God. (The previous dialogues have 'recorded' a dispute, though how Alciphron feels he is doing is open to question.) The speaker may have gone down to tease the atheist, merely to mimic fear. The voice would then be satiric, mocking the atheist for his 'deep thought'. He is *only* a 'man', yet trying to disprove God: the word 'man' becomes changed, mockingly, yet 'man' had seemed neutral. The writing would invite us to laugh, the passage would address us as sharers of the joke against atheists.

One passage may narrate impersonally, argue philosophically, remember personally, and mock satirically. Each process addresses the reader in a different voice. These 'voices' may overlap, even if we cannot hear them all at the same time; it is possible to sound half-nervous and half-mocking ('Alciphron will never convince me that God does not exist, of course, but . . .'). Telling a story may overlap with arguing a case generally: indeed, that is one of the powers of address. Words can also slip between 'impersonal' voices and personal feelings – one moment the sound is that of narration in general, the next moment 'my' feelings are audible. Trying to identify the voices is one way of interpreting the text. What voices are addressing us? Whose words are these? These questions are important for deciding what a text or utterance *means*. 'Meaning' refers to the sense that must be followed, and to the ideas which must be discovered: the 'levels' will not separate. Trying to identify the voices which need the phrase 'all the signs . . .' we follow the passage *and* discover the ideas 'behind' it. The 'I' steps aside, saying that he will record the story:

> [I will] take notes of all that passeth during this memorable *event* . . . (Our italics)

The 'event' will be Alciphron trying to disprove God: that may be 'memorable' because it is absurd, or because it is striking, or because of counter-proofs which defeat the atheist. The word 'event' makes clear that a story is being told – dispute is still something which happens, it is still an action. 'Event' may mock Alciphron as well, because he has inflated ideas about what will happen. (Nevertheless things which are memorable do happen, though not as Alciphron wishes.) Characters arrive, as in a novel or other narratives:

> As we were engaged in this discourse, Crito and Euphranor joined us . . .

Euphranor will argue 'for God'. What is going to happen? There is conflict, there is suspense, there is the promise of an 'event', which may be a comic event or an impressive one or both . . .

The episode has begun: now come the middle and the ending. The Dialogue does divide into phases, clearly: when Euphranor arrives, the beginning is over. The middle is Euphranor arguing with Alciphron, while 'I . . . take notes'. Yet this 'I' has introduced one of the terms which Euphranor needs, having anticipated his use of 'signs', and so the 'I' also feels like the controlling power, setting up the right case. This 'I' is the mouthpiece of the 'author', as well as merely transcribing other voices. Alciphron loses; the middle is over when he gives up, after the others accuse him of 'prejudice' against God. The atheist is angry:

> ALCIPHRON: I disdain the suspicion of prejudice. And I do not speak only for myself.

The 'I' then joins in to suppress the troublemaker, and an episode comes to a close (although the Dialogue has a few after-words).

The narrative keeps asking us questions about how to identify the voices. The beginning poses the problem about 'I' and the arguments. The ending suggests that Alciphron's words *represent* the views of a group, an important group even:

> And I do not speak only for myself. I know a club of most ingenious men, the freest from prejudice of any men alive, who abhor the notion of a God . . .

Alciphron is wriggling: he means to insist that these 'ingenious' men would defeat the believers. Instead, what he says identifies his voice with a movement, a modern philosophy; he has lost, therefore that movement has lost. Euphranor has replied to Alciphron successfully: an atheist tendency has been answered in the process. But Euphranor seems to represent the 'I's' view, and even the story's view. Berkeley's story answers Alciphron, and replies to modern philosophers of the time. The whole story is a reply: that is one way of reading it.

Consider the middle of the story, which is where either side may win, and it is unclear still how victory will emerge. Aristotle argued that stories have a beginning, middle and ending: that principle can help when thinking about voices – provided the principle is used flexibly. Voices do address us differently at different stages of a story: we need to know 'where' a voice is speaking, as well as what may be motivating the words, or what type of process is producing them (arguing, remembering . . .). These words address us from the middle of a story:

ALCIPHRON: Prove therefore your opinion [that God exists]; or, if you cannot, you may indeed remain in possession of it, but you will only be possessed of a prejudice.

EUPHRANOR: O Alciphron, to content you we must prove, it seems, and we must prove upon your own terms.

The characters address each other; but the exchange addresses us. They address each other in a way which establishes conflict; the effect is to invite the readers (us) to think forwards, to anticipate, and wonder. These are 'middle' voices, both because they are joining battle and because the effect is to throw the reader's mind forwards, tensely. (Middle voices can be of different kinds – this is only one example. Many stories play with beginning, middle and end: stories can mislead, they can put voices in where they would not be expected, addressing us as if from an ending at the start, or as if from a middle at the end.)

Alciphron is confident: '. . . you will only be possessed of a prejudice', he challenges the believers. His words will rebound on the atheist, who ends by having to 'disdain the suspicion of prejudice'. The word 'prejudice' turns round: Alciphron throws it at the others, then he receives it back. The voice which accused the others of prejudice becomes the voice accused and defending itself. 'Alciphron's' voice can be identified as 'an accusing voice' and then as 'an accused voice'. The dispute becomes comparable to a contest in law; arguing about philosophy shades into prosecuting and defending, the charge being 'suspicion of prejudice'. In Berkeley's court the roles of prosecutor and defender are slippery, and the plaintiff/prosecutor is liable to end up in the dock. Legal roles are another way to identify the voices. A voice can be identified as accusatory or accused, as speaking from the middle or the beginning or the ending, and as 'Alciphron' or 'Euphranor'. The same words may be accusatory, speaking from the middle, Alciphron's, and representing 'ingenious men'.

Yet voices are audible, humanly audible: 'O Alciphron, to content you . . .', Euphranor exclaims, irritably, or amusedly, or with a touch of both feelings. He may be saying 'to *content* you': 'to keep you quiet . . .'; or 'to content *you*': 'no one else here is worried, but still to keep *you* happy . . .'; perhaps both stresses are there. Perhaps Euphranor is emphasizing that '*we* must prove . . .', although 'you' might be expected to do some proving yourself; or again, he could be accepting wearily that 'we *must* prove . . .', or is he pointing out that 'we must *prove* . . .' now what many people would believe without proof? The voice is speaking to another position, saying that it is demanding or lazy, or unreasonable about proof and faith. The other's words are even present: 'prove' comes from Alciphron.

The whole work must have a voice; as well as identifying the voices within the dialogue, the reader needs to identify the voice of the whole. By what are we being addressed? The question applies to the entire experience of reading, and the answer is as tricky as when passages are being considered individually. Here is an argument, within a story, within a philosophical treatise; or a philosophical theory, within a dispute, within a story. These are questions of interpretation: we decide how to identify voices, and that involves stressing meanings differently. But positions can address us, by addressing each other, even while we interpret voices individually, and the voice of the work as a whole.

The plot thickens, the dispute intensifies. Alciphron defines what he will accept as proof that any being exists, whether a human being or a deity:

> I have found that nothing so much convinces me of the existence of another person as *his speaking to me*.

The atheist thinks he is safe: he can tell that people exist because of their 'speaking to me'. What about God, in that case? If God is not audibly 'speaking to me', then why should 'I', Alciphron, believe in Him? 'Speaking to . . .' becomes central to the dispute, and so the issue is Rhetorical in our terms. The experience of being addressed is the crux, both for the story of the dispute, and for the philosophy. Recognizing that the issue is now stated, Euphranor is eager:

But what if it should appear that God really speaks to man; would this content you?

'Content' is barbed: would Alciphron accept *that* as proof? He would have to concede, and so be 'content' in that sense; he would hardly be 'content' in the sense of being pleased, since he would lose the argument. Euphranor is suggesting that his opponent is in bad faith. Alciphron does not want to be convinced: that is why he has picked 'speaking to me' as a proof that a being exists. The philosophy approaches the idea which will count, the idea for proving God using 'speaking to' and 'signs' to underpin the proof. Yet the story does not fall away – on the contrary.

We *hear* two voices, and can interpret their feelings as well as their ideas. Euphranor is half-angry, half-delighted (in advance); Alciphron is sly, conceited, and mischievous. Here the story comes together with the philosophy most significantly. Many things might convince you of the existence of another person – his 'speaking to me' is not an obvious thing to choose. Indeed Alciphron is being difficult. Yet the Dialogue does convince *us* that these 'people' exist, by showing that they exist for each other. How does the writing show that they exist for each other? By presenting Alciphron 'speaking to' Euphranor, and then Euphranor replying. There is a wonderful moment in which the story slips round the philosophy: having people 'speaking to' each other is one way a story convinces readers that characters exist. Further, we can hear Alciphron and Euphranor 'speaking to' us as well: the feelings, the tones, are audible. The joke is that Alciphron is giving *just* the right reason for the existence of a character in a Dialogue: that is how we are convinced that he exists. If a voice in a Dialogue says that 'nothing so much convinces me of the existence of another person as his speaking to me', that is another way of identifying the voice, the voice which demands that proof is one which belongs to a character in a Dialogue, where all existence is in terms of 'speaking to' (and being addressed).

The words also belong to the main thesis: 'his speaking to me' is the rationale which the Dialogue is waiting to use for showing that God exists. Euphranor has to define language before clinching the case. He says that 'speaking' depends on people being able to understand 'signs'. These 'signs' are 'sensible', meaning that they are audible to our ears (speech), and visible to our eyes (writing). 'Sensible signs' convey meaning – in words, in sentences. But the signs are nothing like what they mean: signs do not resemble what they convey, language does not imitate meaning. 'Speaking' is

> . . . the arbitrary use of sensible signs, which have no
> similitude or necessary connection with the things
> signified . . .

Now Euphranor has to show that God addresses 'men', using 'sensible signs . . .', and so speaks to people. The proof depends upon a parallel between being addressed by words and looking at the world. That parallel results from the theory of 'signs' and 'speaking to'. When we are addressed, we experience 'signs' that have 'No . . . necessary connection with the things signified'. People make sense of what others have said to them by learning the ideas associated with 'signs'. But what about looking? Euphranor argues that we see 'signs' and decode them, translating the 'sign' into 'the thing signified'. We see a 'sign' and *learn* to read that sign as a tree or a hill. We never see the object itself, we only see the sign directly, and the sign does not have any 'necessary connection' with what we learn to read off from it. (This is the idea anticipated by 'all the signs of a man in deep thought'.) But 'signs' must be part of a message – there must be a speaker or author who is responsible for the signs from which we read off the world, who is sending out the 'sensible signs' that we use to discover the world. Looking is really being addressed:

> the Author of Nature [God] constantly speaks to the eyes of
> all mankind . . .

When we look, we are experiencing

> Language, addressed to our eyes . . .

No wonder Alciphron feels tricked: the game is unfair. He is a character in a Dialogue: therefore, of course, he chooses 'speaking to me' as a proof that people exist. Now God seems to have been proved. Euphranor speaks the replies to Alciphron; but the whole story enacts the replying, really – from the narration about 'all the signs of a man' to the form of the Dialogue, to the audibility of the voices 'speaking to' us and so convincing us that people exist to argue about how you tell that people exist . . .

Berkeley's *Alciphron* (Fourth Dialogue) can be interpreted as a story, a story which involves philosophy; or the work can be seen as philosophy which involves a story. Either way, the philosophical ideas connect profoundly with the 'memorable event', Euphranor and Alciphron arguing. Interpreting stories is a process, and processes overlap with each other: Rhetoric can recognize the way interpreting a story overlaps with following an argument, the way hearing characters overlaps with connecting ideas. 'Story' becomes one way of thinking about a text (or an utterance): there is no need to make 'narrative' a category which is closed, a category which excludes everything that is 'not-story'. How do meanings become available to readers (and listeners)? We are asking that question rather than the question 'What defines narrative?' People interpret stories as part of the giving of meaning to the world – a wider process which includes philosophizing and following philosophy, theorizing and following theory.

How do meanings become available? That is not a question to be answered, finally answered. What matters is to explore how the question can be *asked*, rather than to state how it could be answered. Rhetoric is one way of asking questions; that is its function when most alive, when properly revived.

But what about philosophy's claims to reveal the truth? Are we animating Rhetoric at the expense of philosophy – by debunking its hope of being underwritten by truth? Nothing so reductive. To interpret Berkeley's story Rhetorically does involve looking at how meanings become possible rather than testing the logic. That would only be debunking if we were suggesting Rhetoric as the only approach to philosophy, but we have no such ambitions. Rhetoric is no more the only way of thinking about Berkeley than it is the only way of thinking about television news. The point is that when Rhetoric is in play, then claims to truth are not being tested, either factually or logically. Instead Rhetoric is a way of thinking about meaning, and specifically about how meaning comprises persuasive force and playful energy. News and philosophy both tell stories which need to be tested in terms of their truth – but there are many other dimensions to our experience of such stories, dimensions of meaning which need to be explored in their own terms.

Reviving Rhetoric

George Kennedy summarizes what happened to classical Rhetoric:

> . . . there were serious dangers inherent in rhetoric. It was dynamic, it was systematic, and it became traditional . . .

Rhetoric succeeded too well: that is Kennedy's verdict. Rhetoric was a powerful way of studying language, and an energizing way of using language. But the approach was systematic as well as dynamic, and systems became rigid:

> In rhetorical theory the trend towards systemization produced a body of rules and exercises which were more and more abstracted . . .

Rhetoric only became systematic by first being dynamic: but system expelled dynamism in the end. Rules prevailed, and rules always become abstracted when their ruling system goes unquestioned. Yet Aristotle had explicitly warned against imposing rules where no rules are possible (Chapter 3); Gorgias had insisted that language's powers remain necessarily magical and mysterious (Chapter 5); Rhetorically-inclined thinkers reached differing conclusions about politics (Chapter 3). Play and pleasure complicate persuasion in the works of Aristotle, of Cicero, and of other leading Rhetoricians. Even *Ad Herennium*, which *is* a handbook, finely respects the gap between general categories and particular examples. System is there as well, of course; but being systematic is less important than being dynamic.

What we are proposing is precisely a shift in the character of Rhetoric, from the systematic to the dynamic, a shift which is radical in that it demands a return towards origins. Shifting from being systematic towards a dynamic approach: that corresponds to certain moves in related fields. Here Raymond Williams has relevant arguments about analytic method generally. He criticizes the idea that analysts should try to stand above an experience that is being analysed. For Williams, the time is past when cultural analysts could assume a right to stand apart from culture:

> . . . the assumption of an explanatory method which can be taken as *a priori* 'above' all other social experiences and cultural production is itself, when analysed, a fact in the sociology of a particular phase.

The analyst belongs inside the processes. A Rhetorical revival might encourage the analyst to recognize that fact of belonging, of being inside.

By engaging with Williams, we reach again, inevitably, ideology – which is a concept both important and elusive. Williams sifts the senses of 'ideology', and he emphasizes one sense strongly:

> the characteristic world-view or general perspective of a class or other social group, which will include formal and conscious beliefs but also less conscious, less formulated attitudes . . . even unconscious assumptions.

There is a nice generosity about 'class or other social group' which we wish to emphasize here, particularly having considered news Rhetorically, but also in relation to the chapters on language, utterance and society (Chapters 1, 2, and 4). Williams also helps by linking 'formal and conscious beliefs' with 'less formulated attitudes' and 'even unconscious assumptions'. Watching the news (or reading a novel, or listening to a lecture) does engage the mind at different depths – as our approach demonstrates. Again Williams has a feeling for how experience is many-layered: he tries to acknowledge as far as possible how richly people experience the world, how profoundly people make meanings. We feel that our analysis of stories, including news and philosophy, corresponds to the rich texture of experience in Williams's world, though the terms differ.

Finally, then, the interpreting of stories leads back to the problems of belief. Many theories claim to show how values are imposed, how what people perceive is shaped; yet these theories often offer little when it comes to exploring how people create meanings, how people give meaning to their worlds at all. In this context, John Thompson warns that what people say or write

> is not only . . . culturally and historically situated . . . but is

also an expression which claims to say something . . . which must be grasped by interpretation.

Thompson assesses the work in the Marxist tradition of Castoriadis and Lefort, for instance. He agrees that they are right to emphasize that there are

. . . forms which define what, for a given society, is 'real'.

But he criticizes Castoriadis and Lefort, and their tradition as a whole, for failing to consider the actual processes by which meaning is produced, or discovered, or created. Ultimately, Thompson does give priority to

the ways in which meaning . . . serves to sustain relations of domination.

Following the story analyses, we would endorse Thompson's sense of meaning as something that is real, something that shares the same world in which power also operates. But Rhetoric *need not subordinate meaning to power* as Thompson automatically does – the question remains open and differing answers are possible. Or, rather, Rhetoric retains a fuller sense of 'power' than simply 'domination': the creation of meaning is as much a power as the imposing of social hierarchy. The power of address is involved with social power, but cannot be reduced to it: that is why we need Rhetoric.

Notes and further reading

The news bulletin about the release of the American hostages was broadcast on BBC 1 at 9.10 on 30 June 1985.

The references to George Berkeley are from *The Works of George Berkeley*, Vol. II (1901 edition). The Fourth Dialogue of *Alciphron, or the Minute Philosopher* is divided into sections, referred to as follows: section 1 for 'the next morning' and taking notes, section 3 for 'we must prove', section 6 for 'his speaking to me' and 7 for 'God really speaks to men' and 'sensible signs', section 11 for 'the Author', section 13 for 'suspicion of prejudice', and section 15 for 'addressed to our eyes'. The comments on Berkeley and controversies are from Geoffrey Hill (1984), the fine essay on language and judgement entitled 'Our word is our bond'.

Kennedy (1963), Chapter 1, 'The nature of rhetoric' is essential for the tradition and its dangers. Gramsci (1985 translation) Part II, 'Problems of criticism' (p. 91) provides ideas on revival. Russell and

Winterbottom (1972) give Lucian's *How to Write History* and also Aristotle's *Poetics*, in which Chapter 1 concerns modes of narration and Chapter 2 the story as a 'whole'. Aristotle on 'the true' is in *Rhetoric*, I, i. The *Rhetorica ad Herennium* is quoted in the Loeb edition and translation by H. Caplan. The work is listed in the bibliography under Anon., having previously been ascribed to Cicero but subsequently considered of unknown authorship. The references are : I, iv on winning hearers; I, ix on ordering; II, xviii-xix on motives; II, xxiv on weak reasons; II, xxx on commonplaces and foul crimes.

Kenneth Burke's magnificent *Attitudes Toward History* discusses codes in Part I, Chapter 1 ('William James, Whitman and Emerson') and considers Epic in Chapter 2 on 'Poetic categories'. Raymond Williams's *Culture* (1981) is vital for thinking about communication in context: p. 13 for 'signifying system', p. 30 for 'explanatory method', p. 26 for 'ideology'. Thompson (1984), Chapter 1, 'Ideology and the social imaginary' discusses Castoriadis and Lefort, and Chapter 2, 'Symbolic violence', gives the warning on language, context, and meaning.

Raymond Williams is a major influence on the book as a whole, and therefore a particular presence in this chapter on Rhetoric and revival. For further reading in this context, we recommend: *The Long Revolution* (1961), *Communications* (1976) and *Marxism and Literature* (1977). Chapter 1 of *Communications*, 'Definitions', is a wonderful account of models of communication in few pages, and Chapter 4 on 'Controversies' is a fine meditation on traditional values and new contexts. Part I of *Marxism and Literature* gives helpful accounts of 'culture', 'language', 'literature' and 'ideology', the last being especially valuable for its charting of ambiguities in a concept.

On television and media, we found Davis and Walton (1983) a helpful collection of essays, particularly the work by Davis and Walton on 'Death of a Premier: consensus and closure in international news', and by Lerman on 'Dominant discourse: the institutional voice and control of topic'. Glasgow Media Group (1976) is polemical and challenging on television news and political values. Said (1981) is controversial and essential reading on news coverage of 'Islam'. McLuhan (1959) is a historically important article, and perhaps these ideas are now being undervalued after a period of the reverse: McLuhan is certainly interesting as a thinker who connects classical ideas with the problems of modern culture, especially Plato's ideas on writing and on myth from *Phaedrus*. Pateman (1980a) gives a helpful account of theories of language and their relation to the understanding of images.

On Rhetorical tradition, along with Kennedy (1963), we recommend Curtius (1953 translation), particularly Chapters 1-5, 8, 16. Vickers (1988) is a new history of Rhetoric as system-in-transition and argues a very different position on the relation between Rhetoric and modern criticism, well worth consulting as a contrast to the arguments put forward here.

On philosophy and Rhetoric, Habermas (1987 translation) has a challenging essay on 'Levelling the Genre Distinction between Literature and Philosophy'. Habermas disputes what he sees as the over-easy eliding of philosophy with prevailing ideas of literature, and he re-emphasizes argumentation, although we would contend that he underestimates the extent to which argument and literature overlap. Derrida (1982 translation) includes a rich reaction to Plato and philosophical dialogue; Gadamer (1980 translation) is a more sober approach. Rée (1987) is an entertaining and accessible view of philosophy and narrative.

Finally, Derrida (1983) is a polemical reflection on thinking and the academic context.

Theoretical postscript

Every species of literary criticism or linguistic analysis, every act of interpretation, involves either explicitly or implicitly a theory of language. What is its relationship to 'reality', to its author or speaker, to its addressee or reader, to the linguistic system itself? Generally speaking, particular traditions of criticism or interpretation tend to focus on just one of these relationships. Thus the criticism inspired by the dominant idea of the Romantic movement stresses the author as the *originator* of an utterance: it is seen as the expression of a uniquely talented individual. Formalist analysis on the other hand tends to privilege the 'text' as the object of study: it is seen as autonomous, to be understood either in terms of its internal relationships, or in relation to the general system of choices available in the language system as a whole. Whereas Formalist approaches find their most articulate expression in the twentieth century, there has also been a very long tradition, stretching back to the era of Plato, of seeing language as capable of representing an outer reality, of imitating or 'miming' what is 'out there'. From this derives a notion of the possibility of 'neutral' or even 'exact' description of states, processes, objects, and events that are felt to exist independently of language and which are capable of faithful representation by it. It is this expectation that many people bring to descriptions in novels, for instance. And finally, there is another tradition – equally long-standing – of studying utterances in relation to their effects (either actual or intended) on audiences or readers.

To a large extent these relationships – between utterance on the one hand and author, universe, addressee and language-system on

241

the other – are reflected in the model of language functions proposed by Roman Jakobson. For Jakobson, every utterance has a primary focus: the attitudes or feelings of the speaker (he calls this the *emotive* function), getting some response from the addressee (*conative* function), or making a statement about externally verifiable 'facts' (*referential* function); or it may focus principally on itself as an utterance of a fixed and highly patterned form (*poetic* function). The overlap between these four foci and the relationships discussed in the paragraph above should be clear. But Jakobson also lists two other functions. The *phatic* (see glossary) function labels utterances which serve to maintain or establish social contact rather than express feelings, refer to some extra-linguistic reality, or whatever. And the *metalingual* (see glossary) function labels utterances which refer to language itself as a system or – to use Jakobson's own term – 'code' (as when we enquire about the spelling of a word or its meaning).

Many of Jakobson's terms are injudicious or even misleading, so that in the course of this book we have renamed them. But before we discuss the alternative terms, it is necessary to acknowledge that there are also ways in which the entire model is misleading. It depends on a rather naive view of communication, in which the speaker appears to have already decided what to say to someone else: he or she then simply chooses from among the available items and patterns in the appropriate code (in this case language), and whatever is said is 'decoded' by the listener in a relatively unproblematical way. Both speaker and hearer, then, are conceived as 'individuals' existing outside of, and prior to, the code (which in turn exists for the purposes of communication). But as we have argued throughout this book, it is actually we, as speakers and hearers, who are pre-dated by language, which to a large extent makes sense of exterior reality, even a sense of oneself as an individual, possible in the first place. It is language, furthermore, that largely sets up for us the possibilities of meaning, rather than simply reflecting a meaning or meanings already given.

One consequence of accepting this view of language, which can loosely be called a structuralist one, is that language is seen as a kind of straitjacket – even, as Frederick Jameson calls it, a prison-house. While this view may be somewhat extreme, it does at least alert us to what we have called the materiality of language, its opaqueness. As we have seen, language itself can be said largely to constitute many different social practices. It is therefore not clear where so-called institutional utterances (for example, those of religion and law) fit into Jakobson's model. As has so often been pointed out, an utterance such as 'I name this ship Amelia', when accompanied by appropriate actions (such as breaking a bottle of champagne against the bows of the ship in question), is actually constitutive of the act of naming. And it is very difficult to assign a dominant function to an utterance such as the Lord's Prayer when spoken in unison by a congregation in church. It may be *poetic* (deriving from the power of the fixed form, often repeated), *phatic* (deriving from a sense of shared worship) or even *conative* (a plea to God to fulfil certain needs).

The model is also defective in not allowing sufficient space for the variety of verbal games we discuss in this book. For this reason the term 'poetic' (with its rather narrow and reverential connotations) might better be replaced by 'ludic', a term capable of including the sense of 'aesthetic' but also capturing the wider possibilities of verbal play (it also has the advantage of evoking the notion of 'play' by virtue of its customary translation). But verbal play is more than just the acknowledgement of language's material properties. It is also an assertion of the freedom of both speakers and listeners (and writers and readers) to interpret in ways that are not bounded by notions of referentiality or, more important, intentionality. During the last two decades or so there has been an increasing interest within literary criticism and theory in the reader and the act of reading as the site of critical and analytical attention. In their very different ways the work of Barthes in *S/Z*, with its endlessly playful quest for meaning, and of Fish, with his insistence that the 'only game in town' is, ultimately, interpretation, have influenced our thinking. And it is only fair to add that something of the same spirit can be traced back through the writings of an earlier, and perhaps even more influential, critic, William Empson, and beyond, as far back as the classical ages of both Greece and Rome, where language was always a source of delight.

At this point it may be useful to reproduce Jakobson's model in his own chosen form, a diagram, but with our amended terminology (the capitalized terms indicate Jakobson's component of the communicative act):

243

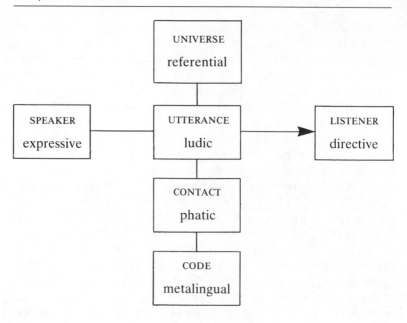

As can be seen we have replaced 'emotive' by 'expressive' and 'conative' by 'directive' (we use both terms extensively throughout the book). Our choice of terms is motivated partly by a desire to economize, partly because we want to find connections between Jakobson's model and concepts drawn from other traditions of enquiry.

Our own approach, in relation to everything discussed so far, can be said to concern itself primarily with the relationship between utterance and addressee. But there are several ways this might be done. Our approach is not the same as the so-called 'reader-response' criticism of theorists like Iser, and neither is it of the kind traditionally associated with Rhetoric, in which an author or speaker uses nameable 'devices' in order to persuade an audience. The effects of such devices are not so predictable, the intentions of speakers or writers not so easily realized. Our own attitude to utterances is to see them as irreducibly social, not in the conventional sense of being opposed to the personal or individual (we would reject the opposition) but in that they always face towards addressees and the wider 'public' culture. This insight has in the twentieth century been most forcefully articulated by the Russian linguist and poetician Mikhail Bakhtin: his influence pervades the whole book. But there is another, and vital, aspect of that social dimension. Language not only constructs, in large measure, our reality for us, it reflects, and helps to create, the interests and ideas of dominant social groups. But rather than see that feature as an immutable part of language as a 'system', we prefer to see language as something realized as utterances by real people, partly as an expression of interest (in both material and ideological senses), social position, and loyalty. It must not be forgotten that though language may pre-date us as creatures of a particular time and place it remains something made by humans, and is therefore capable of being changed. Since in our view language is not a static system but a dynamic *process*, it allows us the space to put new utterances together, the products of different and perhaps opposed interpretations of the world. To see language as dialogue is to acknowledge that there is always space for a reply.

But to say this is only to state the problem, not to offer a solution. To emphasize dialogue is to acknowledge where we have to start; it is not to prescribe a remedy for all the world's ills. We are not trying to revive the comfortable notion that everything will be all right as long as people keep talking to each other. Instead, we argue that no useful account of how language works, how meanings are created, can ignore the dialogic character of language. In arguing this we are asserting a continuity with the past, a tradition which includes what we see as the spirit of Rhetoric, and, with the inspiration of Raymond Williams, a hope for the future.

Glossary of linguistic terms

To keep this Glossary brief we have included only those terms which are given a technical meaning in linguistics. We assume they are unfamiliar to most readers. Some, like *coda*, have however been borrowed from other fields of study; one of them, *ludic*, is our own formulation.

adjacency pair: a term drawn from the sociological tradition of conversational analysis, relating to how speakers 'take turns' in conversation. Some utterances, like offers, questions and greetings, are 'paired' with corresponding responses (acceptances, answers and returned greetings) in a predictable way; departures from the expected response (e.g. the rejection of an offer) are termed 'dispreferred'. *See also* **turn-taking**.

antonym: words whose meanings are felt to be 'opposite' are called antonyms e.g. big/small, odd/even, alive/dead. 'Opposition', however, is not always a straightforward concept: the difference between 'odd' and 'even' is not that of 'good' versus 'bad', since there is no gradation between the extremes (if it's not odd, it has to be even). *See* **synonym**.

bald imperative: imperatives, like interrogatives and declaratives, are a category of grammar (known as 'mood') and should not be confused with the notion of command. Imperatives are used to realize many different **speech acts** (e.g., well-wishing, offering, inviting, ordering, exhorting, etc.), as in 'Have a good time!', 'Help yourself', and 'Be whole'. A command expressed unequivocally in the imperative mood ('Sit down and shut up!', 'Stand up!') can be called a bald imperative.

coda: in Labov's analysis of oral narrative the term 'coda' is used to denote the final component in the narrative proper, before the turn-taking sequence is resumed. It brings the chain of actions to a close and often has a conventional form, as in

'So that was that'; sometimes, as in 'I still see him now and again', it restores the listener to the present.

cohesive devices: linguistic forms and patterns that help knit a text together. Internal *reference* includes the use of pronouns to refer back to nouns already mentioned in the text, or forward to material that is coming up (e.g. *He* and *this* in 'John was a farmer. *He* hated ramblers. *This* is what happened to him.'). There are also several kinds of *substitution*, e.g. 'so' stands for a whole clause previously mentioned in 'If *so*, put your hat on'. *Ellipsis* includes omission, for example, of the verb in the second clause in 'I cooked the meat and Jim the vegetables', and *conjunction* a variety of conjunctions and adverbs, e.g. *but, for instance, however, therefore, meanwhile.* Finally, cohesive links are established through the choice of vocabulary, e.g. 'That's his new *guitar*. He's virtually married the *instrument*', where 'instrument' is a more general category than *guitar*. The kinds of cohesive devices used vary according to the genre of text.

connectives: sometimes known as conjunctions or connectors, these play the role of conjunction in text cohesion (see above). Individual conjunctions like 'and' and adverbials like 'so' often have a very wide range of meanings, particularly in speech (whereas in Logic, 'and' and 'if', for instance, have fixed and single meanings). 'And' can imply a simultaneous relation ('he plays guitar *and* I play harmonica'), a temporal one ('he got on his horse *and* rode off') or even a causal one ('Hitler invaded Poland, *and* the Second World War began'). 'Because' means different things in 'He crashed the car *because* he was drunk' and 'He was drunk *because* he crashed the car'. The use of connectives varies with genre: distinctive is the use of 'and' in news broadcasts ('The Lebanon, *and* all the hostages are now safe').

co-ordination: the linking of clauses by such connectives as *and, but* and *then*. As opposed to subordination, co-ordination doesn't impose a hierarchical relationship between propositions in different clauses. Thus 'I was tired *and* I went to bed' presents a state and an action which are simply conjoined, whereas 'I went to bed *because* I was tired' indicates a *causal* relationship, subordinating the explanatory clause to the main clause denoting the action.

declaration: a *speech act*, usually associated with a highly specific institutional setting, in which a new state of affairs is actually brought about by the utterance of certain words (usually formulaic). Thus the actions of naming a ship (I name this ship . . .), arresting someone (I arrest you), or marrying someone (With this ring I thee wed) are declarations.

declarative: a grammatical term denoting sentences which are neither **imperative** nor **interrogative**. Declarative structures are typically used to make statements. Unlike imperatives, they include subjects, which are typically placed before verbs, as in 'That man (subject) cleans our windows' (verb + direct object). In **RP (received pronunciation)** declaratives tend to be accompanied by a falling **intonation** (*windo͞ws*).

deictic: forms whose meaning can only derive from the context of utterance. In '*He*'s over *there now*' the meanings of *he, there* and *now* depend on who is being talked about (President Reagan, Fred next door, Tibbs the cat), his spatial relation to the speaker (three yards away, across the room, on the other side of the river) and when the utterance is made. Deictics include **pronouns** and adverbs of space (*here, there*) and time (*then, now*), etc.

directive: a **speech act** denoting utterances aimed at securing a response from the addressee (e.g. commands, requests, etc.) Jakobson's term 'conative' overlaps this concept in part. In terms of his model of language functions, however, the focus on the addressee would be a dominant one for a Rhetorical approach to utterance.

fall-rise: one of three major patterns of **intonation**, the others being a *fall* (associated with statements, signalling finality and assertion) and a *rise* (associated with certain types of question, signalling openness and a request for confirmation). A fall-rise combines aspects of both: in 'Do you like pop music?' 'Yes', the fall-rise on 'Yes' suggests the meaning 'sometimes', and invites further questions (e.g. 'Which singers?') whereas a falling intonation would tend to close off the exchange.

filler: a term denoting certain forms used in unscripted, informal speech such as hesitation phenomena (um, er, etc.) and phrases such as 'you know' and 'sort of'. Their function may be seen as either allowing the speaker time to think, or affording the listener an adequate level of redundancy (so that he or she is not overloaded with information). Since they have come to be associated with unscripted talk they may also be regarded as markers of informality.

historic present: the use of a simple present tense to refer to actions undertaken and completed in the past. It is found in both oral and written narratives (for example, D. H. Lawrence's *The Rainbow*, Chapter 5, 'Wedding at the Marsh') in a number of different languages. It is conventionally associated with an effect of 'immediacy' in story-telling – 'I *creep* up to bed' being more 'vivid' than 'I *crept* up to bed' – but this view has recently been challenged by Wolfson (*see* Bibliography).

homophonous: forms identical in sound, but having different meanings are homophones (homo = same, phone = sound), e.g. 'peace' and 'piece', both pronounced /pi:s/ in most varieties of English. A species of pun.

imperative: *see* **bald imperative**.

interrogative: the grammatical structure most closely associated with questions. They may be signalled by an inversion of subject and verb (as in 'Has she?'), the presence of a *wh-* word such as *who, what, why, when* (as in *'Why* did they?') or, in speech, a particular intonation (usually rising). *See* **polar** and **tag question**.

intonation: the rise and fall in **pitch** which is an integral part of meaning in the spoken English utterance. In RP, for instance, a rising intonation signals that 'He missed the train' is a question rather than a statement. An emphatic falling intonation on 'He' in 'He likes Beethoven' emphasizes 'he' as opposed to anyone else. Written usage needs to use other devices (word-order variations, underlining, italics, other details of layout) to signal such dimensions of meaning, but there are no simple one-to-one correspondences. The term 'inflection' is sometimes used in popular usage to denote intonation. *See also* **fall-rise, nucleus**, and **pitch**.

left-branching structure: in a sentence containing many clauses there are choices to be made about where to place the main clause (*see* **co-ordination**). If put last, the preceding clauses are accordingly to the left of the main clause. In 'Although I had walked all day, and had had little to eat, having seen neither shop nor habitation, I couldn't sleep' the effect of delaying the main clause 'I couldn't sleep' may be one of suspense. In general, however, left-branching structures are more easily processed by the eye than the ear, so that they tend to be more commonly used in writing than in speech.

ludic: at the most general level, using language as something to be played with, for its own sake, as a source of delight. More specifically, utterances can be enjoyed on account of their material properties (e.g. sound-patterns such as alliteration and rhyme), semantic ambiguities (as in puns) or patterns of regularity in discourse (as in games of repartee, banter, mock-insult, etc.) Readers and listeners can also indulge in games of interpretation, as when we see a gap between a possible interpretation and what we assume was the writer's (or speaker's) intention. The term is intended to be more inclusive than either *aesthetic* or *poetic* (*see* Theoretical postscript).

metalingual: one of the things we often need to talk about is language itself, and for this we need special terminology or *metalanguage*. Utterances like 'How do you pronounce Shrewsbury?' or 'What does "hyperbaton" mean?' have what is called a metalingual function; they are inquiring into the organization of language, or code, as Jakobson termed it (*see* Theoretical postscript).

nasal: a consonant whose pronunciation is accompanied by expelling air not through the mouth but through the nose. /n/ in 'nose',

/m/ in 'mother' and ŋ/ in 'thing' are nasal consonants in
English. In some languages like French certain vowels are
nasalized e.g. *un* (one), where the consonant is not sounded
(unless followed by a vowel). Some accents of English have
a nasal colouring, i.e. a certain amount of air is released nasally
in the general course of articulation.

new information: the 'information' in an utterance can be divided into
what the speaker/writer assumes the audience knows already
(and therefore treats as given) and what is assumed to be new.
New information carries the intonational **nucleus**. In 'He was
talking to me' it is 'He was talking' that is given, and 'me' that
is new. Given information tends to be 'definite' (often
specified by 'the', or pronouns referring back to words already
mentioned – *see* **cohesive devices**) but it is important to note
that the given/new distinction is not *determined* by the forms
of sentences, and that there are different conventions in
different kinds of texts (both spoken and written). It is also
difficult to know how to distinguish information given in the
text from that assumed to be part of someone's general cultural
knowledge.

nucleus: relates to **intonation**, and denotes the syllable to which the
major change in pitch is attached. *See also* **pitch**.

orientation: Labov's term for those clauses which contain information
about the when, where, and who of a story. Thus '*My* old
man . . . when he lived in London (that was about fifty years
ago) . . .' orientates by identifying a protagonist (an old man),
where the action occurred (London) and when (fifty years
ago). Orientating information typically occurs at the
beginning of a narrative but can also be distributed in strategic
places elsewhere. *See* **coda**.

palatalization: in the description of sounds the degree of raising of the
tongue in the mouth, and the part of the tongue raised, are
of great importance. A *palatal* consonant is one where the
front of the tongue is raised against or adjacent to the hard
palate (the roof of the mouth behind the upper teeth-ridge),
e.g. the initial sounds in 'yet', 'shed' and the medial
consonant in 'leisure'.

phatic: a great deal of what we say to others communicates not so
much our ideas, emotions, or 'information' as such, but a
desire to establish or maintain social contact. Small talk at
parties and talking about the weather are classic instances of
such phatic uses of language. It is arguable that this function
– included by Jakobson in his model (*see* Theoretical
postscript) – is constantly undervalued in school and in the
wider society.

phonological: relating to the sound-structure of a particular language
or variety. Most varieties of English have a sound-system of
about forty-four *phonemes*, sounds capable of bringing about

a change in meaning (e.g. /p/ and /b/ in 'pin' and 'bin'). Each phoneme, however, has a variety of possible phonetic realizations, so that the number of actual sounds produced by a speaker may be very large. A major characteristic of verse is the application of a relatively high degree of phonological patterning – of syllables (giving rhythm) and of equivalent sounds (as in rhyme and alliteration).

pitch: almost all speech has a musical quality in that certain syllables have a higher or lower pitch than others (*see* **intonation, fall-rise** and **nucleus**). Physiologically, pitch is related to the rate of vibration of the vocal folds in the larynx, and may vary according to the age and gender of the speaker.

pitch concord: an important function of intonation is the management of an interaction between speakers. Generally speaking, you can signal disagreement with something just said by a rise in pitch on the initial part of your utterance. It has been found, however, that there is a strong tendency to maintain a similar pitch-height between the end of one utterance and the beginning of a response: in other words, *agreement* is expressed. This tendency can be exploited, for instance, in utterances such as 'You'll come, won't you?', where the speaker ends on a pitch between high and low, anticipating an agreement on the part of the listener, whose initial pitch is likely to be in concord with the final pitch of the questioner.

plosive (or *stop*): a consonant made by 'stopping' the air behind a closure of speech organs (tongue, teeth-ridge, lips, etc.) and then releasing it with an explosive impact. The initial consonants of *pill, bill, till, dill, kill* and *gill* (of a fish) are plosives.

polar question: the kind of question structured to invite either a 'yes' or a 'no' in reply, e.g. 'Are you John Roberts?' or 'Has she come home yet?' *See* **interrogative** and **tag-question**.

pragmatic force: usually termed *illocutionary force*, this refers to the action performed by a particular utterance, i.e., the **speech act** with which it is associated. Thus the pragmatic force of 'I'll give you back that fiver tomorrow' may be interpreted as a promise, 'Don't be late' as a warning. The relationship between pragmatic force and grammatical *form* is indirect, and a crucial aspect of learning a language is the interpretation of utterances in terms of the possible actions they may perform.

pre-sequence: when making a request or invitation the face of either the speaker or the listener (or both) can be saved if the speaker uses a pre-sequence. Thus, instead of risking refusal by asking someone outright 'D'you fancy coming out for a drink tonight?' a speaker might ask 'Are you doing anything tonight?' and only if the response is appropriate go on to make the invitation.

pronoun: generally speaking, words which *substitute* for nouns or noun
phrases as in '*He* came in' where 'he' stands for, say 'the bald-
headed man'. The most well-known group of pronouns are the
personal pronouns: first person singular *I, me, my, mine,
myself*, second person singular *you, you, your, yours, yourself*,
third person singular *he/she, him/her, his/her, his/hers,
himself/herself*, and so on. The precise reference of 'you' and
'we' in, say, political discourse is often problematical, and is
worthy of close attention. *See* **deictic**. Other classes of pronoun
are demonstrative (*this, that, those*, etc.), interrogative (*who,
which, what*, etc.) and negative (*none, nobody*, etc.).

proposition: Loosely speaking, whatever is expressed by a **declarative**
sentence. Propositional meaning, however, is only one part of
an utterance's meaning, and it is the one that can be considered
in terms of truth-value (is is true or false?). Thus if I say 'I
was born in England' and then go on to say 'In France, my
birth-place, the weather's better', one of the propositions in
the second sentence contradicts that of the first, and they
therefore cannot both be true. It will be seen that the
proposition embedded in an utterance has an abstract quality,
since the same one can be expressed differently in different
sentences. Logic and philosophy tend to privilege propositional
meaning, and it is often seen as more important than other
kinds of meaning.

referential: the function of language to 'refer' to objects, states, events,
and people in the 'real world'. The notion that this reality is
given, that language is capable of 'reflecting' it in a direct and
unproblematical way, and that this is the major (even sole)
function of language, has now achieved the status of 'common
sense'. The structuralist and post-structuralist view, however,
maintains that 'reality' is actually structured by language.

RP (received pronunciation):   the accent (pronunciation) of English
which traditionally has enjoyed the greatest prestige among
English-speaking people. Historically an accent taught in the
nineteenth-century public schools, it has since come to be
identified in many people's minds with 'Standard English',
from which it should be distinguished. Standard English is
most clearly associated with writing, and is a variety with its
own range of vocabulary and grammatical forms capable of
being spoken in any accent (including, of course, RP, speakers
of which will invariably use the standard forms).

rhotic: accents described as rhotic pronounce /r/ wherever it is found
in the spelt form of a word. Thus rhotic accents distinguish
fort and *lore* from *fought* and *law* since in the case of the first
two words /r/ – before a consonant and in word-final position
respectively – is sounded. Rhotic accents in the British Isles
are found in Ireland, Scotland, and south-western counties

of England, and part of Wales and Lancashire (as well as much of USA and Canada in the wider Anglophone world).

speech act: utterances can be seen as having a **referential** value, but they can also be seen as performing actions such as claiming, asserting, warning, promising, etc. Speech Act theory tries to group such actions under more general categories such as *commissives* (where the speaker undertakes to do something, e.g. promising) and *verdictives* (where the speaker evaluates something, e.g. passing judgement). Others include **declarations** and **directives**. Speech Acts can be seen as more or less direct: compare 'Pass me that spanner' with 'I'd like that spanner', 'Can you pass that spanner?', 'Would you mind passing that spanner', 'I wish I could reach that spanner', etc.

synonym: words similar in meaning, e.g. *hide/conceal, deep/profound*, are called synonyms. In principle, a word ought to be substitutable by its synonym, but in practice no two words ever have exactly the same meaning.

tag-question: a **polar question** 'tagged' to the end of a statement, seeking confirmation of its truth, e.g. 'We went to Spain, didn't we?' or 'Nobody does that, do they?'. In casual, relaxed conversation tag questions may be seen as ways of seeking agreement, of drawing another into the conversation; in other contexts they have been viewed as an index of uncertainty and insecurity.

turn-taking: if language is seen as verbal interaction, or dialogue, the principle of turn-taking will be of obvious importance. In formal settings such as court-rooms and schools the turn-taking sequence is relatively fixed: the powerful participant determines the responses of the less powerful, often by the use of questions. For casual conversations among friends and acquaintances, however, it is less easy to specify how turns are managed: people learn unconsciously a set of non-verbal 'cues' and in general succeed in avoiding too much overlap between speakers. *See* **adjacency pair**.

Bibliography

We have generally tried to use the most recent and accessible editions of the works cited. In all cases the date given is that of the edition used, not the date of publication (although this often has curious-looking effects when classical and literary texts are cited).

Abel, E. (ed.) (1982) *Writing and Sexual Difference*, Brighton: Harvester.

Abrahams, R. (1984) 'The training of the man of words in talking sweet', in R. Bauman (ed.), *Verbal Art as Performance*, Prospect Heights, Ill.: Waveland Press, 117–32.

Abrams, M. H. (1972) 'Orientation of critical theories', in D. Lodge (ed.), *Twentieth-Century Literary Criticism*, London: Longman, 1–26.

Adorno, T. (1981) *Prisms* (trans. S. and S. Weber), Cambridge, Mass.: MIT Press.

Adorno, T. and Horkheimer, M. (1979) *Dialectic of Enlightenment* (trans. J. Cumming), London: Verso.

Aers, D. and Kress, G. (1981) 'The language of social order: individual, society and social process in *King Lear*', in D. Aers, B. Hodge, and G. Kress (eds.), *Literature, Language and Society in England 1580–1680*, Dublin: Gill & MacMillan, 75–99.

Agrippa, H. C. (1575) *Of the Vanitie and Uncertaintie of Artes and Sciences*, London (English translation).

Andersen, F. (1984) *Commonplace and Creativity: the Role of Formulaic Diction in Anglo-Scottish Balladry*, Odense: Odense University Press.

Andersen, F. and Pettitt, T. (1979) 'Mrs Brown of Falkland: a singer of tales?', in *Journal of American Folklore*, XCII, 1–24.

Anon. (1964) *Ad Herennium*, (ed. and trans. H. Caplan), Loeb Classical Library, London: Heinemann.

Arendt, H. (1958) *The Origins of Totalitarianism*, London: Allen & Unwin.
Arendt, H. (1973) *On Revolution*, Harmondsworth: Penguin.
Aristotle (1926) *The 'Art' of Rhetoric* (trans. J. H. Freese), Loeb Classical Library, London: Heinemann.
Atkinson, J. M. (1984) *Our Masters' Voices: The Language and Body Language of Politics*, London: Methuen.
Atkinson J. M. and Drew, P. (1979) *Order in Court; The Organization of Verbal Interaction in Judicial Settings*, London: Macmillan.
Auerbach, E. (1953) *Mimesis: The Representation of Reality in Western Literature*, Princeton, N.J.: Princeton University Press.
Austen, J. (1966) *Emma* (ed. R. Blythe), Harmondsworth: Penguin.
Austin, J. L. (1962) *How to Do Things with Words*, Oxford: Oxford University Press.
Bakhtin, M. M. (1968) *Rabelais and his World* (trans. H. Iswolsky), Cambridge, Mass.: MIT Press.
Bakhtin, M. M. (1981) *The Dialogic Imagination: Four Essays* (ed. M. Holquist, trans. C. Emerson and M. Holquist), Austin: University of Texas Press.
Bakhtin, M. M. (1984) *Problems of Dostoevsky's Poetics* (ed. and trans. C. Emerson), Manchester: Manchester University Press.
Baldick, C. (1983) *The Social Mission of English Studies 1848–1932*, Oxford: Clarendon Press.
Barnett, A. (1982) *Iron Britannia*, London: Allison & Busby.
Barthes, R. (1973) *Mythologies* (ed. and trans. A. Lavers), London: Paladin.
Barthes, R. (1975a), *The Pleasure of the Text* (trans. R. Miller), New York: Hill & Wang.
Barthes, R. (1975b) *S/Z* (trans. R. Miller), London: Cape.
Barthes, R. (1977) *Image – Music – Text* (essays selected and translated by S. Heath), London: Fontana.
Barthes, R. (1986) *The Responsibility of Forms: Critical Essays on Music, Art and Representation* (trans. R. Howard), Oxford: Blackwell.
Barton, J. (1984) *Playing Shakespeare*, London: Methuen.
Bascom, W. E. (1965) 'Four functions of folklore', in A. Dundes (ed.) *The Study of Folklore*, Englewood Cliffs, N.J.: Prentice-Hall, pp. 279–98.
Başgöz, I. (1975) 'The tale-singer and his audience', in D. Ben-Amos and K. Goldstein (eds), *Folklore: Performance and Communication*, The Hague: Mouton, 143–206.
Baudrillard, J. (1983) *Simulations* (trans. P. Foss, P. Patton, and P. Beitchman), New York: Semiotext(e) Inc.
Bauman, R. (ed.) (1984) *Verbal Art as Performance*, Prospect Heights, Ill.: Waveland Press (2nd edn).
Bauman, R. and Sherzer, J. (eds) (1974) *Explorations in the Ethnography of Speaking*, Cambridge: Cambridge University Press.
Belsey, C. (1980) *Critical Practice*, London: Methuen.
Ben Amos, D. (1972) 'Toward a definition of folklore in context', in

A. Paredes and R. Bauman (eds), *Towards New Perspectives in Folklore*, Austin: University of Texas Press, 3–15.

Ben-Amos D. and Goldstein, K. (eds) (1975) *Folklore: Performance and Communication*, The Hague: Mouton.

Bennett, W. L. and Feldman, M. S. (1981) *Reconstructing Reality in the Courtroom*, New Brunswick, N.J.: Rutgers University Press.

Beer, G. (1983) *Darwin's Plots: Evolutionary Narrative in Darwin, George Eliot and Nineteenth-century Fiction*, London: Routledge & Kegan Paul.

Benjamin, W. (1970) *Illuminations* (ed. H. Arendt, trans. H. Zohn), London: Cape.

Berkeley, G. (1901) *The Works of George Berkeley, Vol. II, Philosophical Works 1732–33* (ed. A. C. Fraser), Oxford: Clarendon Press.

Billig, M. (1986) 'Thinking and Arguing', inaugural lecture, Loughborough University, Loughborough: Echo Press.

Billig, M. (1987) *Arguing and Thinking: A Rhetorical Approach to Social Psychology*, Cambridge: Cambridge University Press.

Billig, M. (1988) 'The notion of prejudice: rhetorical and ideological aspects', *Text* 8, 91–110.

Bloch E., Lukács, G., Brecht, B., Benjamin, W., and Adorno, T. (1980) *Aesthetics and Politics* (ed. and trans. R. Taylor), London: Verso.

Bloom, H. (1987) 'From topos to trope', in C. Norris and R. Machin (eds), *Post-Structuralist Readings of English Poetry*, Cambridge: Cambridge University Press.

Booth, M. (1981) *The Experience of Song*, New Haven: Yale University Press.

Booth, W. C. (1974a) *Modern Dogma and the Rhetoric of Assent*, Notre Dame: University of Notre Dame Press.

Booth, W. C. (1974b) *A Rhetoric of Irony*, Chicago: University of Chicago Press.

Booth, W. C. (1983) *The Rhetoric of Fiction*, Chicago: University of Chicago Press (2nd edn).

Boyes, G. (1986) 'New directions – old destinations: a consideration of the role of the tradition-bearer in folksong research', in I. Russell (ed.), *Singer, Song and Scholar*, Sheffield: Sheffield Academic Press, 9–17.

Bronson, B. (1959–72) *The Traditional Tunes of the Child Ballads*, Princeton, N. J.: Princeton University Press.

Bronson, B. (1969) *The Ballad as Song*, Berkeley: University of California Press.

Bronson, B. (1976) *The Singing Tradition of the Child Ballads*, Princeton N. J.: Princeton University Press.

Brown, P. and Levinson, S. (1978) 'Universals in language usage: politeness phenomena' in E. N. Goody (ed.) *Questions and Politeness: Strategies in Social Interaction*, Cambridge: Cambridge University Press, 56–311.

Buchan, D. (1972) *The Ballad and the Folk*, London: Routledge & Kegan Paul.

Burke, K. (1961) *Attitudes Toward History*, Boston: Beacon Press.

Burke, K. (1969) *A Rhetoric of Motives*, Berkeley and Los Angeles: University of Los Angeles Press.

Burrow, J. (1982) *Medieval Writers and their Work*, Oxford: Oxford University Press.

Canovan, M. (1974) *The Political Thought of Hannah Arendt*, London: Dent.

Carr, E. H. (1964) *What is History?* Harmondsworth: Penguin.

Carroll, J. (1986) 'Michael McCarthy, singer and ballad seller', in I. Russell (ed.), *Singer, Song and Scholar*, Sheffield: Sheffield Academic Press, 19–29.

Centre for Contemporary Cultural Studies (1978) *On Ideology*, London: Hutchinson.

Chambers, R. (1984) *Story and Situation: Narrative Seduction and the Power of Fiction*, Manchester: Manchester University Press.

Chatman, S. (1978) *Story and Discourse: Narrative Structure in Fiction and Film*, Ithaca: Cornell University Press.

Chiaromonte, N. (1970) *The Paradox of History*, London: Weidenfeld & Nicholson.

Ci, J. (1988) 'An alternative to Genette's theory of order', *Style* 22, 18–38.

Cicero (1949) *De Inventione, De Optimo Genere Oratorum, Topica* (trans. M. Hubell), Loeb Classical Library, London: Heinemann.

Cicero (1948) *De Oratore*, Books I and II (trans. E. W. Sutton and H. Rackham), London: Heinemann (revised edn.).

Conley, T. (1985) 'Reading ordinary viewing', *Diacritics* 15, Spring, 4–17.

Connor, S. (1985) *Charles Dickens*, Oxford: Blackwell.

Cosslett, T. (1982) *The 'Scientific Movement' and Victorian Literature*, Brighton: Harvester.

Coulthard, M. (1985) *An Introduction to Discourse Analysis*, London: Longman (2nd edn).

Coulthard, M. and Montgomery, M. (1981) 'The structure of monologue', in M. Coulthard and M. Montgomery (eds) *Studies in Discourse Analysis*, London: Routledge & Kegan Paul, 31–9.

Couzins, D. H. (ed.) (1986) *Foucault: A Critical Reader*, Oxford: Blackwell.

Covington, D. (1986) 'Aristotelian rhetorical appeals in the poetry of Matthew Arnold' in *Victorian Poetry* 24, 149–61.

Crystal, D. and Davy, D. (1968) *Investigating English Style*, London: Longman.

Culler, J. (1975) *Structuralist Poetics: Structuralism, Linguistics and the Study of Literature*, London: Routledge & Kegan Paul.

Culler, J. (1981) *The Pursuit of Signs: Semiotics, Literature, Deconstruction*, London: Routledge & Kegan Paul.

Curtius, E. R. (1953) *European Literature and the Latin Middle Ages* (trans. W. R. Trask), London: Routledge & Kegan Paul.

Danet, B. (1980) 'Language in the legal process', *Law and Society Review* 14, pp. 445–565.

Davis, H. and Walton, P. (1983) 'Death of a Premier: consensus and closure in international news', in H. Davis and P. Walton (eds) *Language, Image, Media*, Oxford: Blackwell, pp. 8–49.

de Man, P. (1979) *Allegories of Reading: Figural Language in Rousseau, Nietzsche, Rilke and Proust*, New Haven: Yale University Press.

de Man, P. (1983) *Blindness and Insight*, London: Methuen (2nd edn).

de Man, P. (1984) *The Rhetoric of Romanticism*, New York: Columbia University Press.

Deming, R. H. (1985) 'Discourse, talk, television', *Screen* 26, 6, November/December, 88–93.

De Quincy, T. (1967) *Selected Essays on Rhetoric* (ed. F. Burwick), Carbondale and Edwardsville: Southern Illinois University Press.

Derrida, J. (1982) *Dissemination* (trans. B. Johnson), London: Athlone Press.

Derrida, J. (1983) 'The principle of reason, the university in the eyes of its pupils', *Diacritics* 13, Fall, 3–20.

Dews, P. (1987) *Logics of Disintegration: Post-Structuralist Thought and the Claims of Critical Theory*, London: Verso.

Dickens, C. (1968) *Martin Chuzzlewit* (ed. P. Furbank), Harmondsworth: Penguin.

Dixon, P. (1971) *Rhetoric*, London: Methuen.

Donovan, P. (1974) *Religious Language*, London: Sheldon Press.

Doody, M. (1980) ' "How shall we sing the Lord's song upon an alien soil?" The new Episcopalian liturgy', in L. Michaels and C. Ricks (eds) *The State of the Language*, Berkeley: University of California Press. pp. 108–24.

Douglass, D. (1973) *Pit Talk in County Durham*, History Workshop Pamphlets 10, Ruskin College, Oxford.

Dundes, A. (ed.) (1965) *The Study of Folklore*, Englewood Cliffs, N.J.: Prentice-Hall.

Durant, A. (1984a) *Conditions of Music*, London: Macmillan.

Durant, A. (1984b) 'The concept of secondary orality; observations about speech and text in modern communications media', *Dalhousie Review*, 64, 2, 332–53.

Eagleton, T. (1976) *Criticism and Ideology*, London: Verso.

Eagleton, T. (1981) *Walter Benjamin or Towards a Revolutionary Criticism*, London: Verso.

Eagleton, T. (1983) *Literary Theory: An Introduction*, Oxford: Blackwell.

Eagleton, T. (1984) *The Function of Criticism: From* The Spectator *to Post-Structuralism*, London: Verso.

Easthope, A. (1983) *Poetry as Discourse*, London: Methuen.

Eden, K. (1986) *Poetic and Legal Fiction in the Aristotelian Tradition*, Princeton, N.J.: Princeton University Press.

Elam, K. (1980) *The Semiotics of Theatre and Drama*, London: Methuen.

Elam, K. (1984) *Shakespeare's Universe of Discourse: Language-Games in the Comedies*, Cambridge: Cambridge University Press.

Empson, W. (1951) *The Structure of Complex Words*, London: Chatto & Windus.

Empson, W. (1953) *Seven Types of Ambiguity*, London: Chatto & Windus (3rd edn).

Ennis, S. (1956) 'Some "English" ballads and folk songs recorded in Ireland 1952–4', *Journal of the English Folk Dance and Song Society*, VIII, 16–28.

Faral, E. (1924) *Les Arts poétiques du XIIe et du XIIIe siècle: recherches et documents sur la technique littéraire du Moyen Age*, Paris: Honore Champion.

Felman, S. (1985) 'Postal survival, or the question of the navel', *Yale French Studies* 69, 49–72.

Feyerabend, P. (1987) *Farewell to Reason*, London: Verso.

Fine, E. (1984) *The Folklore Text: From Performance to Print*, Bloomington: Indiana University Press.

Finley, M. I. (1985) *Democracy Ancient and Modern*, London: Hogarth Press.

Finnegan, R. (1977) *Oral Poetry: Its Nature, Significance and Social Context*, Cambridge: Cambridge University Press.

Fish, S. (1967) *Surprised by Sin*, London: Macmillan.

Fish, S. (1980) *Is there a Text in this Class?* Cambridge, Mass.: Harvard University Press.

Fiske, J. and Hartley, J. (1978) *Reading Television*, London: Methuen.

Florescu, R. (1977) *In Search of Frankenstein*, London: New English Library.

Foster, H. (ed.) (1985) *Postmodern Culture*, London: Pluto Press.

Foucault, M. (1987) *The History of Sexuality: An Introduction* (trans. R. Hurley), Harmondsworth: Penguin.

Fowler, D. (1968) *A Literary History of the Popular Ballad*, Durham, North Carolina: Duke University Press.

Fowler, R. (1981) *Literature as Social Discourse: The Practice of Linguistic Criticism*, London: Batsford.

Fowler, R. (1986) *Linguistic Criticism*, Oxford: Oxford University Press.

Fox, M. (1984) 'Linguistic re-analysis and oral transmission', *Poetics* 13, 217–38.

Frye, N. (1982) *The Great Code: The Bible and Literature*, London: Routledge & Kegan Paul.

Furman, N. (1985) 'The politics of language', in G. Greene and C. Kahn (eds), *Making a Difference: Feminist Literary Criticism*, London: Methuen.

Gadamer, H.-G. (1979) *Truth and Method*, London: Sheed & Ward (2nd edn).

Gadamer, H.-G. (1980) *Dialogue and Dialectic: Eight Hermeneutical*

Studies on Plato (trans. P. Smith), New Haven: Yale University Press.

Gallie, W. B. (1960) *Philosophy and the Historical Understanding*, New York: Schocken Books.

Genette, G. (1980) *Narrative Discourse* (trans. J. Lewin), Oxford: Blackwell.

Genette, G. (1982) *Figures of Literary Discourse* (trans. A. Sheridan), Oxford: Blackwell.

Glasgow University Media Group (1976) *Bad News*, London: Routledge & Kegan Paul.

Goffman, E. (1981) *Forms of Talk*, Oxford: Blackwell.

Goodrich, P. (1984a) 'Rhetoric as jurisprudence: an introduction to the politics of legal language', *Oxford Journal of Legal Studies* 4, 88–122.

Goodrich, P. (1984b) 'Law and language: an historical and critical introduction', *Journal of Law and Society* II, 2, Summer, 173–206.

Goodrich, P. (1985) 'Historical aspects of legal interpretation', *Indiana Law Journal* 61, 327–50.

Goodrich, P. (1986) *Reading the Law: A Critical Introduction to Legal Method and Techniques*, Oxford: Blackwell.

Goodrich, P. (1987) *Legal Discourse: Studies in Linguistics, Rhetoric and Legal Analysis*, London: Macmillan.

Goody, E. (ed.) (1978) *Questions and Politeness: Strategies in Social Interaction*, Cambridge: Cambridge University Press.

Gower, H. (1968) 'Jeannie Robertson: portrait of a traditional singer', *Scottish Studies* 12, 113–26.

Gramsci, A. (1957) *The Modern Prince and Other Writings*, (trans. L. Marks) New York: International Publishers.

Gramsci, A. (1985) *Selections from Cultural Writings* (ed. D. Forgacs and G. Nowell Smith, trans. W. Boelhower), London: Lawrence & Wishart.

Greene, G. and Kahn, C. (eds) (1985) *Making a Difference: Feminist Literary Criticism*, London: Methuen.

Griffith, J. (1973) 'Narrative technique and the meaning of history in Benet and MacLeish', *Journal of Narrative Technique* 3, 3–19.

Habermas, J. (1987) *The Philosophical Discourse of Modernity* (trans. C. Lawrence), Cambridge: Polity Press.

Hall, S., Hobson, D., Lowe, A., and Willis, P. (eds) (1980) *Culture, Media, Language*, London: Hutchinson.

Harari, J. (1984) 'The pleasures of science and the pains of philosophy: Balzac's *Quest for the Absolute*', *Yale French Studies* 67, 135–63.

Hardy, B. (1976) *The Moral Art of Dickens*, London: Athlone Press.

Hardy, B. (1985) *Forms of Feeling in Victorian Fiction*, London: Peter Owen.

Harker, D. (1985) *Fakesong: The Manufacture of British 'Folksong' 1700 to the Present Day*, Milton Keynes: Open University Press.

Harris, S. (1984a) 'Questions as a mode of control in magistrates' courts', *International Journal of the Sociology of Language* 49, 4, 5–27.

Harris, S. (1984b) 'The form and function of threats in court', *Language and Communication* 4, 4, 247–71.

Harris, J. and Wilkinson, J. (eds) (1986) *Reading Children's Writing: A Linguistic View*, London: Allen & Unwin.

Hartley, J. (1982) *Understanding News*, London: Methuen.

Hartman, G. (1964) *Wordsworth's Poetry 1787–1814*, New Haven: Yale University Press.

Heidegger, M. (1971) *Poetry, Lanuguage, Thought* (trans. A. Hofstadter), New York: Harper & Row.

Hill, C. (1977) *Milton and the English Revolution*, London: Faber.

Hill, G. (1984) *The Lords of Limit: Essays on Literature and Ideas*, London: Deutsch.

Hoey, M. and Winter, E. (1981), 'Believe me for mine honour', *Language and Style* 14, 4, 315–39.

Horne, D. (1986) *The Public Culture: The Triumph of Industrialism*, London: Pluto Press.

Howell, W. S. (1956) *Logic and Rhetoric in England 1500–1700*, Princeton, N.J.: Princeton University Press.

Hunt, A. (1981) *The Language of Television: Uses and Abuses*, London: Methuen.

Hunter, L. (1984) *Rhetorical Stance in Modern Literature: Allegories of Love and Death*, London: Macmillan.

Hyman, S. E. (1962) *The Tangled Bank: Darwin, Marx, Frazer and Freud as Imaginative Writers*, New York: Atheneum.

Iser, W. (1974) *The Implied Reader: Patterns of Communication in Prose Fiction from Bunyan to Beckett*, Baltimore: Johns Hopkins University Press.

Jackson, R. (1981) *Fantasy: The Literature of Subversion*, London: Methuen.

Jakobson, R. (1960) 'Closing statement: linguistics and poetics', in T. A. Sebeok (ed.), *Style in Language*, Cambridge, Mass.: MIT Press.

Jameson, F. (1972) *The Prison-House of Language*, Princeton, N.J.: Princeton University Press.

Jennings, H. (1985) *Pandaemonium: The Coming of the Machine as seen by Contemporary Observers* (ed. M.-L. Jennings and C. Madge), London: Deutsch.

Johnson, B. (1980) *The Critical Difference; Essays in the Contemporary Rhetoric of Reading*, Baltimore: Johns Hopkins University Press.

Johnson, B. (1985) 'Rigorous unreliability', *Yale French Studies* 69, 73–80.

Jonson, B. (1953) *Timber* (ed. R. Walker), Syracuse: University of Syracuse Press.

Kennedy, G. (1963) *The Art of Persuasion in Greece*, London: Routledge & Kegan Paul.

Kennedy, G. (1972), *The Art of Rhetoric in the Roman World*, Princeton, N.J.: Princeton University Press.

Kennedy, G. (1980) *Classical Rhetoric and its Christian and Secular Tradition from Ancient to Modern Times*, London: Croom Helm.

Kennedy, P. (1975) *The Folk Songs of Britain*, London: Oak.
Kerferd, G. B. (1981) *The Sophistic Movement*, Cambridge: Cambridge University Press.
Kermode, F. (1979) *The Genesis of Secrecy: On the Interpretation of Narrative*, Cambridge, Mass.: Harvard University Press.
Kerrigan, J. (1985) 'Wordsworth and the sonnet: building, dwelling, thinking', *Essays in Criticism* 35, 45–71.
Kershner, R. B. (1986) 'The artist as text: dialogism and incremental repetition in Joyce's *Portrait*', *English Literary History* 53, 881–93.
Kirk, G. S. (1976) *Homer and the Oral Tradition*, Cambridge: Cambridge University Press.
Kirshenblatt-Gimblett, B. (ed.) (1976) *Speech Play*, Philadelphia: University of Pennsylvania Press.
Kress, G. (1982) *Learning to Write*, London: Routledge & Kegan Paul.
Kristeva, J. (1980) *Desire in Language* (ed. L. S. Roudiez, trans. T. Gora, A. Jardine, and L. S. Roudiez), New York: Columbia University Press.
Kristeva, J. (1985) *The Kristeva Reader* (ed. T. Moi), London: Methuen.
Kritzman, L. D. (1984) 'Barthesian free play', *Yale French Studies* 66, 189–210.
Kuhn, T. S. (1970) *The Structure of Scientific Revolutions*, Chicago: Chicago University Press (2nd edn).
Kuhn, T. S. (1977) *The Essential Tension: Selected Studies in Scientific Tradition and Change*, Chicago: University of Chicago Press.
Kurrick, M. J. (1979) *Literature and Negation*, New York: Columbia University Press.
Labov, W. (1972) 'The transformation of experience in narrative syntax', in *Language in the Inner City: Studies in the Black English Vernacular*, Philadelphia: University of Pennsylvania Press, 354–96.
Leavis, F. R. (1975) *The Living Principle: 'English' as a Discipline of Thought*, London: Chatto & Windus.
Leech, G. (1969) *A Linguistic Guide to English Poetry*, London: Longman.
Leech, G. (1983) *Principles of Pragmatics*, London: Longman.
Leech, G. and Short, M. H. (1981) *Style in Fiction*, London: Longman.
Lentricchia, F. (1983) *Criticism and Social Change*, Chicago: University of Chicago Press.
Lerman, C. L. (1983) 'Dominant discourse: the institutional voice and control of topic', in H. Davis and P. Walton (eds), *Language, Image, Media*, Oxford: Blackwell.
Lerner, L. (1985) 'Poetry as the play of signifiers', *Essays in Criticism* 35, 238–59.
Lewis, C. W. (1986) 'Identifications and divisions: Kenneth Burke and the Yale Critics', *Southern Review*, New Series 22, 93–102.
Liebes-Plesner, T. (1984) 'Rhetoric in the service of justice: the sociolinguistic construction of stereotypes in an Israeli rape trail', *Text* 4, 1/3, 173–92.

Límon, J. (1983) 'Western marxism and folklore: a critical introduction', *Journal of American Folklore* 96, 379, 34–52.

Lodge, D. (1966) *The Language of Fiction*, London: Routledge & Kegan Paul.

Lodge, D. (1977) *The Modes of Modern Writing*, London: Edward Arnold.

Lord, A. (1968) *The Singer of Tales*, New York: Atheneum.

Lyotard, J.-F. and Thebaud, J.-L. (1985) *Just Gaming* (trans. W. Godzich), Manchester: Manchester University Press.

Marcus, J. (ed.) (1981) *New Feminist Essays on Virginia Woolf*, London: Macmillan.

Marrou, H. I. (1956) *A History of Education in Antiquity* (trans. G. Lamb), New York: Sheed & Ward.

Masterman, L. (ed.) (1984) *Television Mythologies*, London: Commedia.

McArthur, C. (1980) *Television and History*, London: British Film Institute.

McCloskey, D. (1986) *The Rhetoric of Economics*, Brighton: Wheatsheaf.

McLuhan, M. (1959) 'Myth and mass media', *Daedalus* 88, 339–48.

Messenger, J. C. Jr. (1965) 'The role of proverbs in a Nigerian judicial system', in A. Dundes (ed.), *The Study of Folklore*, Englewood Cliffs, N.J.: Prentice Hall.

Michaels, L. and Ricks, C. (eds) (1980) *The State of the Language*, Berkeley: University of California Press.

Mill, J. S. (1974) *On Liberty* (ed. G. Himmelfarb), Harmondsworth: Penguin.

Miller, J. Hillis (1982) *Fiction and Repetition*, Oxford: Blackwell.

Moi, T. (ed.) (1985) *The Kristeva Reader*, London: Methuen.

Moi, T. (1986) *Sexual–Textual Politics: Feminist Literary Theory*, Oxford: Blackwell.

Mueller-Vollmer, K. (ed.) (1985) *The Hermeneutics Reader: Texts of the German Tradition from the Enlightenment to the Present*, Oxford: Blackwell.

Murdoch, J. E. (1978) 'The development of a critical temper: new approaches and modes of analysis in fourteenth-century philosophy, science and theology', in S. Wenzel (ed.), *Medieval and Renaissance Studies: Proceedings of the South-eastern Institute of Medieval and Renaissance Studies*, M. and R. series 7, Chapel Hill: University of North Carolina Press.

Murphy, J. J. (ed.) (1978) *Medieval Eloquence: Studies in the Theory and Practice of Medieval Rhetoric*, Berkeley: University of California Press.

Needham, J., *see* Ronan, C.

Newman, B. (1986) 'Narratives of seduction and the seduction of narrative: the frame structure of *Frankenstein*', *English Literary History* 53, 141–64.

Ngugi Wa Thiong'o (1965) *The River Between*, London: Heinemann.

Norris, C. (1983) *The Deconstructive Turn: Essays in the Rhetoric of Philosophy*, London: Methuen.

Norris, C. and Machin, R. (eds) (1987) *Post-Structuralist Readings of English Poetry*, Cambridge: Cambridge University Press.

Ochs, E. (1979) 'Transcription as theory', in E. Ochs and B. Schieffelin (eds), *Developmental Pragmatics*, New York: Academic Press, 43–72.

Ochs, E. and Schieffelin, B. (1983) *Acquiring Conversational Competence*, London: Routledge & Kegan Paul.

O'Barr, W. B. (1982) *Linguistic Evidence: Language, Power and Strategy in the Courtroom*, New York: Academic Press.

O'Kane, J. (1985) 'History, performance, counter-cinema – *Die Patriotin*', *Screen*, 26, 6, November/December, pp. 2–17.

Ong, W. J. (1958) *Ramus, Method and the Decay of Dialogue: From the Art of Discourse to the Art of Reason*, Cambridge, Mass.: University of Harvard Press.

Ong, W. J. (1975) 'The writer's audience is always a fiction', *Proceedings of the Modern Language Association* 40, 9–21.

Ong. W. J. (1982) *Orality and Literacy: Technologizing the Word*, London: Methuen.

Opie, I. and P. (1959) *The Lore and Language of Schoolchildren*, Oxford: Oxford University Press.

Paracelsus (and Crollius, O.) (1657) *Philosophy Reformed and Improved in Four Profound Tractates*, London.

Paredes,A. and Bauman, R. (eds) (1972) *Toward New Perspectives in Folklore*, Austin: University of Texas Press.

Pateman, T. (1980a) 'How to do things with images', *Theory and Society* 9, 603–22.

Pateman, T. (1980b) *Language, Truth and Politics: Towards a Radical Theory for Communication*, Sidmouth: Jean Stroud (2nd edn).

Peck, J. (1984) *The Modern Newspeak*, London: Harrap.

Pecora, V. (1985) '*Heart of Darkness* and the phenomenology of narrative voice', *English Literary History* 52, 993–1016.

Perelman, C. and Olbrechts-Tyteca, L. (1969) *The New Rhetoric: A Treatise on Argumentation* (trans. J. Wilkinson and P. Weaver), Notre Dame: Notre Dame University Press.

Plato (1941) *The Republic of Plato* (trans. with introduction and notes by F. M. Cornford), Oxford: Clarendon Press.

Plato (1956) *Protagoras and Meno* (trans. W. K. Guthrie), Harmondsworth: Penguin.

Plato (1971) *Gorgias* (trans. and introduction by W. Hamilton), Harmondsworth: Penguin.

Plato (1973) *Phaedrus* (trans. and introduction by W. Hamilton), Harmondsworth: Penguin.

Polanyi, L. (1979) 'So what's the point?', *Semiotica* 25, 207–41.

Polanyi, L. (1982a) 'Literary complexity in everyday storytelling', in D. Tannen (ed.), *Spoken and Written Language; Exploring Orality and Literacy*, Norwood, N.J.: Ablex, 155–70.

Polanyi, L. (1982b) 'Linguistic and social constraints on storytelling', *Journal of Pragmatics* 6, 5/6, 509–24.

Porter, J. (1976) 'Jeannie Robertson's "My Son David": a conceptual performance model', *Journal of American Folklore* 89, 7–26.

Prince, G. (1988) 'The disnarrated', *Style* 22, 1–8.

Propp, V. (1965) *The Morphology of the Folktale* (trans. L. A. Wagner and A. Dundes) Austin: University of Texas Press.

Punter, D. (1980) *The Literature of Terror*, London: Longman.

Puttenham, G. (1906) *The Arte of English Poesie* (ed. E. Arbor), London: Constable.

Rabkin, N. (1984) *Shakespeare and the Common Understanding*, Chicago: University of Chicago Press.

Radway, J. (1987) *Reading the Romance: Women, Patriarchy and Popular Literature*, London: Verso.

Reboul, O. (1984) *La Rhétorique*, Paris: Presses Universitaires de France.

Rée, J. (1987) *Philosophical Tales*, London, Methuen.

Richards, I. A. (1964) *Practical Criticism*, London: Routledge & Kegan Paul.

Richards, I. A. (1965) *The Philosophy of Rhetoric*, New York: Galaxy Books.

Richards, I. A. (1970) *Poetries and Sciences*, London: Routledge & Kegan Paul.

Ricoeur, P. (1981) *Hermeneutics and the Human Sciences* (ed. and trans. by J. B. Thompson), Cambridge: Cambridge University Press.

Riffaterre, M. (1980) *Semiotics of Poetry*, London: Metheun.

Rimmon-Kenan, S. (1983) *Narrative Fiction: Contemporary Poetics*, London: Methuen.

Robinson, J. A. (1981) 'Personal narratives re-considered', *Journal of American Folklore* 94, 371, 58–85.

Rogers, S. (ed.) (1976) *They Don't Speak our Language*, London: Edward Arnold.

Romaine, S. (1984) *The Language of Children and Adolescents: The Acquisition of Communicative Competence*, Oxford: Blackwell.

Ronan C. and Needham, J. (1978) *The Shorter Science and Civilisation in China, Volume I (An abridgement of J. Needham's original text)*, Cambridge: Cambridge University Press.

Rose, J. (1984) *The Case of Peter Pan: Or The Impossibility of Children's Fiction*, London: Macmillan.

Rosenberg, B. A. (1975) 'Oral sermons and oral narrative', in D. Ben-Amos and K. Goldstein (eds), *Folklore: Performance and Communication*, The Hague: Mouton, 75–101

Russell, D. A. (1967) 'Rhetoric and criticism', *Greece and Rome*, Second Series, 14, 130–49.

Russell, D. A. (1983) *Greek Declamation*, Cambridge: Cambridge University Press.

Russell, D. A. and Winterbottom, M. (eds) (1972) *Ancient Literary*

Criticism: The Principal Texts in New Translations, Oxford: Clarendon Press.

Russell, I. (ed.) (1986) *Singer, Song and Scholar*, Sheffield: Sheffield Academic Press.

Said, E. (1981) *Covering Islam*, London: Routledge & Kegan Paul.

Said, E. (1984) *The World, the Text and the Critic*, London: Faber.

Sanches, M. and Kirshenblatt-Gimblett, B. (1976) 'Children's traditional speech play and child language', in B. Kirshenblatt-Gimblett (ed.), *Speech Play*, Philadelphia: University of Pennsylvania Press, 65–110.

Saville-Troike, M. (1982) *The Ethnography of Communication: An Introduction*, Oxford: Blackwell.

Schlesinger, P., Murdock, G., and Elliott, P. (1983) *Televising Terrorism: Political Violence in Popular Culture*, London: Commedia.

Scholes, R. and Kellogg, R. (1966) *The Nature of Narrative*, Oxford: Oxford University Press.

Screen (1985) 'Acting' 26, 5, September/October, London: SEFT.

Scribner, S. and Cole, M. (1981) *The Psychology of Literacy*, Cambridge: Cambridge University Press.

Shapiro, M. (ed.) (1984) *Language and Politics*, Oxford: Blackwell.

Shelley, M. (1985) *Frankenstein* (ed. M. Hindle), Harmondsworth: Penguin.

Shepard, L. (1962) *The Broadside Ballad*, London: Herbert Jenkins.

Shields, H. (1972) 'The British ballads in Ireland', *Folklife*, 68–103.

Showalter, E. (1982) 'Feminist criticism in the wilderness', in E. Abel (ed.), Writing and Sexual Difference, Brighton: Harvester.

Sinfield, A. (1981) 'Against appropriation', *Essays in Criticism* 31, 181–95.

Sloane, T. O. (1985) *Donne, Milton and the End of Humanist Rhetoric*, Berkeley: University of California Press.

Spacks, P. M. (1975) *The Female Imagination*, New York: Knopf.

Stallybrass, P. and White, A. (1986) *The Politics and Poetics of Transgression*, London: Methuen.

Stanzel, F. K. (1984) *A Theory of Narrative* (trans. C. Goedsche), Cambridge: Cambridge University Press.

Staten, W. (1984) *Wittgenstein and Derrida*, Lincoln: University of Nebraska Press.

Steedman, C. (1983) *The Tidy House: Little Girls Writing*, London: Virago.

Street, B. (1984) *Literacy in Theory and Practice*, Cambridge: Cambridge University Press.

Stubbs, M. (1983) *Discourse Analysis*, Oxford: Blackwell.

Tannen, D. (ed.) (1982) *Spoken and Written Language; Exploring Orality and Literacy*, Norwood, N.J.: Ablex.

Tannen, D. (ed.) (1984) *Coherence in Spoken and Written Discourse*, Norwood, N.J.: Ablex.

Tedlock, D. (1983) 'On the translation of style in oral narrative', in D.

Tedlock, *The Spoken Word and the Work of Interpretation*, Philadelphia: University of Pennsylvania Press, 31–61.

Thomas, J. (1985) 'The language of power: towards a dynamic pragmatics', *Journal of Pragmatics*, 765–83.

Thompson, J. B. (1984) *Studies in the Theory of Ideology*, Cambridge: Polity Press.

Todorov, T. (1977) *The Poetics of Prose* (trans. R. Howard), Ithaca: Cornell University Press.

Todorov, T. (1984) *M. M. Bakhtin: The Dialogical Principle* (trans. W. Godzich), Manchester: Manchester University Press.

Todorov, T. (1988) 'Poetic truth: three interpretations', *Essays in Criticism*, 38, 2, April, 95–113.

Trotter, D. (1984) *The Making of the Reader: Language and Subjectivity in Modern American, English and Irish Poetry*, London: Macmillan.

Trudgill, P. (1982) 'Acts of conflicting identity: the sociolinguistics of British pop-song pronunciation', in P. Trudgill, *On Dialect*, Oxford: Blackwell, 141–60.

Valesio, P. (1977) ' "That glib and oylie art": Cordelia and the rhetoric of anti-rhetoric', *Versus*, 16, 91–117.

Vassbinder, S. H. (1984) *Scientific Attitudes in Mary Shelley's Frankenstein*, Ann Arbor, Michigan: UMI Research Press.

Vattimo, G. (1988) 'The end of (Hi)story', *Chicago Review* 35, 20–30.

Verdicchio, M. (1984) 'A reader like Phaedrus', *Diacritics* 14, Spring, 24–35.

Vickers, B. (1988) *In Defence of Rhetoric*, Oxford: Oxford University Press.

Vygotsky, L. S. (1962) *Thought and Language*, Cambridge, Mass.: MIT Press.

Vygotsky, L. S. (1978) *Mind in Society*, Cambridge, Mass.: Harvard University Press.

Warnke, G. (1984) *Gadamer: Hermeneutics, Tradition and Reason*, Cambridge: Polity Press.

Weimann, R. (1978) *Shakespeare and the Popular Tradition in the Theatre* (trans. R. Schwarz), Baltimore: Johns Hopkins University Press.

Wenzel, S. (ed.) (1978) *Medieval and Renaissance Studies: Proceedings of the South-eastern Institute of Medieval and Renaissance Studies*, M. and R. series 7, Chapel Hill: University of North Carolina Press.

White, H. (1978a) 'Ethnological "lie" and mythical "truth" ', *Diacritics* 8, Spring, 2–9.

White, H. (1978b) *Tropics of Discourse: Essays in Cultural Criticism*, Baltimore: Johns Hopkins University Press.

White, H. and Manuel, F. (1978) *Theories of History*, Los Angeles: William Andrews Clark Memorial Library.

White, H. and Brose, M. (eds) (1982) *Representing Kenneth Burke* (selected papers from the English Institute, new series 6), Baltimore: Johns Hopkins University Press.

Widdowson, J. (1976) 'The language of the child culture: pattern and tradition in language acquisition and socialization', in S. Rogers (ed.) *They Don't Speak Our Language*, London: Edward Arnold, 33–62.

Williams, R. (1961) *The Long Revolution*, London: Chatto & Windus.

Williams, R. (1963) *Culture and Society 1780–1950*, Harmondsworth: Penguin.

Williams, R. (1974) *Television: Technology and Cultural Form*, London: Fontana.

Williams, R. (1975) *The Country and the City*, London: Paladin.

Williams, R. (1976a) *Communications*, Harmondsworth: Penguin (3rd edn).

Williams, R. (1977) *Marxism and Literature*, Oxford: Oxford University Press.

Williams, R. (1981) *Culture*, London: Fontana.

Williams, R. (1982) 'On dramatic dialogue and monologue (particularly in Shakespeare)', in *Writing in Society*, London: Verso, 31–64.

Williams, R. (1983) *Keywords: A Vocabulary of Culture and Society*, London: Fontana (2nd edn).

Williamson, J. (1983) *Decoding Advertisements: Ideology and Meaning in Advertising*, London: Boyars.

Winnicott, D. (1980) *Playing and Reality*, Harmondsworth: Penguin.

Wolfson, N. (1982) *CHP: The Conversational Historical Present in Modern American English Narrative*, Dordrecht: Foris.

Woolf, V. (1977) *A Room of One's Own*, London: Granada.

Woolf, V. (1978) *Between the Acts*, London: Granada.

Yates, F. A. (1966) *The Art of Memory*, London: Routledge & Kegan Paul.

York, R. A. (1986) *The Poem as Utterance*, London: Methuen.

Young-Bruehl, E. (1982) *Hannah Arendt: For Love of the World*, New Haven: Yale University Press.

Index

Name Index

Agrippa, H. C., 168–9
Arendt, H., 102–3
Aristotle, 5, 6, 19, 33, 68, 75, 80, 84, 90, 91, 95, 101, 102, 145, 149, 152, 154, 178–9, 204, 206, 208, 214, 216, 225–6, 236
Atkinson, M., 25
Auerbach, E., 226
Austen, J., 83, 95

Bacon, F., 105, 168, 194
Bakhtin, M., 72, 74, 83, 89, 95–6, 105, 109, 118, 149, 150, 170, 175, 206, 245
Barthes, R., 154, 184, 243
Benveniste, E., 117, 191
Berkeley, G., 224, 225, 231
Billig, M., 105
Booth, M., 43
Booth, W., 226
Bourdieu, P., 210
Brando, M., 63
Brown, A., 55
Burke, K., 83, 90, 95, 110, 178–9, 222
Burrow, J., 153

Carr, E. H., 178–9, 192
Cato, 71
Chekhov, A., 63
Child, F. J., 51
Cicero, 2, 3, 8, 13, 16, 37, 89, 101, 104, 111, 116, 204, 208, 236
Climaticus, 137
Cronin, E., 55
Curtius, E. R., 79, 90

Danet, B., 143
Davis, H., and Walton, P., 207
Davy, H., 165–6
Demosthenes, 89
Derrida, J., 153
Descartes, J., 82

Dickens, C., 155, 174
Dostoevsky, F., 105, 109, 170
Dryden, J., 110
Durant, A., 46

Eden, K., 79, 178, 205, 208, 225
Empson, W., 206, 243

Feyerabend, P., 101, 224
Fish, S., 243
Foucault, M., xiv
Fyre, N., 114, 136

Gadamer, H-G., 102, 150, 187, 205, 224
Genette, G., 79, 151, 153, 177, 191, 205–6
Goffman, E., 10, 13, 14, 17
Goodrich, P., 138, 142
Gorgias, 97, 98, 161, 204, 236
Gramsci, A., 204–5, 222–3

Hall, S., 207
Homer, 48, 145–6, 214, 216
Hooke, R., 163–4, 167
Horace, 110

Iser, W., 244
Isocrates, 97–99, 104

Jakobson, R., 242–4
Jameson, F., 242
Johnson, S., 111
Jonson, B., 51

Kennedy, G., 79, 89, 97, 178, 205, 236
Kerferd, G. B., 205

Lucian, 178, 208, 218

McCloskey, D., 114

269

Subject Index